On Language

By Gao Mingkai

Translated by Yan Haoran

On Language
Author: Gao Mingkai
Translator: Yan Haoran Language: English
Word Count (for space of all pages): 302 thousand words
Publisher: Chicago Academic Press
Number of Pages: 410
ISBN: 978-1-965890-81-3

Publishing	Chicago Academic Press
	5923 N Artesian Ave
	Chicago IL 60659
Email	contact@chicagoacademicpress.com
Website	http://chicagoacademicpress.com/
Book Size	6X9 inches
First Edition	

About the Translator

Yan Haoran graduated in January 2022 from the School of English and International Studies at Beijing Foreign Studies University with a Ph.D. in English Language and Literature. He is currently the deputy director of the Department of English at the School of Foreign Studies, Xi'an University. His primary research areas include theoretical linguistics, stylistics, semiotics, philosophy of language, and translation. His research has been supported by Shaanxi Provincial Social Science Foundation and Shaanxi Provincial Philosophy and Social Science Research Special Project. He has published several papers in major foreign language journals such as *Contemporary Linguistics* and *Journal of Chinese for Social Science*, including "Research on Transcultural Phenomena in Bilingual Publications from the Perspective of Conceptual Integration" "New Developments in Text World Theory: A Review of *World Building: Discourse in the Mind*" "How to Play Language-games with Rules: Rethinking Wittgenstein's Philosophical Views on Language" and "Restructuring Grammatical Metaphor in Chinese Translations of *Sense and Sensibility*—From the Perspective of Functional Stylistics".

About the Revisers

Liu Jielin holds a Ph.D. in Linguistics and Applied Linguistics (2024, Shaanxi Normal University), with a focus on Chinese philology and overseas Sinology, and an M.A. in Linguistics and Applied Linguistics (2014, Beijing Foreign Studies University), specializing in cross-linguistic studies. She is Lecturer and Head of the English Department, School of Foreign Studies, Xi'an University, and serves as a council member of the Shaanxi Association for International Chinese Education and the Xi'an Translators Association. Her research spans applied linguistics, cross-linguistic studies, Chinese philology, and translation, demonstrated through studies of the use of verb–direction constructions by Chinese learners of English, analyses of Macau's urban linguistic landscapes, and research on the Six Scripts theory, also known as Liushu, the traditional classification of Chinese characters. She is committed to connecting Chinese language, script, and culture with a global readership.

Zhan Juan graduated in June 2001 from the School of Foreign Studies at Hebei Teachers University with an M.A. in English Language and Literature. She is currently an associate professor at the School of Foreign Studies, Xi'an University. She is also appointed as Research Supervisor by the School of Foreign Studies, Northwest University. Her primary research interests include narratology, stylistics, cognitive linguistics and translation. She has translated a book titled *The Bilingual Acquisition of English and Mandarin: Chinese Children in Australia* (Chinese version: 《华裔儿童双语习得》) published by The Commercial Press in January,2022. She was one of the compilers of *Specifications for the English Translation of Public Signs* (西安市《公共场所标识语英文译写规范》(DB 6101/T 3101-2021)).

Table of Contents

Part One

The Social Nature of Language

Chapter 1

The Sociality of Language

Section 1 The Mutual Restraint and Dependence Between Language and Society

Marxist understanding of language first and foremost emphasizes the social nature of language. Stalin said, "Language belongs among social phenomena. From the moment society came into being, language has existed."[1] The assertion that language is a social phenomenon represents a specific explanation of its social nature. This principle can be illuminated from three perspectives:

(1) positive proof through the mutual constraint and interdependence between language and society; (2) negative proof by demonstrating that language is neither an individual nor a natural phenomenon; (3) further concrete proof via the social character of linguistic signs.

Language exists in human society. "Outside of society, there is no such thing as language."[2] Embedded in society, language both constrains society and is constrained by it. Without society, language cannot exist; without

1 *Stalin, Marxism and Problems of Linguistics*, People's Publishing House, 1953, p. 20.
2 Ibid.

language, society would collapse. Garkina-Fedoruk once proposed to illustrate this relationship of mutual restraint and mutual dependence between language and society from the following two aspects: (1) The dependence of language on society; (2) The role of language in social life.[1] We might as well discuss the social nature of language positively from these two aspects.

Language is a product created by human society. Marx said, "Use-value, as a determinant of value, is just like language, a product of human society."[2] Without human society, there would be no language. And only human society in the universe has language. Humans are different from other animals in that they are social animals. From the very first day of his existence, he has engaged in collective labor—jointly creating production tools, collectively transforming nature, battling against nature, carrying out production, and acquiring means of subsistence. This collective social labor is coordinated through the use of language, and human language itself emerged precisely in the course of such social labor—in the joint effort of producing material wealth—to coordinate people's productive actions and meet the urgent need for communication. Language could never have emerged if humans had not engaged in communal social labor. It is conceivable that language would never have emerged without collective

1 Cf. Garkina Fedoruk, *Language as a Social Phenomenon*, Times Publishing House, 1956.
2 Marx, *Das Kapital*, People's Publishing House, 1953, Volume I, p. 56.

social labor. Suppose humans "lived and died without ever interacting"—leading isolated lives, merely exploiting nature's ready-made resources to survive like other animals, and never transforming the environment. In such a scenario, the need for language as a tool for collaboration and communication would never have arisen. One can also imagine how drastically human collective labor to transform nature would be hindered without language.

History has preserved records of many languages no longer in use, commonly referred to as "dead languages." Today, we can only engage with these languages through the written scripts that documented them, as they have truly vanished. Their disappearance is largely due to the extinction of the specific social communities that once used them. For example, the Xianbei language vanished alongside the Xianbei ethnic group in ancient China. Although the *Sui Shu's Classics and Records* section still lists titles related to the Xianbei language, its actual form and usage remain lost to us. This illustrates a fundamental truth: language is inseparable from society. A specific language survives only as long as the society that nurtured it. The diversity of languages worldwide today arises from their evolution within distinct social groups. Different environments and cultural contexts have shaped languages into unique systems, each bearing the imprint of its community's history and identity.

Even in the general development of language, the constraint of language by society is extremely evident. As human social groups have increasingly expanded, the objects served by language and the scope of language use have also grown. Due to the aggregation and dispersion of social groups, languages have unified and differentiated accordingly, while contact between social groups can give rise to mutual influence among languages. Even within the same language, the development of productive forces, cultural advancement, changes in social systems, and shifts in ideology within the social group using that language have all caused enormous changes in vocabulary and increasing precision in grammar throughout its historical development. Therefore, whether viewed from the perspective of language's origin or its development, language is dependent on society; its very existence is constrained by society.

Not only is the existence and development of language constrained by society, but the existence and development of society are also constrained by language. This is concretely manifested in the role language plays in social life. At no time or place have we ever encountered a situation where social life could exist without language. Anthropologists note that even today's so-called "primitive peoples", such as Australia's Aboriginal communities, have their own distinct languages. Even the "most primitive humans" known to science today, such as Java Man and Peking Man, had activities related to language functions. Although Java Man and Peking Man could only utter isolated, unconnected words, they were already able to produce definite, slightly differentiated articulatory sounds such as basic vowels, laryngeal consonants, back consonants (posterior tongue consonants), nasal consonants, and implosives, as well as loud cries that were not subject to individual direct intention.[1] In today's society, the situation is even more evident. Whether in Beijing or Moscow, at the Cape of Good Hope or in Sydney, at the foot of Mount Everest or on the slopes of the Alps, wherever human society exists, language exists.

Even between two individuals, social interaction cannot exist without a shared language for mutual understanding. Social life entails far more than mere communal living—while animals may exhibit herd instincts, they lack true social life. Human social life is defined by collective efforts to transform nature, create tools, and engage in production. Without language as a tool for communicating ideas and achieving mutual comprehension, two people cannot coordinate labor to modify the environment, craft tools, or conduct joint productive activities. Admittedly, there may be instances where two individuals collaborate in silence. However, such cooperation invariably relies on prior verbal communication to exchange ideas and make decisions or employs non-linguistic substitutes (e.g., eye contact) during the process. Even gestures like eye signals derive their meaning from social conventions—habits established in society to replace verbal expressions for specific intentions.

1 Cf. Bunak, *The Origin of Man and Ancient Human Distribution* (Russian edition), Moscow, 1951.

It is inconceivable how humans could coordinate collective production activities without language. From the dawn of human society, language has been indispensable for organizing social life. Throughout every subsequent phase of social evolution, it has remained a cornerstone of societal function and a primary catalyst for progress. As both a vehicle for idea exchange and interpersonal communication, and a vessel for abstract thought, language continuously facilitates productive labor, natural transformation, social reform, cultural advancement, and knowledge dissemination. In essence, language preserves and transmits the accumulated labor experience of human. It records the wisdom of past generations, thereby enabling future societies to inherit knowledge amassed over millennia. Language is not merely a vital instrument for sustaining modern social life; it is also a critical tool for accessing and building upon the intellectual achievements of preceding societies or contemporary peers. Humans use language not only to convey mundane daily ideas but also to articulate complex ideologies central to productive, political, and (notably) class struggles, whether for advocacy or critique. Thus, society is fundamentally shaped by language, with its survival and advancement hinging on this indispensable faculty.

Section 2 Language Is Not an Individual or Natural Phenomenon

The proposition that language is a social phenomenon inherently excludes it from being categorized as an individual or natural phenomenon. We can examine the contrast between social phenomena and their opposites, namely individual and natural phenomena, through two dimensions. By definition, individual phenomena and social phenomena are mutually exclusive; the same applies to natural phenomena and social phenomena. Conversely, any phenomenon that is not individualistic by nature must be social, and what is not natural must be social. Therefore, the social nature of language can be further validated by demonstrating that it belongs neither to the realm of individual phenomena nor to that of natural phenomena.

It is self-evident that language is not an individual phenomenon. No single person has ever invented a personal language to communicate with others, nor can language be created by any individual. Instead, individuals must learn language from the society to which they belong—a necessity admitting no exception. Of course, language is articulated and perceived by individuals: it relies on physiological organs for speech and hearing, and on motor and auditory neural processes to govern speaking and listening. But this does not render language an individual phenomenon, just as class struggle, though enacted by individuals, is not thereby proven individualistic. The crux lies as follows: when speaking, individuals must use their physiological and psychological faculties to produce utterances understandable to others; when listening, they must use their own faculties to comprehend others' speech. Language is neither individually created nor passively acquired; it is fundamentally a social institution embedded in communal use and oriented toward sustaining social life.

Of course, individuals do use language in self-talk or silent reflection without interacting with others, but these instances do not prove that language is an individual phenomenon. When speaking to themselves or thinking silently, people often imagine themselves as conversational partners; even in such cases, the language they use remains socially learned and mutually intelligible. Language serves as a tool for communication and abstract thinking. While individuals may use this tool, its status as a social phenomenon does not hinge on individual usage—just as a hunting stone remains a natural (not individual) phenomenon despite being wielded by a person. The social nature of language must be understood through its essential characteristics, not through the individuality of its users. Since communication is a social phenomenon and language was created out of social needs and practices, its development is socially conditioned, and it inherently constitutes a symbolic system with social properties. Thus, language is a social phenomenon, not an individual one, even though individuals may use it privately. Moreover, as social beings, not all individual activities are purely personal. Individuals may indeed contribute to language evolution, but any "creation" of linguistic elements must align with social needs and gain communal acceptance to become part of the language. Therefore, just as individuals can participate in social revolutionary causes without making revolutionary activities individual phenomena, it cannot be argued that language is an individual phenomenon.

Language is a social phenomenon, not an individual one—this is an evident truth. However, under the influence of an individualistic worldview, many linguists emphasize the role of the individual, either intentionally or unintentionally denying the social nature of language and treating it as an individual phenomenon. For instance, the German linguist Karl Vossler is a typical example of modern linguistic schools that adopt an individualistic perspective. In his book *Positivism and Idealism in Linguistics*, Vossler borrowed and expanded upon Wilhelm Von Humboldt's idea that "language is a creative intellectual tool" and Benedetto Croce's theory that language is "the primary expression of the soul." He argued that "language is the expression of the spirit" and thus incorporated linguistics into the realm of aesthetics, elevating stylistics—with its aesthetic qualities—to the foremost position in linguistic research. He believed that through the lens of stylistics, one could easily uncover the connections between linguistic developments and phenomena in cultural and social history. With the aid of stylistics, the influence of individual creativity on language evolution could be clearly demonstrated, and no distinction needed to be made between the language of the people and the language of writers. Instead, he proposed that the process of language development is an act of individual creation. While Vossler acknowledged the relationship between language, culture, and a people's social environment, he deemed such social factors insignificant. He argued that only aesthetic factors, specifically those related to style, could serve as the primary driving force behind linguistic change, which he viewed as an expression of individual creative behavior. He stated: "Style is the individual use of language, distinct from general usage that is essentially nothing more than an approximate aggregate of all or at least the most significant individual linguistic uses. Since linguistic usage becomes a norm through social prescription, it is described by syntax. Yet because linguistic usage is also an individual creation, stylistics must study it. However, induction proceeds from the particular to the general, from individual instances to universal norms; the reverse is impossible. Thus, stylistics precedes syntax. Every expressive device is first an individual, stylistic means before it becomes a normative, syntactic one... In other words, all linguistic elements are stylistic expressive devices."[1] In this way, he affirmatively posits that language is a means of expressing the spirit, created by individuals. As for why language functions as a tool of communication, in his view, this is not because language is social in nature, a product of society, or constrained by society, but merely because individuals share a common linguistic capacity. He claimed: "When people communicate with each other through language, the possibility of such communication is not founded on shared linguistic norms, common linguistic materials, or syntactic structures, but rather on a universal linguistic faculty. In short, the commonality of any language, including dialects, does not actually exist... If two or more individuals from vastly

1 Vossler, *Positivism and Idealism in Linguistics*, pp. 15–16.

different linguistic communities with no shared linguistic rules are brought into contact, their inherent linguistic faculty will enable them to communicate with each other rapidly. This is how English and other languages allegedly originated."[1] In his view, since the communicative function of language stems from human's universal linguistic faculty, language as a communicative tool is not a social phenomenon but merely a collective employment of individual capabilities, akin to how individuals collectively utilize natural phenomena. While social environments seemingly influence language, they serve only as "contact conditions"—nothing more than ordinary catalysts that stimulate language use. He asserted that language cannot be learned; it can only be activated as a spiritual manifestation of human's innate linguistic faculty. He explicitly rejected the notion of language as a system of social norms, stating: "The boundary of linguistics lies where shortcomings emerge and the linguistic faculty stops functioning. To view language as social norms is to adopt a non-scientific perspective." Therefore, he drew the conclusion: "Syntax, akin to morphology, is not a science. The whole of grammatical studies constitutes a grand cemetery built by industrious positivists, where the deceased fragments of language are interred—either piece by piece or en masse—in its elaborate sepulchers, each marked with a number and an

1 Ibid., pp. 37–38.

epitaph."[1]

Vossler claimed that only idealist methodology qualifies as scientific. The idealist fallacies in his individualistic linguistic theory are self-evident, as he inadvertently confesses to them. Thus, merely criticizing him as an idealist does not clarify the precise nature of his errors. We must also provide arguments to dismantle his fantastical doctrines. Vossler argued that language is an expression of the spirit—specifically, a manifestation of the individual psyche. We do not deny that language can express individual psychology, but does this suffice to prove that language is not a social phenomenon but an individual one? To be sure, language can serve as a tool for expressing individual psychology in certain contexts, just as it can serve as a tool for individual thought. However, can we really equate a tool for expressing individual thought with an individual phenomenon or something individually created? Expressing one's psyche is a personal act, but the tool used for this expression is not necessarily an individual phenomenon. Just as hunting can be a personal activity, the stone used for hunting remains a natural phenomenon, not an individual one. The fact that language serves as a tool for expressing individual psychology does not prove it is an individual phenomenon. Perhaps Vossler would argue that he denies language as a social phenomenon because it is individually created. But is language truly a product of individual creation? We do not deny the role

1 Vossler, p.38.

individuals play in linguistic innovation, but this does not mean language itself is individually created. If language were individually created, with over 600 million people in China, there might be 600 million languages. Yet who can deny that China has only languages such as Han, Tibetan, Mongolian, Manchu, Miao, Zhuang, and Uyghur—not 600 million? If language were individually created, so-called linguistic elements invented by individuals should irresistibly enter the linguistic system. But why did terms like Yan Fu's "monad" (monad, a philosophical term he coined) fail to become part of the Chinese vocabulary? If, as Vossler claims, the possibility of communication arises solely from a shared linguistic faculty, this faculty should enable all humans to create a single universal language. Why then did Vossler use German—a language unintelligible to most Han Chinese—to expound his theory of individual linguistic creation? Why do people from different ethnic groups with a shared linguistic faculty still need translation to understand each other? Is it true, as Vossler claimed, that "individuals with no shared linguistic rules... will quickly start conversing with each other upon contact"? Consider the fact that even European sinologists who have studied Chinese for years and become experts may still struggle to converse with native Chinese speakers—is this not evident? If language were not something that can be learned but only activated, why would people study languages in schools? These are all extremely obvious facts. In short, Vossler's individualistic linguistic theory lacks any scientific basis, and it only reinforces our conviction that language is a social phenomenon, not an individual one.

Is language a natural phenomenon? Natural phenomena are products of the natural world, not created by humans. Not only are celestial phenomena like the sun, moon, clouds, and rosy clouds beyond human creation, but even a single grain of sand in nature cannot be created by humans. If people can use natural materials and follow natural laws to create things similar to natural ones, these remain artificial. This is why certain scientific inventions are called "artificial satellites," "artificial silk", and the like. The emergence and development of natural phenomena do not depend on human social factors. Although human society can sometimes accelerate the development of natural phenomena, plants in nature can still grow according to their own laws without human cultivation. The existence, development, and decay of natural phenomena do not depend on the existence, development, or decline of human society; they operate independently of social conditions. Social phenomena, by contrast, are products of human society; their existence, development, and disappearance are inherently tied to those of society, and they are shaped by social conditions. Is language like natural phenomena, capable of emerging and fading without being conditioned by society? Clearly not. No one has ever discovered a language existing outside of society or not created by society. Nor has anyone witnessed a language that does not develop alongside society or vanish with its collapse. It is evident, therefore, that language is not a natural phenomenon.

Yet such self-evident truths have escaped the notice of certain linguists, who persist in claiming that language is a natural phenomenon despite overwhelming evidence to the contrary. This is the perspective of linguistic naturalists. In the early 19th century, the German linguist August Schleicher, a prominent exponent of this school, wrote in his *Sprachvergleichende Untersuchungen* (*Comparative Studies of Language*): "Language has its own future, which in the broad sense of the term may be called history. But the purest form of this history can be found in nature, as in the growth of a plant. Language belongs to the domain of nature, not to that of free mental activity."[1] In many of his works, he furthermore portrayed language as an organism, whose growth embodies linguistic life. He even argued that there is no essential difference between the life of language and that of plants: both have periods of growth and decay. Languages in prehistoric times were in their growth phase, evolving from isolating to agglutinative forms, and from agglutinative to inflectional forms. Sanskrit, termed the "rose of languages", represents language at the zenith of its growth. Historical languages, by contrast, are in a state of senescence—Indo-European languages in the historical period have already entered a declining trajectory. He argued that languages can be classified into types based on the organic structure of their systems and grouped into language families according to

1 Quoted from Cen Qixiang, *Outlines of the History of Linguistics*, Science Press, 1958 ed., p. 242.

their historical development. Each family possesses a proto-language or parent language, akin to a root from which all related languages emerge as branches. This is the so-called "family tree" hypothesis. In the second half of the 19th century, the British linguist F. Max Müller inherited Schleicher's theory and, in his Lectures on the Science of Language, opposed linguistics to history. He argued that linguistics, which studies language as its object, should belong to the natural sciences, while philology, which uses language as a tool to study human society's morality, intelligence, religion, and literature, belongs to historical sciences. Although he acknowledged that "no natural science is as closely related to human history as linguistics",[1] he claimed that all linguistic changes "are not historical changes but merely natural growths; art, science, philosophy, and religion may have histories, but language—or any other product of nature, strictly speaking—has no history, only growth," because "while language is constantly changing, no one can produce or arrest these changes."[2]

This theory of regarding language as a natural phenomenon is extremely erroneous. It is fundamentally flawed to oppose natural phenomena to historical phenomena. Everything in the universe has its development and history, and natural objects are no exception. So-called natural sciences are in fact natural historical sciences. What should stand in

1 Müller, *Lectures on the Science of Language*, London, 1899, Vol. 1, pp. 39–40.
2 Ibid., p. 38.

opposition to natural phenomena are social phenomena. Social sciences are essentially social historical sciences. Even more absurd is the analogy of language to a living organism akin to a biological being. Of course, language undergoes emergence, development, and demise, but these processes are contingent upon the birth, growth, and collapse of society—they are governed by social conditions. In contrast, the emergence, development, and decay of natural objects are independent of social constraints. Moreover, the "birth" of language does not refer to biological generation; no one can explain how a so-called "parent language" could "conceive" or "give birth" to its "daughter languages". The development of language refers only to the addition of new elements and the evolution or disappearance of old elements in its historical progression. So-called "daughter languages" are in reality the result of a "parent language" changing its form in subsequent eras due to such processes; they cannot coexist with the "parent language" like biological offspring, nor does this term refer to biological reproduction. The "death" of a language merely means it ceases to be used, not a biological cessation of functions like a heartbeat or "natural death". As a product of society, language shares no commonality with biological products of the natural world. Müller's claim that "while language is constantly changing, no one can produce or arrest these changes" is precisely a source of his error. Müller observed certain facts and noted that changes in language cannot be willed into existence or halted by any individual. But he failed to note that what cannot be created or halted by any individual is not necessarily a natural phenomenon. Social phenomena also cannot be created or halted by any single person; only society as a whole can do so. While linguistic changes are clearly beyond the control of any individual, they are subject to the influence of society. Since the founding of the People's Republic of China, many changes have occurred in Modern Chinese. New words that did not exist before, such as "cosmic rocket", "armed demonstration", "people's commune", "integration of indigenous and modern methods", "satellite vehicle", "artificial satellite", "politics takes command", etc., have come into being. The creation of these terms was certainly not decided by any individual, but they reflect societal development—they are new coinages created by the masses during social progress. Words that once existed, such as "冰人" (matchmaker), "弄瓦" (birth of a daughter), "令媛" (your daughter), "贵庚" (your age), "台甫" (your honorable name), etc., are no longer used in everyday language. Their disappearance, of course, was not determined by any single individual, but it reflects social transformations and is governed by social conditions. The fact that some languages of "primitive societies" have not developed as Chinese has today is undoubtedly constrained by social factors to some extent. It is evident, therefore, that naturalist linguists who argue that the inability of individuals to determine language's emergence and development proves it is a natural phenomenon are not only committing logical fallacies but also misinterpreting empirical facts.

The fallacy of the naturalist school treating language as a biological natural phenomenon is readily apparent. Many Western linguists have disagreed with this erroneous view, such as W. D. Whitney. However, this does not mean naturalist ideas have not left a pernicious influence on linguistics. Beyond regarding language as a biological natural phenomenon, the naturalist school further advocated studying language using the methods of natural science, explaining linguistic phenomena through physical, mechanical, or biological laws. For example, in the preface to his work *Vergleichende Grammatik der Sanskrit, Zend, Armenischen, Griechischen, Lateinischen, Litauischen, Altslawischen, Gotischen und Deutschen* (*Comparative Grammar of Sanskrit, Zend, Armenian, Greek, Latin, Lithuanian, Old Slavic, Gothic, and German*), F. Buber stated: "In this work, I intend to describe the structural mechanisms of the various languages listed in the title, compare facts of similar nature among them, investigate the physical and mechanical laws governing these languages, and seek the origins of the forms expressing these grammatical relationships." Buber also once explained his use of "physical", "mechanical", and "dynamic" laws in the form of correspondence. He stated: "I primarily interpret 'physical' laws as the law of gravity, particularly the influence of personal endings on the preceding syllable. If, contrary to our view, one agrees with Grimm that the vowel changes in Germanic verb conjugations have grammatical significance—for example, if the *a* in the Gothic preterite *band* ('I just bound') is taken as an expression of past tense, opposing the *i* in the present tense *binda* ('I bind')—one would be justified in saying that this a possesses a dynamic force. By 'physical laws', I refer to other grammatical rules and (especially) phonetic laws. For instance, in Sanskrit, instead of *ad-ti* (from the root ad-, 'to eat'), one says *at-ti*; the change from *d* to *t* has a physical cause."[1] The mechanical imposition of natural science methodologies and laws of natural phenomena onto linguistics marks the genesis of the flawed notion, held by certain linguists—particularly some structuralists—that linguistics belongs to the natural sciences. Even today, this perspective continues to influence some linguists in China who regard linguistics as a natural science. Needless to say, this view is extremely harmful: "It leads people away from the essence of language into a realm of falsity, describing language as 'unrelated to experience' (in the words of V. Hjelmslev), abandoning the 'hypothesis of existence', extracting and isolating 'indissoluble basic units' (unités de base indissociables) from speech, using these units to construct the 'synchronic state' of language, and then arranging 'stratification' (stratification)."[2] Certain structuralists, particularly Hjelmslev of the Danish school, argue that the object of linguistics should be the constants of the linguistic sign system, which in reality are the relationships among language forms. Although they acknowledge language as a social phenomenon, they maintain that it is necessary to study language from within its self-contained system,

1 See the French translation by M. Bréal of *Grammaire comparée des langues indo-europeénnes*, Volume 1, Preface, footnote on page 1.
2 Gerngross, *On the Characteristics of Language Structure*, in *Linguistics Translation Series*, 1960, No. 1, p. 21.

excluding the relationship between language and society from the scope of linguistic inquiry and relegating it to "metalinguistics". By severing language from society in this way, language is effectively conceptualized as a structural system akin to the organization of physical phenomena—in essence, treating it as a natural phenomenon. That some structuralists advocate applying natural science methods used for natural phenomena to study language, while opposing sociocultural approaches, embodies their view of language as a natural phenomenon, despite their verbal acknowledgment of its social character. Treating language in this way naturally leads linguistics down the wrong path, for it causes people to overlook the social essence of language. Studying language while discarding its social nature is akin to examining a living organism in isolation from its physical environment—a practice that, in ancient times, gave rise to superstition—and can only yield unscientific results. Linguists' tendency to view language as a natural phenomenon is undoubtedly linked to its phonological structure. Buber's discussions of "the influence of endings on preceding syllables", the "dynamic force" attributed to "a" in opposition to "i", and changes like "d" to "t" all pertain to phonetics, even as he attempted to explain grammatical phenomena. The phonological structure of language does indeed have a physical dimension, serving as the material substrate through which language is graspable by humans. The rules governing these phonological structures and their historical development or change may well have physiological and physical causes.

As a result, some have come to see language as a natural phenomenon, arguing that it must be studied using the same methods applied to physiological and physical phenomena. In reality, language is neither a physical nor a physiological phenomenon, even though linguistic components have their acoustic aspects, and these sounds are produced by physiological organs. However, sound itself is not language, nor are physiological organs necessarily "language organs". The rustling of grass in the wind, or the sounds made by insects, fish, birds, and animals—none of these constitute language. Newborn human infants also make murmuring sounds, yet we do not therefore claim that infants possess language. Language must be a composite of sound and meaning. This is precisely due to the social essence of language as a tool for human communication, which serves to embody thought or express ideas. Without the meaning it conveys, the sounds produced by the human mouth are not the language that bears abstract thought, nor the language that serves as a communication tool—in short, they are not language. In reality, language is neither a physical nor a physiological phenomenon, even though linguistic components have their acoustic aspects, and these sounds are produced by physiological organs. However, sound itself is not language, nor are physiological organs necessarily "language organs". The rustling of grass in the wind, or the sounds made by insects, fish, birds, and animals—none of these constitute language. Newborn human infants also make murmuring sounds, yet we do not therefore claim that infants possess language. Language must be a composite of sound and meaning. This is precisely due to the social essence of language as a tool for human communication, which serves to embody thought or express ideas. Without the meaning it conveys, the sounds produced by the human mouth are not the language that bears abstract thought, nor the language that serves as a communication tool—in short, they are not language. It is true that language must use sound as its material basis, but sound itself is not language. While the evolution of the phonetic component of language may indeed have physical and physiological causes, these causes do not directly drive phonetic change; rather, they become conditions for such change through social communication. Moreover, sound is not language, and the evolution of language's phonetic component is not equivalent to the evolution of language itself. Thus, the attempt to explain language solely through physical and physiological causes for its structural laws or phonetic evolution—while claiming that language is fundamentally a natural phenomenon—is as flawed as explaining society through the biological structures of individuals and their evolutionary drivers, asserting that society is a natural phenomenon.

Section 3 The Social Nature of Linguistic Signs

Lenin stated, "Language is the most important means of communication for human."[1] Stalin noted, "Language is a tool and weapon

1 *Collected Works of Lenin*, People's Publishing House, 1958, Vol. 20, p. 396.

that people use to communicate with one another, exchange ideas, and achieve mutual understanding." [1] Language serves as a tool for communication between people in human society by facilitating the exchange of ideas and mutual understanding. This characteristic of language is the very source of its social nature and the essence of its social function. However, since language qualifies as a social phenomenon by virtue of being a communication tool, it must possess characteristics that distinguish it from other non-communication social phenomena. As the most important human communication tool, language must also have features that set it apart from other human communication tools. What are these characteristics? Stalin explained: "Language serves society as a tool for human communication, a tool for exchanging ideas in society, and a tool for enabling people to understand one another and coordinate their joint activities in all spheres of life—including the realm of production, economic relations, politics, culture, social life, and daily existence." These characteristics are unique to language alone, and it is precisely because they are exclusive to language that language becomes the object of study for an independent science—linguistics.[2] Language, as the object of linguistic study, differs from other social phenomena because it serves as human's most important communication tool. It enables the exchange of ideas,

1 Stalin, *Marxism and Problems of Linguistics*, p. 20.
2 Ibid., p. 35.

fosters mutual understanding, and coordinates activities in realms such as production, economics, politics, culture, social life, and daily interaction. Moreover, language is the most important among all communication tools precisely because it is a complex system of signs. In reality, language is a complex sign system serving as human's most important means of communication. In terms of language's social function, it is human's most important communication tool; in terms of the internal structure that distinguishes it from other phenomena, it is an extremely complex system of signs. Language serves as a communication tool precisely because of this complex sign system. Without this system, language would be inconceivable and could not function as a communication tool.

Some structuralists and other linguists emphasize that language is a system of signs while intentionally or unintentionally denying the social essence of its role as a communication tool. This is a grave error on their part. However, this does not mean it is mistaken to acknowledge that language is a complex sign system. The problem lies in the fact that these structuralists believe the sign system can exist in isolation from its social context and they view it as a physical, non-social, self-contained entity. In contrast, we maintain that the linguistic sign system itself is a social phenomenon, for language as an entity is nothing other than this complex sign system—one that inherently functions as a communication tool. Since language is a social phenomenon, this sign system is naturally a social phenomenon as well.

But why is this sign system considered a social phenomenon? This requires us to analyze and prove the social nature of linguistic signs.

Linguists have long paid attention to the problem of language as a sign system. In the early 19th century, Wilhelm von Humboldt, while explaining that words are signs of things, pointed out that "People can understand each other not because they master the signs of things, nor because they can correctly understand the same concept through prescribed signs, but because these signs are the same links in the chain of human sensory perception and the internal mechanism of concept formation. Therefore, when naming things, the same strings of the mental instrument are struck, and as a result, each person generates corresponding—though not identical—concepts." The Russian linguist A. A. Potebnya also once stated, "The sound of a word is not a sign but only the shell of a sign, that is, a so-called sign of a sign. Therefore, from the definition of a word as a unity of sound and meaning, it cannot be concluded that a word contains two elements; in reality, there are three." Both discussed the problem of linguistic signs. Although at the time there were various views on the semiotic nature of language, they shared a common tendency: explaining the problem of language as signs through its relationship to speakers' psychological activities.[1] In his *Course in General Linguistics*, Swiss

1 See B. A. Zvegintsev, *The Problem of Language as a Sign System*, in *Selected Translations of Linguistic Essays*, Seventh Volume, Zhonghua Book Company, 1958, pp. 65–66.

linguist F. de Saussure proposed that language is a sign system within the domain of semiotics—alongside social signs like writing, sign languages, symbolic rituals, respectful gestures, and military signals, though a more complex one. This proposition has since drawn significant attention to the semiotic nature of language among linguists. Saussure contended that a sign comprises a signifiant (signifier) and signifié (signified). In linguistic signs, the signifiant (signifier) refers to the auditory impression or sound image, while the signifié (signified) refers to the concept. The combination of an auditory impression and a concept forms a sign; a sign cannot exist without either component. The hallmark of a sign lies in the arbitrariness of the connection between its signifier and signified—this bond is reasonless and unmotivated. Linguistic signs are monodimensional: they unfold sequentially in time rather than extending spatially. Simultaneously, linguistic signs constitute a system, where each sign exists in dependence on the system, and its value is constrained by the system's structure. Due to their arbitrariness, signs are susceptible to change over time—both the signifier and signified can be altered. Yet because of this same arbitrariness, once socially accepted, signs cannot be arbitrarily modified at will. Both the variability and invariance of signs are products of their arbitrariness. Furthermore, because signs are constrained by the system and influenced by their relationships with other signs, the arbitrariness of signs is relative.[1] Saussure's theory of linguistic signs has undergone divergent developments across different linguistic schools, and it remains a topic of lively debate among linguists today. Given that language is a system of signs, varying perspectives on signs inherently reflect divergent conceptions of language. Thus, a correct understanding of the semiotic nature of language is of paramount importance.

What is a symbol? In cognitive activities, when using thing A to represent thing B and borrowing thing A to understand thing B, a symbolic relationship is formed. In this relationship, thing A becomes the "signifier" and thing B becomes the "signified". For example, using a red flag to represent victory—seeing the red flag means recognizing victory. Things inherently exist and have their own characteristics, but when they enter into symbolic relationships, they change in nature and become the "signifier" and "signified" in symbolic relationships. Generally speaking, this "signifier" is called a symbol. In his *Problems of the Symbolism of Language*, Zvegintzev believed that apart from the fundamental characteristic of arbitrariness, symbols also have (1) non-productivity, (2) lack of systematicity, (3) autonomy of symbols and meanings, and (4)

1 See F. de Saussure, *Cours de linguistique générale*, Paris, 1931, pp. 97–113; pp. 180–184.

univocality of symbols.[1] He compares these characteristics with words in language and questions the symbolic nature of words because he believed words do not conform to these characteristics.[2] In fact, the characteristics of symbols described by Zvegintzev are not possessed by all symbols but only by things like flag signals and traffic signals. Therefore, there is insufficient basis for comparing these characteristics with words in language. Although flag signals, traffic signals, etc., are also symbols, they differ greatly from language. Gerngross stated: "The sensory activity evoked by any symbol is different from that evoked by non-symbolic things; the sensory activity evoked by symbols is an activity of understanding or 'intellectual activity'. This belongs to both linguistic symbols and all other symbols that incorporate system components of varying degrees of complexity... However, the activity of understanding language is so much more complex than the sensory activities generated by all other symbols and their systems that we even need to acknowledge, based on the principle of quantitative change leading to qualitative change, that language is fundamentally different in nature from all other symbolic systems..."[3] His argument is correct. Additionally, arbitrariness is not a fundamental characteristic of symbols, because symbols encompass more than just

1 Zvegintzev, *Problems of the Symbolism of Language*, in *Selected Translations of Linguistic Papers*, Seventh Volume, pp. 72–74.
2 Ibid., pp. 75–81.
3 Gerngross, *On the Characteristics of Language Structure*, in *Linguistics Translation Series*, 1960, No. 1, p. 21.

things like flag signals and traffic signals—national flags, emblems, medals, etc., are also symbols, yet these symbols do not possess arbitrariness. In fact, symbols can be divided into two main categories: one is symbolic signs (non-arbitrary symbols), and the other is signaling signs (arbitrary symbols).[1] The relationship between a symbolic sign and its signified is justifiable, serving to "symbolize" or "signify" something: the design of a national flag used to represent a country cannot be arbitrarily stipulated; rather, it must be discussed collectively and determined based on some similarity between the flag's design and the country's characteristics. By contrast, the relationship between a signaling sign and its signified is unjustifiable: why does firing a gun signal the start of a 100-meter race? There is no rational explanation—this is merely a convention among people. Thus, arbitrariness is only a fundamental characteristic of signaling signs within the realm of symbols. The defining feature of symbols in general lies solely in their role as representations in cognition; this cognitive activity is not necessarily an "intellectual activity", as there are also signaling issues in imagistic thinking. Is language a symbol?

Language is clearly a type of symbol, which can be understood from three perspectives: (1) Language serves as the carrier of abstract thinking. It represents abstract thoughts, and we can understand human abstract thinking through their language. (2) Language is a marker of objective

1 Cf. Sandmann, M., *Subject and Predicate*, Edinburgh, 1954, pp. 47–57.

things. It represents the objective world, which enables us to recognize the state of the objective world through human language. (3) Each component of language is a combination of sound and meaning, where pronunciation represents semantic meaning. We can grasp the intended meaning by listening to the sounds others utter. What type of symbol is a linguistic symbol? This question has sparked lively debates among linguists. Some argue that linguistic symbols are arbitrary and therefore belong to signaling signs (arbitrary symbols). Others contend that linguistic symbols are non-arbitrary and thus fall under symbolic signs (non-arbitrary symbols). Galkina-Fedoruk stated: "The phonetic aspect of a word can be understood as a symbol anchored to things, objects, actions, etc.—that is, anchored to the content of the word. ... Every word, as a sound cluster, is a symbol anchored to things and recognized by society."[1] She also quoted Marx's words: "The name of a thing is entirely external to its nature"[2], and explains: "The connection between the word 'fish' and a certain animal living in water is completely conditional; the sound cluster is merely a symbol, not a mirror reflection, an image, or a replica, and unlike the concept of a thing, it does not possess these characteristics."[3] Here, Galkina-Fedoruk viewed linguistic symbols as arbitrary signaling signs, because she regards the

1 Galkina-Fedoruk, *On the Symbolism of Language from the Perspective of Marxist Linguistics*, in Foreign Language Teaching (Russian edition), 1952, No. 2, p. 9.
2 Marx, *Capital*, People's Publishing House, 1953, Volume 1, p. 88.
3 Galkina-Fedoruk, *On the Symbolism of Language from the Perspective of Marxist Linguistics*, in Foreign Language Teaching (Russian edition), 1952, No. 2, p. 8.

connection between a word in language (i.e., the sound cluster as she understands it) and the thing it represents as determined by certain conditions (i.e., social conventions), rather than a symbolic reflection or image. However, in his Introduction to Linguistics, Budagov (P. A. Будаков) stated: "Of course, the connection between a word's sound shell and its concept, as well as the connection between this concept and reality, cannot be simplified or understood from a vulgar sociological perspective like Marr did... But we also cannot endorse the views of linguists like de Saussure, who addressed this issue from an idealist perspective—de Saussure claimed that language has no connection whatsoever with reality, nor even with concepts." Although the sound shell of a word has a certain degree of independence and stability, and is to some extent independent from the word's meaning itself, we must still remember: any word can acquire justifiable grounds for its interpretation through subsequent lexical development.[1] What he means is that the combination of a word's sound and its meaning is not entirely arbitrary, especially in the development of language, where such arbitrariness disappears because the connection between a word's sound and meaning is determined by the word's internal form. For example, today we cannot arbitrarily say "water cannon" to refer

1 Budagov, *Introduction to Linguistics*, Times Publishing House, 1956, pp. 53–54. Here Budagov misinterprets de Saussure's argument. De Saussure never claimed that language is unrelated to concepts; on the contrary, he argued that concepts are an indispensable aspect of linguistic signs, forming linguistic signs together with the other aspect, namely auditory impressions.

to a "rocket"; instead, we use "rocket". In other words, Budagov argued that linguistic symbols are not arbitrary signals but non-arbitrary symbols. We believe the question of language's symbolic nature is complex and requires explaining its characteristics from multiple perspectives. As mentioned above, linguistic symbols can be understood in three ways: language is both a symbol of abstract thinking and of objective things, and each component of language is a sound-meaning complex that uses phonetic forms as symbols. The question of the characteristics of linguistic symbols depends on which aspect we are examining. If we are referring to the relationship between the phonetic form and meaning of linguistic components, then the structure of such linguistic symbols is arbitrary, not symbolic. Budagov's mention of a word's "internal form" cannot serve as a basis for denying the arbitrariness of linguistic symbols, because the internal form of a word is a separate issue, unrelated to whether the relationship between a language's symbol (signifier) and its meaning (signified) is arbitrary. It is true that today we say "huǒjiàn" (火箭, rocket) rather than "shuǐpào" (水炮, water cannon), and the coinage of the word "huǒjiàn" is constrained—but this does not concern whether there is any inherent rationale for the combination of the sound symbol [xuɔ-tgien] and its signified meaning ("a rocket-shaped machine propelled into the air by explosives, flying rapidly through the sky"). Instead, it relates to the non-arbitrary relationship between the sound-meaning complex "[xuɔ-tgien]×火箭(rocket)" and two other sound-meaning complexes "[xuɔ]×火(fire)" and "[tgien]×箭(arrow)". In other words, during word-formation, the combination of this "signifier×signified" is constrained by other arbitrary "signifier×signified" combinations. Regarding the connection between the sound [xuɔ-tgien] and the meaning "rocket", the relationship between signifier and signified remains arbitrary. French linguist Émile Benveniste also claimed that linguistic symbols are entirely non-arbitrary. He argued that symbols in language are necessarily constrained because, for speakers, concepts and phonetic forms are inseparably linked in their intellectual activities and function as a unified whole. Concepts are formed on the basis of phonetic forms, and without corresponding concepts, phonetic forms cannot be accepted by the intellect. [1] His view similarly fails to resolve the issue, as he only demonstrates that concepts and phonetic forms are inseparably linked, not that the relationship between the sound (signifier) and its signified meaning—though inseparable—can be rationally justified. We do not deny the existence of individual "prelinguistic" and "postlinguistic" symbolic signs within the system of language's sound-meaning complexes. For example, onomatopoeic words are "prelinguistic" symbolic signs, while metaphors are "postlinguistic" symbolic signs. The former can function as signs representing their referents before becoming linguistic components (e.g., using the sound ja to represent "duck"), while the latter involve

1 Benveniste, *Nature du Signe linguistique* (*The Nature of the Linguistic Sign*), in *Acta Linguistica, I*, 1939, pp. 23–29.

comparing meanings after linguistic components have formed (e.g., using the existing words “水” (water) and “龙头” (dragon head) to metaphorically denote a faucet as “水龙头”). However, these structures do not undermine the principle of arbitrariness in such signs. For prelinguistic symbolic signs like “鸭” (duck), the connection between the phonetic and semantic components is only relatively symbolic. It can change across different societies and eras, losing its symbolic nature. As for postlinguistic symbolic signs like “水龙头”), the combination of its sound [sui luŋt*ou] and meaning remains arbitrary. No one can rationally explain why this pure sound cluster is associated with the concept of a faucet. Certainly, the sound structures of various components in language are influenced by the sound system and constrained by the phonetic value system. However, such influences and constraints still do not undermine the arbitrariness of the sign relationship between sound and meaning. It is true that due to the influence of the phonetic system, the original *nim* (您) in Chinese became *nin*, and this was inevitable. But whether it is *nim* or *nin*, the relationship between these sounds and the meaning of “you” (polite form) is rationally unjustifiable and entirely arbitrary. Therefore, in terms of the relationship between the signifier and signified in language’s sound-meaning complexes, the connection between the sound (as the signifier) and the meaning (as the signified) embodies a signaling sign relationship, with arbitrariness as its fundamental characteristic.

Precisely because this relationship is arbitrary, the determination of which sound represents which meaning does not rely on the physical attributes of the sound but on social conventions. This is a concrete manifestation of the social nature of such linguistic symbols. In fact, the connection between the sound and meaning of any linguistic component is established by members of society during shared labor processes, shaped by specific social conditions. This is essentially a social conditioned reflex. The reason language serves as a stimulus for the second signal system—and differs from stimuli of the first signal system—is not only that it acts as a stimulus for abstract thinking rather than imagistic thinking, but also that it possesses sociality, which first-signal-system stimuli lack. Without social conditioned reflexes, the sound components of language could not become "signifiers" in symbolic relationships, and thus could not constitute linguistic symbols. Therefore, the sound part of language—the signifier in linguistic symbols—is inherently a social phenomenon. It is neither an individual nor a natural phenomenon. This aligns with the principle of "conventional establishment" described by Xunzi.

We can also regard the entire sound-meaning complex in language as the "signifier"—a signifier of thought—and view thought as the "signified" in this symbolic relationship. In this case, linguistic symbols refer to language components that contain meaning, such as words and morphemes[1].

[1] Morphemes are generally translated into Chinese as "词素" (Ci Su, elements of words, on which I formerly agreed. For the sake of theoretical consistency and systematicity of the current discussion, I intend to rename it "形位" (Xing Wei, morphological location).

Pavlov's theory of the second signal system holds that words do not serve as stimuli for the second signal system merely through sound materials; they function as such through sound materials imbued with meaning. Thus, language as the carrier of abstract thought and as a stimulus (i.e., symbol) of the second signal system acts as a symbol of thought in the form of sound-meaning complexes. From this perspective, the characteristic of linguistic symbols lies in their relative arbitrariness. The primary meaning component of language elements is essentially the manifestation of concepts in thought within language elements, constrained by concepts. Therefore, the relationship between meaning (as one component of the symbol) and its signified (concept) is not arbitrary. However, in this symbolic relationship of language, there is not only a meaning component but also a sound component—and the latter, due to its materiality, is more critical. The relationship between sound and concept is arbitrary. For this reason, we argue that the symbolic relationship of language exhibits only relative arbitrariness. Benveniste's mistake lies in his misidentification of the symbolic relationship of language (i.e., the relationship between sound-meaning complexes and concepts) as the symbolic relationship between the sound and meaning components within linguistic elements. This symbolic relationship of language also equally demonstrates the social nature of language. It should be noted that meaning differs from concepts precisely because meaning represents how society members express concepts in language under conditions of social communication, and meaning is in fact formed through specific social conditions. In this symbolic relationship of language, the sound component is social, the meaning component is also social, and the combination of sound and meaning is determined by social conditions—thus, the entire language element as a sound-meaning complex is a social phenomenon. It is an extremely erroneous view for some linguists to regard meaning as an individual psychological activity. In fact, from the perspective of the symbolic relationship between language and thought, language elements as symbols of thought (i.e., the structure of sound-meaning complexes) also concretely illustrate the principle that language is a social phenomenon.

Language can also be understood as a symbol of objective things, for it serves as a marker of objective reality and is capable of establishing a symbolic relationship with the objects it denotes (i.e., things) in the role of a signifier. The reason language can function as a marker of objective things is that it consolidates or expresses the outcomes of thinking—outcomes that reflect and are determined by objective things—within language as its semantic component. In other words, it becomes a symbol (signifier) of objective things indirectly through thinking's reflection of the objective world. Thinking itself is a social phenomenon, and the relationship between language and thinking involves a complex combining social phenomena of phonetics and semantics as symbols of thought. In the symbolic relationship between language and objective things, the relative arbitrariness and sociality of linguistic symbols are equally evident.

In summary, from any perspective, linguistic symbols are inherently social. This constitutes one of the primary arguments incompatible with the views of certain structuralists. Language itself is such a system of symbols; beyond this, language can also be understood as a symbol of objective reality, for it serves as a marker of objective things and can establish a symbolic relationship with the objects it denotes (i.e., things) as a signifier. The reason language can function as a marker of objective things is that it consolidates and expresses within itself the outcomes of thinking—outcomes that reflect and are determined by objective things—as its semantic component. In other words, it becomes a symbol (signifier) of objective things indirectly through thinking's reflection of the objective world. Thinking itself is a social phenomenon, and the relationship between language and thinking involves a composite of social phenomena—phonetics and semantics—as symbols of thought. In the symbolic relationship between language and objective things, the relative arbitrariness and sociality of linguistic symbols are equally evident.

If linguistic symbols lacked sociality, empty discourse about the social nature of language would be meaningless. In fact, linguistic symbols inherently possess evident sociality, which serves as a concrete manifestation of language's social essence. Language functions as a communication tool precisely because every one of its components is a symbol established and employed by society as part of a communicative system.

Chapter 2

The Functions of Language

Section 1 The Communicative Function of Language

Since language is classified as a social phenomenon in its capacity as "the most important means of communication for mankind," it possesses a communicative function. In other words, language enables people to engage in communication within human social life. The communicative function of language is self-evident. Everyone can appreciate that when interacting with other members of society, they use language to communicate—even the most basic so-called "small talk" relies on language. For this reason, wherever social life exists and wherever there are interactions between people, language is necessary. We can observe language serving people's social lives and interpersonal communication not only in today's culturally advanced societies but also in some extremely underdeveloped societies today, such as certain aboriginal societies in Australia. Moreover, language has existed from the very first day of human society. As Stalin stated: "There has never been a human society in history, even the most backward, that could do without its own spoken language."[1] For without language, communication among people would be rendered impossible, and so too would social life. The emergence of language was precisely spurred by the need for communication. Had people not had a need for communication, they would not have created language.

However, despite the fact that the communicative function of language is a palpable reality, certain linguists, wittingly or unwittingly, distort the truth and overlook this characteristic of language. For instance, in his essay *Language and the World of Objective Things*, E. Cassirer contended that the most crucial function of language lies not in communication but in creating the objective world. He stated, "Language does not enter into the perception of pre-existing, clearly-demarcated objective things merely by affixing 'names', that is, purely external and arbitrary symbols, to each of them; rather, it is itself the medium through which these objective things are created. In a sense, it is the pre-eminent medium, the most vital and precious tool for conquering and structuring a genuine world of objective things."[2] Cassirer's theory is an application of Kant's idealist philosophy in linguistics. This German linguist, influenced by the neo-Kantian phenomenology, held that the objective world is constructed by the subjective synthesizing ability of human beings. He opposes the theory of

1 Stalin, *Marxism and Problems of Linguistics*, p. 46.
2 Cassirer, *Le langage et le monde des objets* (*Language and the World of Objects*), in *Psychologie du langage* (*Psychology of Language*), Paris, 1933, p. 23.

reflection. Instead of believing that human knowledge is a reflection of objective things in the human brain, he contends that, on the contrary, the objective world is constructed by the synthetic ability of the human brain, and language serves as a medium or tool for the human brain to construct objective things. In his view, without language, objective things could not exist. He attempted to "prove" his argument by citing the languages of children and those of primitive societies. He argued that when children are learning language and knowledge, they ask what a thing is, rather than what it is called. In the eyes of children, names and knowledge are both tools for constructing the world. He further posited that in primitive societies, people often fail to distinguish between things and their names. They consider names to be an objective component of things and a genuine essential characteristic of them. Since the synthetic function of the human brain can construct objective things from the materials of representations, words that combine various representations also participate in the construction of the objective world. Cassirer also held that language is not only the constructor of the world of objective things, but also of the inner world of human beings, namely, the self - world (including emotions, morals, sensations, etc.) and the social world. He stated, "In truth, beyond the world of 'external' things and the self-world, the social world is gradually opened up and conquered by language."[1] Cassirer did touch upon the role of language in human social life, yet instead of regarding the function of language as facilitating communication among people, he views it as helping people construct society. He claimed that the first step in people's understanding of the external world is to recognize the existence of "you". Therefore, people initially regard all objective things as "you". It is language that enables people to participate in the lives of others and sense the existence of "you". He quoted Humboldt as saying, "In all things that stir the emotions, especially in emotionally-charged language, there is not only an awareness of unity and universality, but also an intuition, a heartfelt conviction that, despite being divided into many different individuals and small groups, human is essentially and in its ultimate destiny an indivisible whole...". He also believed that a child initially has only his or her own idiosyncratic language, and only through the subsequent recognition of "you" does he or she gradually come to recognize the existence of a commonly-used language. Thus, society is constructed, for language is a necessary process that leads people to acquire the concepts of "society" and even "human being".[2]

Cassirer's understanding of language's function represents a concrete manifestation of subjective idealism in linguistics. His aim is nothing more

1 Cassirer, *Language and the World of Objects*, in *Psychology of Language*, Paris, 1933, p. 33.
2 Ibid., pp. 18–44.

than to demonstrate that the objective world (whether natural or social) is constructed and determined by the subjective capabilities of the human brain. This theory stands in fundamental opposition to the Marxist view of language. Like all idealists, Cassirer subjectively seeks to portray the objective world as created by the synthetic powers of the human brain with the aid of language. However, his arguments are untenable. It is true that in the process of cognitive development, children and members of primitive societies struggle to distinguish between things (in both the natural and social realms) and language. But this fact does not prove that the objective world is constituted by the brain's synthetic abilities through language; on the contrary, it demonstrates that people can only gradually understand the objective world through continuous engagement with objective reality. If the synthetic ability is inherent in humans and the objective world is constructed by this ability, then humans should be able to construct the objective world from birth without continuous engagement with it. However, Cassirer cannot but admit that humans cannot construct the objective world at birth. This reveals the groundlessness of his theory. The truth is: humans do possess a high degree of synthetic ability, but the very reason this ability can function is determined by the synthetic stimulation of various characteristics of objective things on the human brain. People are compelled to make different syntheses in the face of different things, which sufficiently demonstrates that such syntheses operate under the determination of objective things. Moreover, synthetic ability is a function of the human brain, not of language. Even if, as Kant and Machists argued (and this is only a hypothesis), the human brain's synthetic ability could construct the objective world, the objective world would still not be constructible by language. Language certainly plays a role in social life, but this role is not to help people construct society; rather, it is to facilitate communication in social life and make human social life possible. The emergence of society is determined by the needs of production. When we say there can be no society without language, we do not mean that the objectively existing society is constructed by the synthetic abilities of the human brain with the help of language. Rather, we mean that the communicative function of language is a necessary condition for the existence of society. It should be noted that Cassirer's claim about the role of language in social formation refers to language assisting thought in creating the natural and social worlds. Thus, his theory treats language and thought as primary determinants of the objective world. In contrast, when Marxists say there can be no society without language, they are referring to the indispensable communicative role of language in connecting members of society within social life. The two perspectives share no common ground. Language certainly plays a role in people's cognition of objective things and social life, but this role is limited to being the carrier of abstract thought. By enabling abstract thought to be realized, language allows for the recognition and reflection of the objective world in its essence, rather than assisting thought in creating it. Since Cassirer inherited Kant's philosophy, which held that subjective synthetic abilities can create the objective world, he naturally misinterpreted the function of language. In reality, language can neither create the natural world nor the social world. It is merely an indispensable condition for social life, serving as a communicative tool and fulfilling its communicative function within society.

Section 2 The Function of Language in Embodying Thought

Cassirer's view of language as "the most vital and precious tool for conquering and creating a genuine world of objective things" is not without reason. As a follower of Kant's subjective idealist philosophy, Cassirer conceptualized the synthetic ability of the human brain (i.e., thinking ability) as the "matrix" for creating the objective world. Naturally, he regards language—closely intertwined with thought—as a tool by which subjective thinking constructs the objective world. The crux lies in the fact that while language and thought are indeed inseparably linked, this connection does not serve to aid thought in creating the objective world; rather, it enables thought to be embodied and fulfills thought's function of reflecting the objective world. Although language and thought are indissolubly connected, they are not identical. Thus, the functions of thought are not those of language: we cannot claim that language helps thought create the objective world, nor that the function of language lies in directly reflecting the objective world. Nevertheless, precisely because language is inseparably bound to thought, it plays a role in the generation of thought. Therefore, in addition to its communicative function, language also has the function of embodying thought.

The close connection between language and thought is a truth long recognized by scholars, but how this relationship manifests in terms of language's functions remains a matter of debate. Many linguists consider language a tool for expressing thoughts. They therefore argue that it has an expressive function. Since the so-called communicative function of language precisely refers to what Stalin described as "people using it to communicate with each other, exchange ideas, and achieve mutual understanding"[1], scholars held differing views on the relationship between language's expressive function and its communicative function. In his *Comments on "Some Theoretical Questions in Linguistics (Introduction)*", Chikobava stated: "Language (as a tool of communication) is a unique social phenomenon. Soviet linguistics defined language by its functions as a tool for communication and mutual understanding, and thus also as a tool for expressing thoughts (language, as the bearer of these functions, is a system of symbols); the communicative function is primary, while the expressive function (of thought) is subordinate, for if language ceases to be a tool of communication, it gradually loses its expressive function and no

1 Stalin, *Marxism and Problems of Linguistics*, p. 20.

longer remains a tool of thought."[1] He argued that language has both a communicative function and an expressive function, with the former being dominant and the latter subordinate. Budagov stated: "As in many of his previous works, the author [referring to himself] does not view language as 'hypothetical symbols', but as a tool through which people can communicate with one another, expressing their thoughts and emotions. The author is convinced that only this formulation of the problem can yield scientific results. Apart from the unity of the communicative function and the function of expressing thought, there can be no language and no science of linguistics. However, in recent times, linguists—both in foreign and Soviet linguistics—have largely tended to study language as a unique, closed system of 'communicative signs'. As a result, the most critical problem in linguistics—the relationship between language and thought—remains unilluminated, with almost no research being conducted on it. This book not only attempts to 'restore the balance' between the two most important functions of language—the communicative function and the function of expressing thought—but also seeks to demonstrate their constant and profound interaction. The author intends, throughout the entire scope of this book, to employ all his strength and resources to clarify the essence of language's fundamental functions and their interplay."[2] Here,

1 Chikobava, *Comments on "Some Theoretical Questions in Linguistics (Introduction)"*, in *Chinese Language*, No. 5, 1960, p. 229.
2 Budagov, *Introduction to the Science of Language*, Moscow, 1958, p. 3.

Budagov regarded both communication and thought-expression as fundamental functions of language, assigning them equal importance and denying any hierarchical dependence. His perspective clearly diverges from Chikobava's. In this context, how should we understand the issue?

As early as the beginning of the 19th century, Humboldt stated that language is a tool for expressing thoughts, but linguists have long held a vague understanding of this function of language. When explaining that language is a tool for expressing thoughts, linguists often regard both the act of verbalizing thoughts aloud and the act of silently contemplating thoughts without verbalizing or writing them down as instances of language expressing thoughts. This obscures the issue. In reality, verbalizing thoughts aloud is an act of expressing thoughts, while silently contemplating thoughts without verbalizing or writing them down using language cannot be called expressing thoughts, because "expressing" implies "making something manifest externally" and "reaching others". Silent contemplation involves neither manifestation nor reaching others, and thus does not actually express thoughts; it is merely the silent use of language for thinking. The phenomena of expressing thoughts and thinking without expressing thoughts are two distinct phenomena. Expressing thoughts is indeed an indispensable factor in communication. It is unimaginable to have communication using language as a tool without the expression of thoughts. The process of communication using language as a tool is essentially a process of expressing thoughts. "Exchanging ideas and achieving mutual understanding" constitutes the specific content of communicative activities that use language as a tool, and this communicative process is inseparable from the expression of thoughts. When thoughts are not expressed, communicative activities using language as a tool do not exist. However, there are instances—such as when a person recites aloud alone—where there is an act of expressing thoughts without actual communication taking place. Therefore, we can say that in any situation, the communicative function of language is always accompanied by its expressive function, but the expressive function of language is not necessarily always accompanied by communicative function. Nevertheless, cases of using language to express thoughts without engaging in communication are rare; they are in fact preparatory actions for communication (e.g., practicing a speech aloud) or unintentional vocalizations of language-based, non-communicative thought processes. In most cases, thought activities that use language as a tool involve the formation of inner speech—a process of employing language without vocalization—and preparatory actions for communication should not be confused with communication itself. The act of expressing thoughts without engaging in communication should be regarded as an occasional phenomenon of thought embodiment. In reality, regarding the relationship between language and thought, language serves both to express and embody thoughts. As the material foundation or "material shell" of thought, language is a necessary tool for thought to occur, be realized, or be embodied; without language, thought could not be embodied. However, thought itself is not a communicative activity; it is an internal mental process through which humans reflect the objective world, and it does not need to be expressed or conveyed to others at all times. More often than not, it proceeds in a silent state. People only need to express their thoughts to make them understood by others during communicative activities of "exchanging ideas and achieving mutual understanding". In our daily lives, we often observe situations where people think through problems while conversing with others, and the words spoken during such conversations do not necessarily represent the full content of their thoughts. This shows that expressing thoughts and embodying thoughts are two distinct activities, and the roles or functions of language in these two activities are also different. In her book *Judgment and Sentence*, Galkina-Fedoruk once stated: "To understand language as a tool of communication, it is necessary to distinguish between the embodiment and expression of sensations and emotions in language. Suppose someone feels a severe headache but does not think about it at all, merely crying out in pain: ǒu—ǒu—ǒu—ox—ox—ox. Is this a judgment? No, these cries are not sentences and do not express a judgment."[1] Although she discusses the distinction between expressing and embodying feelings and sensations rather than thoughts, her words inspire us to recognize that "expression" and "embodiment" are two different concepts representing distinct activities. Just as embodying

1 Galkina-Fedoruk, *Judgment and Sentence*, Moscow, 1956, p. 58.

feelings without communicating them to others does not constitute expressing feelings, merely embodying thoughts through mental activity without communicating them to others cannot be regarded as expressing thoughts. In the latter case, if there is no silent contemplation but rather solitary speech—speech that does not involve communication—what appears superficially as a non-communicative act of expressing thoughts is actually no different in nature from silent contemplation: it is a vocalized act of embodying thoughts. Therefore, such seemingly expressed mental activities should essentially be viewed as embodiments of thought. In short, when understanding the functions of language, it is necessary to distinguish between the roles of expressing and embodying thoughts. The function of expressing thoughts is in fact an indispensable adjunct to the communicative function, whereas the function of embodying thoughts is a separate matter. Based on this understanding, we can agree with Chikobava's argument that although the communicative function and the expressive function of language differ, the latter is merely an adjunct of the former. However, what Chikobava refers to as the expressive function encompasses what we call the function of embodying thoughts. From this perspective, we cannot agree with Chikobava's view that this function of embodiment should also be regarded as an adjunct to the communicative function. We can also agree with Budagov's argument that the communicative function and the expressive function of language are two distinct functions, both of which are fundamental to language—for his concept of the expressive function also subsumes what we call the function of embodying thoughts. However, Budagov's "expressive function" does not include what we define as the expressive function. From this standpoint, we cannot endorse Budagov's position of treating the expressive function—understood as subordinate to the communicative function—as fundamentally distinct from the communicative function. In other words, we also recognize two fundamental functions of language, but our understanding of these functions is that they are the communicative function and the function of embodying thoughts. These are the two functions performed by language as both a tool of communication and a tool of thought. For expressing thoughts is in fact the specific content of communication, making it an adjunct within the scope of the communicative function; it cannot be equated with the communicative function nor conflated with the function of embodying thoughts.

The function of language in embodying thought involves the distinction between thinking and thought. "Thinking" refers to the faculty of the human brain to reflect the objective world, as well as the activities of this faculty and the laws governing these activities. In general understanding, concepts and logical rules directly formed by this faculty are categorized under the scope of thinking. "Thought", on the other hand, refers to people's specific application of thinking—i.e., the activity of using concepts and logical rules in thinking as means to organize products such as judgments or inferences, and the products themselves. Thinking activities are the direct operations of the thinking faculty, while thought activities are the specific applications of this faculty. For example, the reasoning "All human actions in a class society carry class imprints; writing by humans in a class society is an action of individuals within social classes; therefore, writing by humans in a class society carries class imprints" is a product formed by people's specific application of numerous concepts and logical rules in thought activities, namely an inference. Does language have the function of embodying abstract thinking, or the function of embodying thought? Or does it have both? Separately speaking, language has both the function of embodying abstract thinking and the function of embodying thought. Language not only enables human abstract thinking activities to take place and be realized but also enables human thoughts to be actualized. As the material shell of concepts and logical rules, language makes abstract thinking possible; by turning concepts and logical rules into practical means for organizing thoughts, language serves as a medium for embodying thought. Without language as a material basis, naked abstract thinking could not exist. Since abstract thinking cannot be realized without language as its material substance, thought activities and their products based on abstract thinking would also be unfeasible. Therefore, language is both the embodier of abstract thinking and the embodier of thought. Precisely for this reason, scholars sometimes say that language embodies thinking, and sometimes that it embodies thought. When analyzing the issue in detail, we can certainly distinguish between language's functions of embodying abstract thinking and embodying thought, though this distinction does not frame the two as opposites. In reality, the function of embodying thought is integrated with the function of embodying abstract thinking. When language embodies abstract thinking, it simultaneously serves as a tool for embodying thought. These two should be regarded as two aspects—two inseparable aspects—of the same phenomenon. When people speak of language embodying abstract thinking, they are also implicitly addressing its role in embodying thought; when they speak of language embodying thought, they likewise imply its role in embodying abstract thinking.

The same applies to the expression of thinking and the expression of thought. Expressing thinking refers to conveying concepts and logical rules, while expressing thought involves conveying things like judgments or inferences—there is a distinction between the two. However, due to their inseparable connection, these are merely two aspects of the same process. Therefore, the distinction between them does not imply opposition or isolation. Thus, when people speak of language expressing abstract thinking, they inherently also refer to its role in expressing thought; when they speak of language expressing thought, they simultaneously imply its function in expressing abstract thinking. This issue will be further discussed when we examine the relationship between language and thinking; for now, based on general understanding, it suffices to note that the functions of language in embodying and expressing abstract thinking inherently encompass the functions of embodying and expressing thought.

Section 3 Other Functions of Language

Apart from the functions of communication and embodying thinking, does language have other functions? Since modern linguistics began addressing challenges like translation automation and summarization of scientific/technical documents (e.g., developing automatic translators and information machines), as well as designing self-reading machines, automatic stenographers, and language-controlled automated production devices, and improving communication capacity in wired/wireless circuits through efficient information coding, some linguists have argued that language also has a technical communication function. We do not deny that language plays a role in technical communication, but this role is in fact a specific manifestation of language's broader communicative function, for technical communication is a form of human communication. Therefore, we believe there is no need to list a separate "technical communication function" for language alongside its general communicative function, as the former is already subsumed within the latter.

What deserves discussion is the so-called representative function of language. In the 1930s, the German linguist K. Bühler proposed the idea that language has a representative function.[1] His proposition once sparked discussions in the linguistic community. In his article "Onomatopoeia and the Representative Function of Language"[2], he discusses the representative function of language through certain onomatopoeic phenomena in language. Bühler argued that "the tendency to depict through sounds exists not only in poetry but also universally in ordinary language. Overall, this is nothing more than a manifestation of people's efforts to use other tools in culture to eliminate the indirect characteristics inherent in ordinary language."[3] He stated that people always have a longing to establish a direct connection with the sensory world they perceive, and even feel the need to directly immerse themselves in the immediate sensory world. Generally speaking, language can only connect humans indirectly with the sensory world. Those who have learned to use sounds to interpret or make sense of the objective world deeply feel that the tools constructed by language and its specific rules isolate them from what their eyes can see, ears can hear, and hands can touch. They constantly seek to restore this intuition of the objective world without rejecting the use of sounds for representation. Therefore,

1 Bühler's term *Darstellungsfunktion* was translated as "function of exposition" by Cen Qixiang in his *General Linguistics* (Science Press, 1957, p. 79). The German word Darstellung inherently has two meanings: "exposition" and "representation", but in Bühler's original work, this term carries no connotation of "exposition" and instead refers to "representation". It is therefore revised here as "representative function".

2 According to the author's note, this essay is a chapter from his *Sprachtheorie* (Jena, 1933). The text appears in *Language Psychology*, pp. 101–119.

3 Bühler, *L'onomatopée et la fonction representative du langage*, in *Language Psychology*, p. 101.

Bühler argued that linguistic theories should recognize and explain where and how this return to the sensory world can be achieved without destroying language itself, and should explore whether and how such a sensory return is possible while remaining within the scope of language. To address his own questions, he posited that gaps allowing for this exist within language's structure, and only by integrating these scattered gaps can people form a unified field of representation (Darstellungsfeld). There are primary and secondary fields of representation (Darstellungsfeld), with onomatopoeic elements existing between them. Onomatopoeic elements also possess a representative function but do not form a complete field. If such a field were fully realized, language would cease to be language as we know it; however, language can permit at its margins a kind of auxiliary force—namely, onomatopoeic elements characterized by depicting objective sensations. Bühler argued that we may hypothesize that sound initially served the purpose of depiction, and that the sounds produced by humans inherently possess onomatopoeic capacity. Human voices have a rich timbre, far more varied than individual musical instruments (each of which has only one timbre), and they also exhibit numerous variations in length, pitch, and stress. The objective world has an auditory dimension, just as it has a visual one. Sounds surround us and are characteristic of many things that interest us. To recognize familiar objects, we do not always need to look out the window; our ears can inform us of what is happening outside. Thus, sound has a representational role. However, in language, sound cannot universally function as representation, for the formation of linguistic components is not fundamentally based on onomatopoeia. The connection between word meanings and sounds in vocabulary, as well as the formation of grammatical elements, are largely independent of onomatopoeic principles. Even from a linguistic perspective, phonemes in language follow specific rules: to express diverse meanings, a finite number of phonemes and their combinatorial patterns cannot adhere to an onomatopoeic principle. Nevertheless, phoneme theory offers an insight: the same phoneme can have multiple allophones. These allophones do not disrupt a language's phonological structure but leave room for people to use them to depict objective sensations or construct "sound pictures". This precisely constitutes a gap within or at the margins of language where the depictive function of sound can be employed to represent objective phenomena. He cited an example once given by Werner, noting that the German word Seife ("soap") exhibits a representational function. Soap is a gelatinous and foamy substance, and when analyzing the sounds of Seife, we can discern that the phonemes S, ei, and f each contribute to a kind of "sound picture". Each phoneme leaves a certain latitude for people to use it to depict the sensory representation of soap. This analysis can only be conducted after examining the phonological structure and its corresponding meaning. Seife designates "soap" through the phonological structure of the entire word; its connection to this meaning is determined by linguistic rules, not onomatopoeic principles. However, after analyzing the word's internal structure, we can examine how each phoneme, within the range of its allophones, serves a representational role. Of course, if we replaced ei with au to form Saufe, it might seem more "representational", but this is not permitted in language—for the similar word Saufen means "to get drunk", and the sound au does not represent the sensory characteristics of "drunkenness". Therefore, we can only say that at the margins of language, there is a role that allows people to use the onomatopoeic principle to represent direct sensations, and it is only in this context that onomatopoeic elements possess a representational function.[1] Bühler also discussed primary and secondary Darstellungsfelder (fields of representation), but he did not explicitly clarify in this paper what these fields entail. Nevertheless, many linguists still argue that language has a representational function, namely the function of expressing imagistic thinking. For example, the German Young Grammarian Paul (H. Paul) once argued that a sentence in language is "a sign through which certain representations or groups of representations are realized in the speaker's mind, and also a tool for evoking the same combination of these representations in the listener's mind."[2] The German linguist Wundt held a similar view.[3] What attitude should we take toward this theory?

1 Bühler, *"Onomatopoeia and the Representative Function of Language"*, in *Language Psychology*, pp. 101–110.
2 Paul, *Prinzipien der Sprachgeschichte* (*Principles of the History of Language*).
3 Wundt, *Völkerpsychologie* (*Ethnic Psychology*).

We do not deny that language has the function of expressing or embodying imagistic thinking, including sensations, perceptions, and mental representations. This function is manifested not only in the onomatopoeic elements discussed by Bühler but also in the semantic coloring of linguistic components. Metaphors used in language, for example, evoke imagistic thinking in both speakers and listeners through semantic analogy. Take the metaphor "Imperialism is a paper tiger" for example: it triggers imagistic thinking by linking the characteristics of imperialism with the image of a paper tiger. Ordinary linguistic expressions describing concrete images also powerfully convey or embody the imagistic thinking of both speakers and listeners. For instance, when we say, "Water was poured on my back; it was icy cold, and I felt uncomfortable," we clearly convey and express our own sensations, while also evoking similar feelings in the listener. These are precisely the characteristics of so-called "imaginative language". However, does this phenomenon warrant our treating the function of expressing or embodying imagistic thinking as a special function of language, equally as important as the communicative function (or the function of expressing thought) and the function of embodying thought? Our answer is no. It should be noted that one of the essential characteristics of language is its role as the carrier of abstract thinking; imagistic thinking is not necessarily embodied by language, and a large portion of it is not expressed through language. However, abstract thinking must be embodied or expressed by language, and language does not universally need to express or embody imagistic thinking—it only incidentally does so. As the carrier of abstract thinking, words in language always serve as embodiments or expressions of concepts in thought, while sentences composed of linguistic elements always serve as embodiments or expressions of judgments in thought. Without this function, words would cease to be linguistic components, and sentences would cease to be speech units composed of linguistic elements. Even in so-called onomatopoeic words or other imagistic words, the word first embodies or expresses a concept, with the expression or embodiment of imagistic thinking serving only as an incidental function. For example, in the sentence "Imperialism is a paper tiger", the term "paper tiger" first embodies or expresses the concept of "paper tiger"—a concept derived from our abstract thinking. When uttering this sentence, our primary intent is to convey our perspective on imperialism or our judgment about its characteristics, with "paper tiger" serving as the predicate of this judgment. However, in communicating our judgment, we intend for ourselves or others to derive or imagine the image of "paper tiger" from the objective concrete entity denoted by this concept. This phenomenon occurs because human abstract thinking is intertwined with imagistic thinking, and abstract thinking is in fact generalized from imagistic thinking. When a word in language embodies a concept directly generalized from the image of a concrete object in the objective world, the word can evoke both the concept and the corresponding image of the concrete object in the speaker or listener. This is precisely why, when literary works are written in language, the use of many such words denoting concrete objects to form sentences can evoke in readers both an understanding of the author's abstract portrayal of these objects and the specific images of the objects denoted by these words—hence why literary works are felt to possess "imagistic language". However, the so-called "imagistic language" does not mean it lacks abstract thinking; rather, it is that a layer of concrete imagery is more prominently presented against the backdrop of abstract thinking. Some literary theorists argue that the language of literary works is purely for expressing or embodying imagery, not abstract thinking. This view is incorrect. Although language can express or embody imagistic thinking, this is not an essential characteristic of language; moreover, imagistic thinking does not rely solely on language for existence or expression. Moreover, language does not necessarily have to express or embody imagistic thinking; when it does so, it is merely incidental to its expression or embodiment of abstract thinking. Therefore, the function of expressing or embodying imagery is not a fundamental role of language. It is only a byproduct of language's communicative function, which primarily involves expressing or embodying abstract thinking. We should not mistake this byproduct for one of language's basic functions, even though we do not deny that language can express or embody imagery in certain contexts.

That language has the function of expressing emotions and will is also acknowledged by linguists, but does this mean we can argue that expressing or embodying emotions and will is one of language's basic functions? Emotions and will are not forms of imagistic thinking, but rather conditioned reflexes controlled by the brain centers of the first signal system, and they are also intertwined with imagistic thinking. Due to the interweaving of imagistic and abstract thinking, words in language can express or embody judgments through their meanings—even the objective concrete objects reflected by these judgments and their contained concepts, or certain relationships between them—thereby expressing or evoking emotions in the speaker regarding these objects or relationships, or inducing similar emotions in listeners. Will is essentially a specific type of emotion, posing no unique theoretical challenges. In short, language does indeed have the function of expressing emotions and will. However, just as expressing or embodying imagistic thinking is a byproduct of language's function to express or embody abstract thinking, the function of expressing or embodying emotions and will is also a byproduct of language's core role in expressing or embodying abstract thinking. It cannot be regarded as a fundamental function of language.

Section 4 The Relationship Between the Communicative Function of Language and Other Functions of Language

Although language has many functions, there are only two

fundamental functions: the communicative function and the function of embodying thought. All other functions of language are in fact subsidiaries or byproducts of these two core functions. The function of expressing thought is a subsidiary of the communicative function and a specific mode of the function of embodying thought, as expressing thought is an indispensable component of communication. The function of expressing imagistic thought is a byproduct of the function of expressing abstract thought. The function of embodying imagistic thought is a byproduct of the function of embodying abstract thought. The function of expressing emotions or will is a byproduct of the function of expressing abstract thought. The function of embodying emotions or will is a byproduct of the function of embodying thought. The communicative function of language in its technical sense (e.g., in signaling or formal communication) is merely a specific manifestation of the broader communicative function.

So, what is the relationship between the communicative function of language and the function of embodying thought? Although the communicative function of language and the function of expressing thought are distinct, they are closely interconnected. Communicative activities that use language as a tool are simultaneously processes of expressing thought and ideas, for such communication is centered on “exchanging ideas to achieve mutual understanding”. The process of expression is also a mode of embodying thought and ideas, even though embodying thought and ideas does not always equate to expressing them. Thought appears to occur within an individual's mind, but it is fundamentally a social phenomenon. Thought is a social phenomenon because it arises from social labor, serves social labor, and proceeds on the basis of the intellectual achievements of others in society. The reason we seek to reflect objective things more profoundly is that we aim to understand them more deeply, so as to grasp their laws and engage in social labor to transform the world. Social labor also compels us to interact with various aspects of objective things, enhancing our cognitive abilities. Although individuals can engage in silent thought, and although thought may appear superficially to be carried out by each individual, it actually proceeds on the basis of an individual acquiring the intellectual achievements of others—the concepts others have already obtained. So-called individual thinking cannot occur in isolation from this foundation. Precisely for this reason, any so-called individual knowledge is in fact collective knowledge, for it is acquired by building on the achievements of others' thought and generating knowledge that benefits the thought of others. However, since the function of thinking is after all distinct from the communicative function—and since thinking can indeed take the form of individual activity (even though such individual thinking remains social in nature)—when language aids individuals in silent contemplation in non-communicative contexts, the function performed by language is not communicative but rather the embodiment of thought. The communicative function and the function of embodying thought are two irreducible functions of language. Nevertheless, communication using language as a tool is precisely concerned with the intellectual outcomes embodied in language, giving rise to a close connection between thinking and communication—and by extension, between the communicative function of language and its function of embodying thought. For the process of expressing ideas in communication is in fact a mode of embodying thought (a mode that embodies thought outwardly in communicative situations), such that the communicative function of language merges with its function of embodying thought in these contexts. It is only in the case of silent contemplation that the function of embodying thought does not coincide with the communicative function. In communicative situations, the communicative function combines with one mode of the function of embodying thought, and the function of embodying thought can also exist in non-communicative situations. It may seem that the communicative function is subsumed within the function of embodying thought, but when viewed from an essential perspective, the situation is the opposite. The language people use when thinking is the same as the language they use when communicating. Although people proficient in several languages may use a different language for thinking than for daily communication (for example, Chinese students studying in the Soviet Union who communicate in Russian on the streets of Moscow but think in Chinese in the dormitories of Moscow University), the language they use for thinking must always be a specific language that is used in some communicative context. So, what exactly is this language? It must be a language created by the people of a certain social group and understandable to all members of that society. In other words, it is a language that people can understand in specific communicative situations. There is no language, either in ancient or modern times, at home or abroad, that is specifically used for thinking and detached from the language used in communicative situations. Evidently, it is primarily the communicative function that makes language what it is; without communication, language would not be what it is today. The differences among various languages mainly stem from different communicative environments, rather than different ways of thinking. Different social groups have different communicative settings, but they do not have different thinking faculties or laws of thinking. Therefore, it is the communicative function that determines the formation of language and its role in social life in the first place. Viewed from this perspective, and in terms of the social nature of language, the communicative function is the more fundamental one. However, we cannot thereby claim that the function of embodying thought is not a basic function of language. Because when viewed from another angle, namely, that communication is in fact a way of embodying thought (i.e., expressing ideas), the function of language in embodying thought becomes extremely important. For without embodying thought, language would cease to be a tool for communication. Nevertheless, among these two basic and non-reducible functions, there is still a distinction between primary and secondary. The communicative function of language is more fundamental. This is because language, as a thing that can serve both as a communication tool and a thinking tool, with its specific linguistic, semantic, lexical, and grammatical structures, and its development into various variants (such as regional dialects and social dialects), depends more on the communicative environment than on the thinking environment. Moreover, what is expressed or embodied (thoughts) is precisely the specific content of communication, and in many cases, the embodiment of non-expressive thought serves as preparation for communication. Although thought is distinct from communication, it provides content for communication. The reason humans engage in thinking is to reflect objective laws, enabling the exchange of ideas and experiences in communicative contexts accompanied by social labor. Communication must be accompanied by thought, while thought, on the one hand, does not necessarily require the accompaniment of communication and, on the other hand, serves to provide content for communication. Thus, the formation of a symbolic system that can function both as a tool for communication and thought depends on communication. This is because a system capable of fulfilling the communicative function can simultaneously fulfill the function of embodying thought, whereas a symbolic system designed solely to embody thought without the communicative function cannot sustain itself as language. In conclusion, while we recognize that both communication and the embodiment of thought are fundamental functions of language—distinct in nature and irreducible to one another—they are closely interconnected. Among the two, the communicative function is more fundamental.

Section 5 The Role of Language's Functions in the Struggle for Production and Class Struggle

The communicative function and the function of embodying thought of language play a significant role in social life. The reason people use language in social life lies in its ability to embody thought, enabling thinking activities that reflect objective laws (whether natural or social) to take place, thus allowing people to grasp these laws and engage in the struggle for production and class struggle. At the same time, it lies in the ability to achieve mutual understanding and collaboration through the expression of ideas in specific communicative situations, so as to carry out the struggle for production and class struggle—even using this tool to conduct direct class struggle between different classes.

Although language is not a productive tool, it serves as an instrument in the struggle for production. While it cannot directly produce wealth like productive tools, it enables people to embody productive activities or acquire the knowledge necessary for the struggle for production. It allows for the exchange of ideas and knowledge, thereby promoting production, and facilitates collaboration among people in specific productive activities. Without language, human social labor would be unimaginable. Thus, Stalin stated: "In this sense, language is both a tool of communication and a tool for social struggle and development."[1] That language is a tool for the struggle for production is an easily understandable argument, but the idea that language is a tool for class struggle is generally misunderstood by most people. Due to language's lack of class character and its role as a communicative tool, many assume it serves only as a means of communication between different classes, not as a tool for struggle between them. This standpoint is incorrect. Certainly, language has no class character, but this does not mean that people of different classes cannot use this classless language to engage in class struggle—just as different classes use classless guns and artillery to wage class struggle. Language is undoubtedly a tool for communication between classes, but such communication can itself be a form of class struggle. In class-based societies, struggles between classes are constant, differing only in their forms. While the use of violence is obviously class struggle, "peaceful negotiations" can also constitute class struggle. When opposing classes are intricately linked, the forms of class struggle become diverse. Even communication that appears on the surface to be mere "etiquette" can serve as a form of class struggle. Therefore, even though language itself has no class character, among different classes that use the same language, what is commonly understood as ordinary communication can actually be a specific manifestation of class struggle. People use language to embody thought activities that reflect objective laws

1 Stalin, *Marxism and Problems of Linguistics*, p. 21.

and to impart various kinds of knowledge, all of which serve the purpose of class struggle. When members of the same class use language to communicate with each other, exchange ideas, and cooperate, it more clearly demonstrates the significant role of language in uniting and educating the members of the class for class struggle or coordinating the steps of class struggle. In 1940, Stalin, in connection with the national question, put forward the proposition that the language of one's own nation should be used as a tool for national development and for the struggle against national oppression and class rulers. Chairman Mao Zedong, the great leader of the Chinese people, further elaborated on the role of language in class struggle and developed this important thesis in Marxist language theory. He has pointed out more than once that language is a weapon in revolutionary struggle. He said, "We are revolutionaries working for the masses. If we do not learn the language of the masses, we will fail to do our work well."[1] He also stated, "*China Workers* will use popular language to explain many principles to the working masses, report on the realities of the working class's anti-Japanese struggle, summarize its experiences, and strive to fulfill its mission."[2] Guided by Chairman Mao Zedong's perspective on language, the June 6, 1951 editorial in *People's Daily* declared: "The correct use of language to express ideas holds great

1 Mao Zedong, *Oppose Stereotyped Party Writing*, in *Selected Works of Mao Zedong*, Volume 3, People's Publishing House, 1st edition, Beijing, February 1953, p. 858.
2 Mao Zedong, *Foreword to "China Workers"*, in *Selected Works of Mao Zedong*, Volume 2, People's Publishing House, 1st edition, Beijing, March 1952, p. 700.

political significance today in all the work led by the Communist Party.... Every document, report, newspaper, and publication of Party organizations and government agencies exists to propagate truth to the masses and indicate tasks and methods. They wield tremendous influence among the people; therefore, it is essential that all documents, reports, newspapers, and publications use proper language to express ideas, so as to ensure that these ideas are correctly grasped by the masses—only then can they generate proper material force."

In conclusion, as Stalin put it, "…individual social groups and classes are far from being indifferent to language. They try their best to use language to serve their own interests."[1] Although language has no class character, it is a powerful tool in class struggle.

The roles of language as a tool in the struggle for production and in class struggle are the specific manifestations in social life of language's functions of communication and thought reflection. When understanding these two basic functions of language, we should attach importance to such roles of language in social life. This is an important argument in Marxist language theory and also an important development of Mao Zedong Thought in Marxist language theory.

1 Stalin, *Marxism and Problems of Linguistics*, p. 10.

Chapter 3

Language and Communication

Section 1 Language and the Universal Social Unit

Since language has a communicative function, it becomes an indispensable tool in human social life and is simultaneously constrained by the social communication environment. Therefore, we must discuss certain characteristics of language from the nature of the social communication environment.

Language is a communicative tool used by people in their daily lives without interruption. Due to its close relationship with daily life, people living together must share a common language. Otherwise, if everyone spoke differently, communication would become difficult, and social life as we know it would be impossible. For this reason, a universal social unit often has only one language, which thus becomes a communicative tool commonly used by all members of that social unit.

But what exactly is a universal social unit? Generally speaking, it refers to a social group that lives together in a specific region due to production-related connections and other factors, shares a common psychological makeup, common customs and habits, and possesses independence. A universal social unit denotes the largest independent social complex formed at a certain stage in the developmental history of human society. When individuals live together, social life emerges. However, social complexes vary in nature. For example, the workers at the Shijingshan Iron and Steel Factory live together in the factory and form a social complex, but this complex is not a universal society; it is merely a small social group within the universal society. However, the Han nationality is a universal social unit, as it consists of an independent, largest social unit composed of men, women, and children who generally live in a specific region at the current stage of historical development and share common psychological characteristics (cultural traits) and customs. We say that the Han nationality is an independent largest social complex at the present stage because it cannot be subsumed within other ethnic groups such as the Zhuang nationality. The people of the Han nationality differ from those of the Zhuang, Tibetan, Yao, Miao, and other ethnic groups in psychological makeup and customs, and they all serve as independent social units (not politically independent entities). At the same time, we cannot identify a larger independent social group that includes the Han nationality and shares commonalities in psychological characteristics, customs, and living regions. Some may argue that the Han nationality is an ethnic group within the People's Republic of China, and the complex composed of all the people of China (people of all ethnic groups) is the independent and largest social complex. Of course, the People's Republic of China is a big family composed of many fraternal ethnic groups, but its unity is a political one, not a purely social combination. Although political units and social units are closely related, they also have their differences. Due to certain political reasons, different social units that have never lived together can suddenly become part of the same country, while people from the same social unit can belong to different countries. For example, the Korean people living in northern Korea form the Democratic People's Republic of Korea, while those living in China are citizens of the People's Republic of China. From the perspective of social integration, the Han nationality is the largest independent complex. Even citizens of American nationality living in Chinatown, New York, are still members of the Han national social unit. When we say a universal social unit is independent, this contains two meanings: (1) it is independent in terms of psychological makeup (cultural characteristics) and customs, and is not the same as other universal social units in these aspects; (2) it is not subordinate to other social units. The Han and Zhuang nationalities are independent from each other in psychological makeup and customs, and the Han nationality is not subsumed within any other social unit with the same psychological makeup and customs. Therefore, it is a universal social unit. As members of a universal society share commonalities in psychological makeup and customs, they also have various close connections in their lives. For the purpose of mutual communication, exchanging ideas, and achieving mutual understanding, they often use the same language, which thus becomes an important factor sustaining this complex. Therefore, Stalin stated: "Language, as a tool for people's communication in society, is unified and common to the entire society; it serves all members of society equally regardless of their social status."[1] He also said: "History tells us that a national language is not class-based but universal. It is a language common to the members of the nation and unified for the entire nation."[2]

Of course, universal social units belong to the category of history. In different historical periods, the conditions of universal social units vary. The organization of social units has both a formal aspect and a substantive aspect. These two aspects are interconnected and both develop as the wheel of history turns. The progression of society from primitive communist society to slave society, then from slave society to feudal society, from feudal society to capitalist society, from capitalist society to socialist society, and even to communist society—this represents changes in the substantive content of social organization, that is, qualitative transformations in social organization. However, society can also undergo changes in its organizational form, developing from primitive clan society to tribal society, from tribal society to tribal union society, and from tribal union society to nation-state society.... However, the term "nation" can be understood in both broad and narrow senses. In its broad sense, any largest social unit or

1 Stalin, *Marxism and Problems of Linguistics*, p. 9.
2 Stalin, *Marxism and Problems of Linguistics*, p. 10.

universal society in any era—including clans, tribes, and tribal unions—can be called a nation. In its narrow sense, only the further-developed largest universal unit of social organization that emerges after tribal union society is termed a nation. Of course, the qualitative changes in social organization are linked to its formal changes. Generally speaking, clan society is the organizational form of primitive communist society, while tribal union society is the organizational form of feudal society. However, because these are after all different aspects, there may be overlapping cases; for example, tribal society could belong to either slave society or feudal society. Universal social units are explained from the perspective of social organizational forms; therefore, with the development of society, universal social units may differ across different eras. Clans, tribes, tribal unions, and nations with different psychological characteristics and customs represent distinct universal social units across various eras. To meet the communication needs of all members within these different universal social units of each era, there emerged corresponding clan languages, tribal languages, tribal union languages, and national languages. These languages are all universal, as they serve as collective communicative tools for all members of their respective social units. Even within the same universal social unit, qualitative and formal changes may occur during historical development according to its specific conditions, and its language will evolve from clan language to tribal language, then from tribal language to tribal union language, and further to national language along with the transformation of social organizational forms.

Of course, there are various special circumstances in the process of historical development. For example, a universal social unit may split into many semi-independent units for certain reasons, while independent social units may also be unified within the same political entity due to specific factors. In such cases, language exhibits unique characteristics. In the first scenario, this can give rise to numerous regional dialects. Take the society of medieval Han China, for instance: feudal separatism led to the emergence of various local dialects. In the second scenario, a common communicative language may develop. For example, within China's socialist big family, the language of the dominant ethnic group (the Chinese language) serves not only as the common language of the Han nationality but also as a shared means of communication among all fraternal ethnic groups. However, these circumstances do not undermine the universality of language or its role as a universal communicative tool. Even if semi-independent social units emerge in different regions, and the local population speaks only regional dialects rather than a common language, this does not deny the universality of language. When a universal society splits into semi-independent regional groups, language naturally diversifies into different local dialects along with changes in the scope of communication. When language differentiates into local dialects, these dialects are essentially regional variants of the universal common language—the regional embodiments of the national tongue. In fact, a local dialect serves as the universal communicative tool within its region, thereby demonstrating the universality of language; it is precisely through such regional embodiments that language expresses its universality. However, because a region is a semi-independent social unit and a local dialect is a regional variant of the language, the regional society is only a quasi-universal society, and the local dialect thus only possesses quasi-universal characteristics.

It is obvious that language derives its universality from the scope of communication. However, some linguists deny this irrefutable fact and hold a skeptical attitude toward universal language. For example, in his *A. Hardy Pereunial: The problem of la langue and la parole*, N. O. W. Spence argued that there is no such thing as a language shared by all members of society. He stated, "The study of *la langue* (everywhere interpreted as the true object of linguistic study) is practically impossible, for one cannot hope to master 'the sum total of linguistic imprints stored in all individual minds.'"[1] He uses the differing ways of speaking between educated and uneducated English speakers, as well as between Parisians and Savoyard French speakers (who do not speak regional dialects), to prove that a universal language does not exist. He concludes, "Language is affirmed as a system of expressive tools potentially existing in the minds of all members of a linguistic society. However, even if we could explore 'the sum total of

1 N. O. W. Spence. *A. Hardy Pereunial: The problem of la langue and la parole*. In *Archivum Linguisticum*, 1957, 9 (1), pp. 6-7.

linguistic imprints stored in all individual minds', these imprints would not form a harmonious system of expressive tools, but rather what Roger calls *ein rein additives Gebilde* (a purely additive construct)."[1] This argument questioning the existence of a universal common language is a concrete manifestation of the scholar's agnosticism. If the fact that educated and uneducated English speakers speak differently proves that there is no common English language, then can anything in the world be proven to exist? Any individual or specific thing has its unique characteristics that distinguish it from the general characteristics of its broader category. This is precisely the inevitable manifestation of the dialectical relationship between the general and the specific. Spence is British and obviously looks different from us, but can we therefore claim that a common "human" does not exist? Linguistic elements reside in the speech of all members of a universal society: they are expressive means generalized from the utterances of these members, and language is the system of expression composed of these elements. The speech of individual members may contain certain unique linguistic elements that differ from those in others' speech, but this does not undermine the existence of a universal language. These unique elements are merely extreme exceptions and do not prevent individuals from using the universal common language to communicate

1 N. O. W. Spence. *A. Hardy Pereunial: The problem of la langue and la parole.* In *Archivum Linguisticum*, 1957, 9 (1), p. 20.

with others in society. The issue is clear: people use language for communication, and a language that is not understandable to all members cannot serve as a communicative tool for a universal society. If there were no universal common language, communication within a universal society would be impossible. Facts contradict Spence's claims, for they show that the very language Spence uses to articulate his arguments is understandable not only to all members of the English nation but even to a Han Chinese speaker like myself who has learned English. Everyone feels that they speak according to the language they acquired from society, even though they may occasionally coin a new word or grammatical element to construct their own expressions, or make mistakes in using vocabulary and sentence-formation rules. There may be minor differences in how individuals use language, but these personal idiosyncrasies are not the language itself. Linguists can study the entire system of the non-personal, universal common language and even attempt to establish its norms according to the internal laws of linguistic development. Therefore, the existence of a universal common language and the universality of language are beyond doubt.

Section 2 Language and Social Classes

The universality of language also explains why it has no class character. As a communicative tool shared by all members of society, language cannot be class-specific. This is because opposing classes within a universal society must rely on a common language to interact and conduct class struggle. It should be noted that universal societies do not necessarily have class divisions—for example, the clan societies of primitive communism had no internal class stratification. "It is evident that in classless societies, there is no such thing as a class-based language. The primitive clan commune system was classless, so naturally there could be no so-called class-based language; at that time, language was common and unified for the entire group of people."[1] Then, in class societies, does language have class character? If language were class-based, its emergence, development, decline, and structure would be governed by class rather than by the universal society. However, history shows that languages in all eras and places have formed with the emergence of universal social units, developed with the growth of universal societies, declined with their disintegration, and acquired a unified structure alongside them. They have never risen or fallen with the rise and fall of classes, nor developed different structures due to class distinctions. The Chinese language has been created and developed over thousands of years by our ancestors and the entire Han people throughout historical development. It was not invented or exclusively used by any particular class in Han society, nor has it declined with the historical disappearance of certain classes among the Han people, nor developed different structures due to class divisions within the Han ethnicity. The Chinese language has historically served as a tool for communication and a

1 Stalin, *Marxism and Problems of Linguistics*, p. 9.

common language between feudal dynasties and oppressed peasants. Although the feudal class of the Han ethnic group has vanished with the passage of historical development, the language they once used did not die out as a result. Despite being a newly emerging class in capitalist society, the bourgeoisie has not refused to use the language passed down through history. Every language has its unique phonological system, semantic system, grammatical structure, and basic vocabulary. However, we have never seen such things as a "Han bourgeois grammar", a "Han bourgeois phonological system", or a "Han bourgeois basic vocabulary". We have never encountered a language that belongs not to any universal social unit but solely to a particular international class. Although the proletariat of Russia and that of the Han ethnic group are both part of the international proletariat, the Russian proletariat does not use the same language as the Han proletariat. On the contrary, the Russian proletariat uses the same Russian language as the former Russian bourgeoisie, and the Han proletariat uses the same Chinese language as the Han bourgeoisie.

That language has no class character seems like an obvious truth, yet some linguists—including those of the Marr school—argue that language is class-based. The French linguist Antoine Meillet once depicted the ancient Indo-European peoples as a "conquering nation with an aristocratic structure," sending out "enterprising individuals to wage wars and establish the rule of chiefs using Indo-European dialects in increasingly new regions."[1] He stated, "The unity of the Indo-European languages remains evident, as the chiefs of the Indo-European nations felt a deep sense of unity toward their people and generally spoke similar languages. The unity of the Indo-European languages reflects the unity of the aristocracy."[2] Meillet further argued that there were "social distinctions" within the common Indo-European language, which reflected the social divisions between the aristocratic class and the general populace of the "Indo-European nations." He divided Indo-European vocabulary into "noble terms" used by "chieftains" and "elders" as part of an "aristocratic" lexicon and "vulgar" colloquial words belonging to the lower classes. He also attempted to establish morphological distinctions between these two vocabularies, attributing most words and roots expressing the most important concepts to the "noble terms" of the aristocracy.[3] He claimed that the "Indo-European aristocratic language" was characterized by strictly regulated morphological types in word-formation, as well as regular alternations of the vowels e/o and zero forms. In contrast, he argued that the vulgar vocabulary of the lower classes was marked by expressive word-formation techniques such as consonant reduplication and "anomalous" prefixation. Most of the words he classified as "folk vocabulary" or "vulgar vocabulary" contained the vowel a, which he viewed as a regular vowel outside the

1 Meillet, *The Current State of Comparative Grammar*, in *Historical Linguistics and General Linguistics*, Second Series, Paris, 1938, p. 163.
2 Ibid., pp. 164–165.
3 Ibid., pp. 165–166.

alternation system. J. Vendryès also proposed the theory that modern French originated from the language of the Parisian bourgeoisie. He stated, "The formation of the French common language and its geographical development are closely linked to the political, economic, and social history of our country; the former cannot be understood without recognizing the latter. However, the French common language developed from the capital city and emerged within it from a specific social class: the bourgeoisie. Brunot has provided an excellent account of this fact: our common language, standardized in its seventeenth-century form, was the language of the Parisian bourgeoisie, the 'urban' language. The court first adopted it, followed by the provinces, and in using it, great writers endowed it with a force that eventually prevailed and endured..."[1]

Marxist linguist N. Ya. Marr plagiarized such views from Western European linguists to formulate his theory of language's class character, asserting that "until now, there has been no language outside of class"[2], "Japhetic linguistics denies the existence of languages outside of class; all languages, including those of European and Caucasian peoples—we repeat—are class-based, and not just later, but from the very beginning"[3], "There has never been a language outside of class; since the emergence of

1 Vendryès, *Le langage*, Paris, 1921, pp. 310–311.
2 Marr, *Baku Conference on Japhetic Studies and Marxism* (Russian edition), 1932, p. 17.
3 Ibid., p. 18.

vocal language, language has been class-based, serving as the language of the class that possessed all the means of production (including magical production) of that era"[1]. Marr regarded language as part of the superstructure, stating: "It follows that linear language, and especially vocal language, generally fall under the category of the superstructure based on the relations of production"[2], "Language, like fine arts and art in general, is a social value of the superstructure"[3]. He argued that all languages originated from the same source and shared the same beginning. The reason they have now become morphologically distinct is solely due to their respective backgrounds, that is, different degrees of social evolution. Marr strongly emphasized how language reflects the "society" of its time, claiming that specific facts of Japhetic languages could prove that all elements in language are determined by class and reflect the institutions of class society. He believed that sounds in language—not only vowels but also consonants—could sometimes be light and weak, easily transforming into similar sounds; at other times, they could be strong and hard, more stable. They could also have rising and falling tones, which, like corresponding social phenomena, signify the ebb and flow of "liveliness" among them, as well as the increase or decrease of "vitality" and "initiative". He stated: "All changes and interrelations of sounds, for spoken language

1 Ibid., p. 10.
2 Ibid., p. 25.
3 Marr, *General Course on Linguistic Theory,* in *Collected Works of Marr* (Russian edition), 1928, Vol. 2, p. 107.

as a tool of communication, derive their significance not as physiological phenomena but as manifestations of the relationships of social phenomena. Thus, the three stages of the pronunciation of T (T—d—d) signify its development in three successive eras: first within the same economic group, then within the same class, and later within the same clan system. Similarly, the rise and fall of tones also originated within the same economic groups and subsequent blood-related clan systems. The substitution of s and š represents a 'harmony' between two adjacent linguistic groups, akin to a consonance between two economic groups, two classes, or two ethnicities."[1] This is true of phonetics, and even more so of grammar. Marr argued that the earliest part of speech to emerge was the noun. In primitive times, even adjectives were uninflected "nouns". However, the formation of nouns themselves and verbs gave rise to various new forms, which emerged not only with the help of nouns that had become suffixes and markers but also through pronouns. Pronouns appeared simultaneously with the concept of private property; they were "possessive" nouns indicating personhood. The grammatical category of "gender" only emerged in language after the development of family and kinship terms (including bilateral or broader blood relations). Even in later eras, the human concept of blood relations remained tied to the concrete noun "brother". In prehistoric times, the conjunction *kaj* ("and") meant "brother". "Dog and

1 Cited in A. P. Andreyev, *Marr's Theory of Language*, Popular Bookstore, 1950, p. 26.

chicken" even means "dog brother chicken" in the languages of nations aware of blood relations, because he discovered that in the Georgian language, *da* means both "and" and "sister". He also argued that the distinction between direct and indirect cases in language reflects the class relations between dominators and the dominated, while the three degrees of adjectives (positive, comparative, superlative) reflect class titles—the positive degree representing the lower class, the comparative the middle class, and the superlative the upper class. In his view, therefore, the relationship between grammar and society proves that language is class-based. As for vocabulary reflecting social institutions and possessing class character, this seemed even more self-evident to him. Marr argued that during a prehistoric period, the word-formation process was "cosmic": at that time, there were few words that concretely represented all conceptualized cosmic forces, and each of them simultaneously signified many related conceptualized objects. For example, the word "bird" was understood in primitive times as "sky" or "a part of the sky"; its original meaning was literally "sky" or "many skies", and it was only through repeated semantic narrowing that it evolved into "small sky". Meanwhile, the word "bird" could also be interpreted as "cloud", "torch", "height", "blue", "mountain", "head", "pine tree", "beginning", "end", and so on. It was not until this "cosmic worldview"—in which, according to Marr, humans saw themselves as microcosms and regarded the limbs and organs of their bodies as parts of the surrounding world—passed that the process of "differentiating sounds" and associating meanings with sounds began. And this process of differentiation evolved in tandem with the progression of societal worldviews—from cosmic to ethnic and class-based. In short, according to the Marrist school, "there has never been, anywhere or at any time, any non-class-based vocal language. Consequently, it is unscientific and unrealistic to regard a language belonging to a so-called 'national culture' as the general parent tongue of the entire nation: 'a non-class-based national language remains a fiction'. In other words, all languages are class-based, and classless languages can only exist in classless societies."[1]

These are the arguments put forward by the Marrist school to support the claim that language has class character. While this conclusion may initially appear compelling, its underlying reasoning is so frail and unpersuasive that it collapses under even cursory scrutiny. For instance, what does it prove when sounds are sometimes soft and weak, sometimes hard and strong, with tonal variations allegedly signifying "liveliness"? Which class corresponds to soft and weak sounds, and which to hard and strong ones? Marr's assertion that the phonetic development of T through three stages "T—d—d'" reflects the progression of three class-based eras (T for the initial homogeneous economic group, d for the subsequent homogeneous class, and d' for the later clan system) is equally questionable. Why should d be designated as the pronunciation of the "subsequent

1 A. P. Andreyev, *Marr's Theory of Language*, pp. 33–34.

homogeneous class" era? Furthermore, in modern European languages, the phonemic contrast between /T/ and /d/ persists, with both sounds functioning within the same linguistic framework. Is this evidence that two different eras exist simultaneously? Can two distinct eras coexist? Some Chinese dialects distinguish between the phonemes /T/ and /d/, while others do not—does this prove they are products of different eras or classes? If pronouns are symbols of private property concepts, why do they still exist in Russian and Chinese today, long after the abolition of private ownership in the Soviet Union and China? Can we imagine that in a communist society, we would cease to use pronouns like "I", "you", "he", "we", "you", or "they"? Even if the prehistoric conjunction *kaj* meant "brother", what does this have to do with social systems or class? Is "brother" a term unique to a specific social system or class? And to which historical period does this so-called "cosmic worldview" supposedly belong? Which class does this worldview belong to after all? In China's Han Dynasty, there was the philosophical idea of "the unity of heaven and man", which is precisely a concrete manifestation of this "cosmic worldview". Did the Han people have to wait for this worldview to pass before they could begin to "differentiate sounds" and associate meanings with them? In short, all these arguments are extremely forced. No wonder Chikobava said: "When people assert that language is a class phenomenon, what exactly do they mean? Where, after all, have people observed the class character of language? This is unclear: the advocates of class character have not specified the criteria for class character. Those who claim that language has class character lack objective criteria sufficient to determine the class character of language."[1] In reality, the Marrist school never proved that language has class character. The reasons they advocated for the class nature of language included mistaking class dialects such as "aristocratic language" or "drawing-room language" for language itself upon observing their existence; assuming language has class character because it serves as a tool for class struggle and caters to class interests; or claiming that, like culture and ideology, language belongs to the superstructure and possesses class character due to their inseparable connection. In fact, these views are nothing but misunderstandings, not valid arguments.

In class societies, as each class strives to make language serve its own interests, class dialects emerge, along with special words and expressions. For example, in ancient China, scholar officials (士大夫) would intersperse their speech with so-called "书腔" (scholarly tones). They referred to their own wives as "拙荆" (my humble thorn-bush, a self-deprecating term) or "贱内" (my lowly inner one), while addressing others' wives as "嫂夫人" (Madame Sister-in-Law) or "尊夫人" (Esteemed Madame). Their own parents were called "家严" (my strict father) and "家慈" (my kind mother), whereas others' parents were addressed as "令尊" (your honorable father)

1 A. C. Chikobava, *Introduction to Linguistics*, Higher Education Press, 1954, Part I, Volume I, p. 33.

and "令堂" (your honorable mother). Other examples include "寒舍" (my humble abode), "府上" (your esteemed residence), "马齿" (horse teeth, a polite term for age), "高足" (noble disciple), "足下" ("you", literally "under your feet"), "清玩" (refined curios), and "雅量" (generous tolerance)—the list is endless. Some writers have termed this phenomenon "士大夫语言" (scholar-official language) and labeled such specialized vocabulary used by nobles, capitalists, workers, and farmers as "aristocratic language", "bourgeois language", "worker language", and "peasant language". Proponents of the class language theory thus argue that language has class character. In reality, however, such phenomena belong only to "class dialects", not to language itself. These terms are merely special additions to the common language of the Han ethnic group, just as individuals may introduce personal idiosyncratic words into the common language without leading anyone to claim that language is a personal phenomenon. Therefore, we cannot assert that each class has its own distinct language. As Engels stated: "The workers speak a different patois (i.e., 'class dialect') than the bourgeoisie, have different ideas, concepts, customs, and moral principles, a different religion and politics."[1] This shows that he clearly identified these as class dialects, not languages. Class dialects are merely branches or variants of a language, emerging from its differentiation but never evolving

1 Engels, *The Condition of the Working Class in England*, cited in Stalin, *Marxism and Problems of Linguistics*, pp. 12–13.

into independent languages. They lack their own grammatical structures and basic vocabulary, and are not uniformly used by all members of the same class within a social unit. We have never denied that the language spoken by the Han working class is Chinese, even though we sometimes metaphorically refer to this working-class dialect as "worker language". As Lafargue stated: "The artificial language mastered by the nobility... is derived from the national language spoken by both property owners and artisans, urban dwellers and rural residents."[1] His explanation is explicit. Thus, regarding the class character of class dialects as evidence for the class nature of language itself is a misunderstanding.

In class societies, class struggle is indeed ruthless and intense. It permeates all human activities, including the use of language. Language is undoubtedly a powerful tool in class struggle. However, this does not mean that language itself is class-based. Class struggle and the tools of class struggle are two distinct concepts. In class struggle, people employ everything at their disposal to fight, yet not everything used in class struggle possesses class nature. When China's proletariat conducted class struggles, they once utilized guns, water, fire, stones, wooden sticks, donkeys, horses, dogs, rabbits, and other such things, none of which have class attributes. Not only do natural objects used as weapons in struggle lack class nature, but even certain social phenomena employed as combat tools may be non-

1 Stalin, *Marxism and Problems of Linguistics*, p. 14.

class-based. For example, leveraging locally observed customs to engage in class struggle. Thus, we cannot conclude that language has class nature merely because it serves as a tool in class struggle. Whether something has class nature depends on whether its emergence, development, and decline are determined by classes, whether it is exclusive to one class and rejected by another, and whether it has a structure that caters to the special interests of a class. The birth, development, and disappearance of language are not determined by classes but by the entire society (including the role played by classes). Moreover, as a tool for communication, language serves as both a means of interaction and struggle among classes within the same societal unit of the entire population. Class struggle does not imply the complete fragmentation of society. As Stalin noted: "These comrades mistake the opposition between bourgeois and proletarian interests, and the fierce class struggle between them, for a complete split in society, for the severance of all ties between two hostile classes. They argue that since society is divided and there is no longer a unified society—only classes—there is no need for a unified language for the whole society or a national language." If society is completely divided and there is no national language for the entire population, what remains? Only classes and "class languages". Naturally, each "class language" would have its own "class-specific" grammar: "proletarian" grammar and "bourgeois" grammar. In reality, such grammars do not exist anywhere in the world. Yet this does not embarrass these comrades; they believe such grammars will surely emerge.[1] Thus, the communicative function of language and the scope of its communicative role determine that it cannot have class nature. As a tool for communication, language is commonly used by opposing classes with "countless economic ties" within the same societal unit to interact and engage in class struggle. This very characteristic of language is a fundamental reason why it lacks class nature and possesses a national, all-people character.

Language is indeed inseparably linked to culture and thought. However, language does not acquire class nature merely because culture and thought are class-based. Although language is intertwined with culture, it is not identical to culture. Whether language has class nature depends on whether its own essential characteristics are class-based, not on whether the things associated with it are class-based. As Stalin stated: "These comrades cite Lenin's words about two cultures under capitalism, apparently hoping to convince readers that since there exist two cultures in society—bourgeois and proletarian—there should also be two languages, as language is linked to culture. They conclude from this that Lenin denied the necessity of a unified national language and thus advocated for 'class-based' languages. The error here is that these comrades equate language with culture and confuse the two. In reality, culture and language are distinct: culture can be bourgeois or socialist, but language, as a tool of communication, is always

1 Stalin, *Marxism and Problems of Linguistics*, pp. 15–16.

national and all-people in character. It can serve both bourgeois culture and socialist culture."[1] Language is certainly closely connected to thought, but it is merely the embodiment or expression of thought, not thought itself. Therefore, the class nature of thought does not dictate that language must also have class nature. We will elaborate on this issue further below, so we will not dwell on it here.

In summary, because language serves as a tool for communication and there is a necessity for communication between classes, language becomes a means of interaction among all classes. As a result, it possesses a universal character. Language is not a class phenomenon, even though classes can use it to engage in class struggle.

Section 3 Language and the Superstructure

Those who argue that language has class nature believe they can prove their point by citing two facts: language serves as the embodiment or expresser of thought, and the ideological component of thought belongs to the class-based superstructure. In reality, however, such so-called "evidence" is unconvincing. It is true that the superstructure and ideology are class-based, but the close connection between language and thought (ideology) or the superstructure does not endow language with class nature. The crux of the matter lies in the fact that language is neither equivalent to the

1 Stalin, *Marxism and Problems of Linguistics*, p. 7.

superstructure nor to ideology. It is merely the embodiment or expressive means of the ideological elements within the superstructure, constituting a distinct entity that is linked to but different from ideology. Two closely related things can each possess unique characteristics; they are not necessarily bound to share the same essential traits. Whether language has class nature should be determined by its own attributes, rather than being arbitrarily inferred from the class nature of the entities with which it is associated.

Language and the superstructure have many different characteristics. The superstructure consists of society's views on politics, law, religion, art, philosophy, as well as the political and legal institutions suited to these views, and it has a distinct class nature. Every base has a corresponding superstructure. When the base changes or is eliminated, the superstructure will change and be eliminated along with it; when a new base is about to emerge, a new superstructure will also arise. However, language is not like this. Of course, language also develops with the development of society, but unlike the superstructure, it does not undergo qualitative changes with the transformation of the base. After the founding of the People's Republic of China, the economic base of our country underwent qualitative changes, and so did the superstructure. However, the Chinese language did not undergo qualitative changes. Although many new words were added and many old words were eliminated, the basic vocabulary and grammatical structure of Chinese did not undergo complete transformation.

Fundamentally, the Chinese language remains the same as it was before the founding of the People's Republic of China. The superstructure is not merely a reflection of the base; it is not passive or neutral, nor is it indifferent to the fate of its own base, the fate of classes, or the nature of the social system. On the contrary, once the superstructure emerges, it becomes a powerful active force that aids in the formation and consolidation of the economic base, employing all means to help the new system destroy and eliminate the old base and old classes. Today, the struggle between the proletariat and the bourgeoisie in China on the political and ideological fronts serves precisely to consolidate and develop the socialist base and facilitate the arrival of the communist base. However, language is not generated by any specific old or new base within a society. Instead, it is the product of the entire historical process of society and the economic base over thousands of years. As a communicative tool for the entire population, language does not serve a single class but the entire society. It can serve both old declining systems and new rising systems, as well as both old and new economic bases. Modern Chinese once served the base of semi-feudal, semi-colonial bureaucratic capitalist old China and is now serving China's socialist construction, playing an even greater role in communication. The superstructure is a product of the era alongside the economic base from its emergence to its active period or shortly after its demise, existing concurrently with the class it serves in all aspects. Its lifespan is short. By contrast, language is the product of many eras, far outlasting any economic base or superstructure. In the historical development of the Han ethnic group, there have been several changes in the economic base and the superstructure, yet the Chinese language has existed for thousands of years without undergoing a qualitative transformation of the entire language. The superstructure has no direct connection with production or human productive activities. It is only indirectly linked to production through the intermediaries of the economy and the economic base. The political program of the superstructure can only alter the nature of production and productive activities through revolution—overthrowing the old economic system and establishing a new economic base. The superstructure does not directly or immediately reflect changes in the level of productive forces; instead, through the "refraction" of productive changes onto various modifications of the base, it reflects such changes only after the economic base has been transformed. For example, in the United States, changes in production levels have not been immediately reflected in the superstructure due to the absence of a revolutionary transformation of the economic base, whereas in China, the revolutionary transformation of the base has led to obvious reflections of production-level changes in the superstructure. By contrast, language is directly linked to human productive activities and even all other human behaviors. Therefore, language reflects changes in production directly and instantaneously. For example, with the invention of steam operations in production, the language immediately reflected this change, giving rise to words such as "steam engine".[1] Since language and the superstructure differ in so many fundamental aspects, language cannot be categorized as part of the superstructure. Therefore, the fact that the superstructure has class nature cannot prove that language has class nature. One type of superstructure serves only a specific class within the entire society and belongs to that class, emerging, developing, and dying out along with the class's birth, growth, and demise. However, as a communicative tool for all of society, this very characteristic of language determines the distinction between language and the superstructure.

Section 4 The Essence of Language Characteristics

Because communication is language's most fundamental function and language employs a symbolic system to fulfill this role, the universality of language is inherently reflected in its symbolic structure. Language symbols are universal, as they are to be used by all members of society. Of course, when individuals learn a language, they may not master all the symbols within it. However, this does not deny the universality of language symbols. Universality refers to the inherent property of language symbols, not whether they have been fully mastered or utilized by the entire population. For example, atomic nuclei have the property or characteristic of being

1 See Stalin, *Marxism and Problems of Linguistics*, pp. 1-8.

capable of a powerful explosion. This characteristic existed even before it was discovered by humans. Whether atomic nuclei have the property of powerful explosion does not depend on whether someone has discovered or utilized it. Similarly, the symbols in a language are universal, not because they are necessarily mastered or used by all members of society, but because they possess the inherent capacity to be mastered and used by all members of society. The class-specific vocabulary of class dialects possesses class nature rather than universality not because it is mastered or used by all members of a particular class (in reality, not every lexical item in a class dialect is mastered or used by all class members), but because it has the inherent capacity to be mastered or used by all members of that class—and the capacity to remain unmastered or unused by members of another class. Even if members of a hostile class become aware of the special terms in an opposing class's dialect, they will not use them, and may even refuse to do so. For this very reason, the special terms of class dialects or individual speech characteristics do not belong to the symbolic system of language, but rather fall within the scope of language's special variants. All linguistic elements within the language's symbolic system (including symbols from various language variants that have entered the language) are universal, because language is a communicative tool for the entire population. Cen Qixiang stated in his General Linguistics: "The vocabulary of a language is the sum total of all the words in that language." However, words in a language are of various types: some are exclusive to certain professions, some to specific disciplines, some to particular social groups, and others are class idioms (i.e., class dialects). These are all what we refer to as social idioms[1]. In addition, there are words used universally by all people in the same society regardless of profession, social stratum, or educational level—these constitute what we call the basic vocabulary. Generally speaking, the basic vocabulary is narrower in scope than the total vocabulary, has a longer lifespan, and has the capacity to form new words; it is universal in nature.[2] Here, Cen Qixiang argues that only basic vocabulary possesses universality, while other words do not, yet they are still members of the language's vocabulary. This view is clearly problematic. We agree that words in the basic vocabulary are universal. But does the universality of basic vocabulary stem from the fact that they are commonly used by all people? No one can guarantee that they have used or mastered all the words in the basic vocabulary. However, words in the basic vocabulary remain part of the basic vocabulary because they possess the inherent capacity to be mastered or used by the entire population, and they also have other characteristics that will be explained below. It is not just the words in the basic vocabulary; even words outside the basic vocabulary are not necessarily lacking in universality. Only the special terms of community dialects or individual idiolects lack universality.

1 "Social idioms" are what we refer to as "community dialects".
2 Cen Qixiang, *General Linguistics*, Science Press, 1957, p. 83.

The language symbol system is in fact the sum of lexical and grammatical components and their structural relationships. Not only do lexical components have universality, but grammatical components also possess it. Only extremely individual special grammatical elements lack universality. The universality of language symbols is a necessary byproduct of the language's universality. Since language is a communicative tool for the entire population, its various symbols naturally exhibit universality. If this were not the case, they could not fulfill their function as a communicative tool for all.

However, since the universal communicative roles played by various symbols in language are unbalanced, and their functions within the linguistic structure also differ in significance, the symbols in language can be classified into categories based on their distinct roles in public communication. Grammatical structure is an indispensable component of linguistic structure, which is consistently utilized by all language users in communication irrespective of conveyed content. As it is constantly employed in communication, it is the most stable and least prone to change. Basic vocabulary is also frequently used by communicators, making it highly stable and less likely to undergo changes. Other lexical components in language, while universal, are not regularly used by the general public. Consequently, they are more prone to change and exhibit greater fluidity. Because language uses a system of symbols as its communicative tool, symbolicity is also an essential characteristic of language. This, however, refers to the general properties of language. When it comes to why language can be distinguished from other symbol systems and why specific languages can be differentiated from one another, their essential characteristic lies in the fixed and rule-governed structure formed by the constant exercise of their communicative function—the basic vocabulary and grammatical structure that enable a language to exist as a language and differentiate it from other languages. Basic vocabulary and grammatical structure are the structures within language that make it a fixed, rule-governed symbol system distinct from other symbol systems. They are the structures of the linguistic symbol system that allow languages to differ from one another, and they constitute the foundation of language—why language is language, and why each individual language is distinct from others. Stalin stated, "The grammatical structure (i.e., syntactic structure) and basic vocabulary of a language are its foundation and the essence of its characteristics."[1] By "the essence of language characteristics" is meant that, regarding language as a special symbol system and the distinctions between specific languages, these are essential characteristics. Every language has its own "essence of characteristics", which differ from those of other languages. When there is eventually only one language for all humans, this "essence of characteristics" will remain the fundamental factor distinguishing language from other symbol systems or phenomena.

1 Stalin, *Marxism and Problems of Linguistics*, p. 24.

The grammatical structure of language is familiar to linguists and requires no elaboration. What, then, is the basic vocabulary of a language? Generally, it is considered that the basic vocabulary of a language consists of a collection of stable, productive, and universal words, with root words at its core. Some argue that basic vocabulary also has the characteristic of "neutrality", meaning words without stylistic coloring. However, whether a word belongs to the basic vocabulary cannot be determined by its stylistic coloring. Style is a historical category that emerges only at a certain stage of language development.[1] Yet basic vocabulary exists at all times in the history of a language. This shows that stylistic coloring cannot serve as a criterion for whether a word belongs to the basic vocabulary. Moreover, certain words with stylistic coloring, such as "妈妈" (māma, mommy) and "母亲" (mǔqīn, mother), can hardly be excluded from the basic vocabulary. The words of the basic vocabulary are indeed those with a long history and greater stability, and they are also words with strong productivity. However, the most crucial characteristic of basic vocabulary lies in its universal and frequent usage by all members of society. Cen Qixiang argues that the defining feature of basic vocabulary is its universality[2]. We contend that universality alone is insufficient to explain the characteristics of basic vocabulary. As a communicative tool for all, even the general vocabulary of

1 Cf. Gao Mingkai, *The Content and Tasks of Linguistic Stylistics*, in Linguistic Essays, Fourth Series, Shanghai Educational Publishing House, 1960, pp. 187–188.
2 Cen Qixiang, *General Linguistics*, p. 83.

a language possesses universality. The key distinction is that basic vocabulary is constantly used by the entire population. Words not frequently used cannot play a special role in communication and thus cannot serve as the foundation of language or its "essential characteristics". Universal and frequent usage is, in fact, the primary feature of basic vocabulary. Precisely because basic vocabulary is used frequently, it exhibits great stability and is slow to change. The things it designates (e.g., natural phenomena like "mountain", "water", "tree", "wood"; production tools like "knife", "axe"; social relationships like "father", "mother", "son", "daughter", etc.) are everyday concepts that people have consistently needed to describe throughout history, deeply intertwined with the fabric of life over time. Precisely because basic vocabulary is frequently used, many other words are derived from it. In other words, the reason why basic vocabulary becomes the foundation of a language is due to the communicative function of language. Words that are frequently used in communication become the basic vocabulary of a language. Needless to say, the core of basic vocabulary-root words, which serve as the basis for derived words-is the part with the longest history among the words that are frequently used by the entire population. Owing to their long-standing frequent usage, these root words naturally become the most stable and productive words. Since the main characteristic of basic vocabulary lies in its universal and frequent usage by all members of society, during the process of historical development, words that do not have a long history but have the characteristic of likely existing for a long time due to frequent usage, along with their related derived words, may become components of basic vocabulary. Words such as "cadre" and "proletariat" in Modern Chinese, although not having a long-standing history, are nevertheless of the nature of components of the basic vocabulary of Modern Chinese.

Both the basic vocabulary and the grammatical structure in a language are highly stable and not easily subject to change. The stability of these essential parts of a language, which represent its fundamental characteristics, reflects the overall stability of the language, despite the fact that the general vocabulary in a language can change rapidly. This stability of language is manifested in its characteristic of gradual change, in its characteristic of "being realized through the gradual accumulation of new-quality elements... and the gradual decline of old-quality elements"[1], and in its characteristic of expanding and improving basic components. In fact, these characteristics are all derived from the social essence of language as a universal communicative tool. The basic vocabulary and grammatical structure in a language do not simply refer to basic words and grammatical components. Basic vocabulary is a collection of basic words, and grammatical structure is a system composed of grammatical components. Individual words in the basic vocabulary can be changed, and individual grammatical components in the grammatical structure can be modified, but

1 Stalin, *Marxism and Problems of Linguistics*, p. 26.

this does not mean that the basic vocabulary and grammatical structure have undergone a qualitative change. In recent years, undoubtedly, certain individual grammatical components in Modern Chinese have been modified. For example, structures like "作为……的……" (as...) have emerged. Also, undoubtedly, some individual basic words have been added or changed. However, this is insufficient to demonstrate that the grammatical structure and basic vocabulary of Modern Chinese have undergone a qualitative change, and thus that the Chinese language has undergone a qualitative change. In *A Draft History of the Chinese Language*, Wang Li holds that "if the development of a language represents a qualitative change, it should be considered that a historical period has been transformed"[1]. Subsequently, he divides the historical development of the Chinese language into the ancient period, the medieval period, the modern period, and the contemporary period. He believes that "the characteristics of the ancient period are: (1) the copula had not emerged; (2) in negative and interrogative sentences, the object pronoun was placed before the verb; (3) there were two types of entering tones (one of which changed to departing tones in later generations), and so on." The characteristics of the medieval period are: (1) the emergence of copulas; (2) the development of causative and dispositional constructions; (3) the rise of the passive construction with "被"

1 Wang Li, *A Draft of the History of Chinese Language* (Volume I), Science Press, 1957, p. 33.

(bèi); (4) the appearance of suffixes such as "儿" (ér), "子" (zi), "了" (le), and "着" (zhe); (5) the origin of falling tone characters, etc. The characteristics of Modern Chinese (late imperial period) include: (1) the disappearance of voiced obstruent initials in northern dialects; (2) the loss of final [-m] in northern dialects; (3) the extinction of entering tones in northern dialects, etc. The characteristics of contemporary Chinese are: (1) the appropriate absorption of Western grammatical structures; (2) the substantial increase in disyllabic and multi-syllabic words, etc.[1] We argue that while individual linguistic components can indeed change, the alteration of each component does not equate to a change in the language as a whole. The qualitative change or leap of an entire language is achieved precisely through the accumulation of changes or qualitative shifts in its individual components. Since the essence of linguistic characteristics lies in its grammatical structure and basic vocabulary, whether a language has changed in nature depends on the degree to which its "new qualitative elements" have accumulated and the degree to which the decline of "old qualitative elements" has accumulated. It depends on whether the result of this accumulation has caused changes in the overall appearance of the language's basic vocabulary (not individual basic words) and grammatical structure (not individual grammatical components). Wang Li only cites a few changes, some of which are merely phonetic changes, and these

1 Ibid., p. 35.

changes hardly prove that Chinese has undergone three qualitative changes in its historical development. Wang Li agreed with Sanxiyev's proposition, arguing that "to determine the moment when a language transitions from one quality to another, one must first rely on changes occurring in the grammatical structure of that language"[1]. Since grammatical structure is the most stable part of a language, we also agree that observing qualitative changes in language should take the qualitative change of grammatical structure as the primary criterion. However, Sanxiyev did not claim that qualitative changes in just a few grammatical components would signify a qualitative change in grammatical structure or, by extension, a qualitative change in the language itself. We also agree to divide the history of Chinese into four periods: ancient, medieval, modern, and contemporary. However, the criteria for periodization are not necessarily all based on qualitative changes in the language, although they are related to the qualitative changes in linguistic components. Just as dividing the history of the Soviet Union into the Lenin era and the Stalin era does not imply that Soviet society underwent another qualitative change or revolution, why, then, should the division of Chinese linguistic history into four periods—Ancient, Medieval, Early Modern, and Modern—necessarily imply that Chinese has experienced three qualitative shifts or leaps?

1 Sanxiyev, *On the Characteristics of Qualitative Change in Language*, in *Philosophical Problems in Stalin's Linguistic Works (Sequel)*, p. 108.

Does the essence of linguistic characteristics include phonological structure? Stalin did not discuss phonological structure, but this does not mean he ignored phonetic issues. Every component in language is a combination of phonetic form and semantic meaning; lexical and grammatical components are both unities of sound and meaning. When discussing vocabulary and grammar, we inherently address phonetics, as no lexical or grammatical component can exist without a phonetic form—even a phonetic zero form. Certainly, the rules of phonological structure in language have their own independent characteristics, but these characteristics are also analyzed from lexical and grammatical components and are simultaneously reflected in the phonetic forms of these components. Therefore, when stating that basic vocabulary and grammatical structure constitute the essence of linguistic characteristics, we in fact include the phonetic features of basic vocabulary and grammatical structure. However, mere phonetic changes do not signify qualitative changes in lexical or grammatical components. Consequently, we cannot conclude that a language has undergone qualitative change solely due to pure phonetic shifts.

In summary, the basic vocabulary and grammatical structure of a language constitute its stable core—the very essence that defines language as such and distinguishes one specific language from another. Their status as stable elements and the defining features of language is determined by language's communicative function and its universality across society.

Since these components are constantly used in public communication, they cannot undergo wholesale changes at will; a complete transformation would cause language to lose its communicative role.

Chapter 4

Language and Thinking

Section 1 The Unity of Language and Thinking

Since language has the function of embodying thinking, language and thinking are extremely closely related. Marx and Engels long ago stated that language is the material "intertwined with" the spirit.[1] Stalin also once said: "No matter what kind of thoughts arise in a person's mind, or when these thoughts arise, they can only be generated and exist on the basis of linguistic materials, linguistic terms, and words. There is no such thing as naked thought completely devoid of linguistic materials and the 'natural substance' of language."[2]

Before clarifying the relationship between language and thinking, we must first provide a brief explanation of what "language" and "thinking" denote. As Rubinstein noted, "The problem of the mutual relationship between language and thinking, speech and thinking, belongs to the most complex and controversial issues. The difficulty in solving these problems stems largely from the fact that the formulation of the problem sometimes refers to thinking (as a process, an action), and at other times to thoughts

1 See Marx and Engels, *The German Ideology*, People's Publishing House, 1961, p. 24.
2 Stalin, *Marxism and Problems of Linguistics*, pp. 38–39.

(as the product of this action); sometimes it refers to langue, and at other times to parole."[1] Without clarifying the specific meanings of "language" and "thinking", it is difficult to elucidate the relationship between the two. Language is the most important communicative tool for humans and also a tool for embodying thinking. As a communicative tool, it cannot be confused with communicative behavior or content; rather, it is an entity that people use in communicative situations to engage in communication and exchange ideas. Since it is a tool for embodying thinking, it cannot be confused with thinking itself; it is merely an entity used by humans to express thoughts. This entity is the sum total of a language's lexical system and grammatical system—for example, the combined lexical and grammatical systems of Chinese. It is not the specific utterances (such as sentences composed of lexical and grammatical components) that people use in communicative situations or when forming ideas, because utterances already constitute the communicative content generated by communicative acts, not the tool of communication itself. The reason language is classless is precisely that the lexical and grammatical systems within it are classless. However, utterances do have class character: in class societies, the utterances of individuals bear a profound class orientation. "Thinking" refers to a property of matter organized in a special way, that is, a function

1 C. Л. Rubinstein, *On the Problems of Language, Speech, and Thought*, in *Linguistics Translation Series*, 1959.

of the human brain. The essence of this function lies in its indirect or generalized reflection of the objective world. It also refers to the activity of this function and its laws. In a general sense, people include the concepts and logical rules directly formed by this function within the scope of thinking. The specific application of concepts and logical rules to organize products such as judgments or inferences constitutes "thoughts". However, "thoughts" and "thinking" are two distinct concepts. We can speak of bourgeois thoughts, but we cannot speak of bourgeois thinking, because everyone, regardless of class, possesses the same basic concepts and logical rules, and everyone has the faculty of thinking. However, the thoughts formed by the specific application of concepts and logical rules clearly bear a class character. Although "thinking" and "thoughts" are distinct, the two are closely intertwined, as thoughts are precisely the activities and products that emerge alongside thinking and are grounded in it. Without thinking, there can be no thoughts; without the activity of thought, thinking remains merely potential. Thought is also a human activity that requires both the faculty of thinking as a foundation and its own starting point for operation. The smallest unit of thought lies in forming judgments: to engage in a thought process, one must always make a judgment, as a thought activity without judgment is an incomplete one. Therefore, the smallest unit of the products formed by this activity is the judgment. We can also say that the act of making a judgment is the smallest unit of thinking activity, and the judgment is the smallest unit of thought. When engaging in thought, concepts must serve as the starting point. A judgment is composed of concepts. Each act of thinking involves combining several concepts or creating new concepts to combine with existing ones. Concepts are the achievements of past thought activities—the new elements created by previous thinking and embedded in judgments—and they also serve as the starting points for subsequent thought activities. Later thoughts use these concepts as materials for thinking. Because thought activities represent the concrete application of the faculty of thinking—along with the concepts and logic directly generated by it—and arise in tandem with thinking processes, people generally use the term "thinking activities" to collectively refer to both the operations of the thinking faculty and the processes of thought. Meanwhile, the products formed through these activities—such as judgments or inferences—are termed "thoughts".

"Thinking" generally refers to abstract thinking, and the distinction between abstract thinking and imaginative thinking represents a new perspective in modern psychology. What traditional psychology calls "thinking" is precisely abstract thinking. Therefore, in common usage, people often use the term "thinking" exclusively to denote abstract thinking. To ensure clarity, we must both clarify that the term "thinking" as commonly understood refers to abstract thinking and note that there are times when it is necessary to divide thinking into two types (abstract thinking and imaginative thinking), with distinctions made in the context.

Language and thinking are inseparably intertwined and mutually dependent. Neither can exist in isolation: thinking cannot exist without language, nor can language exist without thinking. In reality, language and thinking form two opposing yet interdependent aspects of the same unity: language constitutes the form of this unity, while thinking constitutes its content. For this reason, many linguists describe language as the form of thought and thought as the content of language. However, this formulation is imprecise, as it blurs the distinct natures of language and thinking, as well as the nuances of their relationship. It is important to note that all things have form and content, which are the two internal opposing aspects of any entity. As a social phenomenon, language itself has formal and contentual components: its formal aspect is phonological (sound structure), and its contentual aspect is semantic (meaning), which are not identical to the concepts or logical relationships in thinking, for linguistic meaning is not equivalent to the conceptual or logical constructs of thought.

Thinking itself also has its form and content, but the formal aspect of thinking is not phonetic, nor is the content aspect of thinking equivalent to linguistic meaning. Therefore, we cannot simply assert that language is the form of thinking and thinking is the content of language. A more reasonable formulation is to regard language and thinking as the formal and contentual components of a unity composed of these two entities. As Shedrovitsky stated in his essay *Thinking in Language and Its Analysis*, "Thus, when we set out to study thinking and language as the embodiment of thinking, we must from the outset refrain from treating language and thinking as isolated entities. Instead, we should view them as a unity—externally appearing as a single aspect, but internally an inseparable whole encompassing both language and thinking. We call this entirety 'thinking in language' to particularly emphasize its inseparable existence."[1]

To more clearly define this relationship between language and thinking, we argue that the term "thinking in language" is still insufficiently precise. It is preferable to call this unity "language-thinking", for since language and thinking are two aspects within this unity, they are not subordinate to each other but rather inseparable parallel opposites. Within this unity, language constitutes the formal component, while thinking constitutes the content. Specifically, the lexical and grammatical components of language form the formal aspect of the "language-thinking" unity, while the concepts serving as materials for thinking activities and the logical relationships governing thinking processes constitute its content. When language is used, it exists in utterances; when thinking is in process, it forms thoughts. The combination of linguistic elements in utterances and the thoughts composed of concepts and logical rules also constitute a unity. In this unity, the arrangement of linguistic elements in utterances is the formal part, while the thoughts formed by combining concepts are the content part. What linguistics refers

1 Г. П. Shedrovitsky, *Linguistic Thought and Its Analysis*, in *Linguistics Translation Series*, 1959, No. 1, p. 48.

to as "parole" is precisely this kind of utterance.[1] "Parole" is composed of linguistic elements combined with certain non-linguistic expressive means, which forms a complex of meanings in terms of content. This complex of meanings precisely represents the thoughts constituted by thinking. Parole and thought also form a unity, where "parole" is the formal component of the "parole-thought" unity, and thought is its content component. Although the relationship between language and thinking generally refers to the relationship between the lexical and grammatical elements of language and the materials of thinking (concepts) and the rules of thinking (logic), it also involves the relationship between parole and thought—though it is necessary to distinguish between different scenarios—because language exists concretely in parole, and thinking concretely constitutes thoughts.

Language and thinking, as two opposing aspects existing within the "language-thinking" unity, are both inseparably unified and distinct from each other. This is because the formal part and the content part of any entity are simultaneously interconnected yet different. Thus, the relationship between language and thinking is one of unity-in-difference.

1 For the distinction between langue and parole, see the discussion in Chapter 5 of Part One.

Section 2 The Inseparable Dependence Between Language and Thinking

The inseparable unity between language and thinking is manifested in their mutual dependence. Language and thinking are two inseparable entities, which highlights their mutual reliance. However, to understand this relationship of mutual dependence, detailed argumentation is required, as there are divergent views between idealism and dialectical materialism regarding this fundamental postulate. Without meticulous scientific reasoning, it is impossible to critique the erroneous perspectives of idealism or correctly grasp the Marxist view on this issue.

Why is it said that language and thinking are interdependent? First, language arises through thinking, and thinking also arises through language. In other words, from the very first day of their emergence, language and thinking have depended on each other for existence. Without thinking, language could not have been generated; without language, thinking could not have been generated. Humans and other animals can all produce sounds through their vocal organs. Other higher animals, such as apes, can even emit more than thirty different sounds. However, apart from humans, no other higher animals possess language. This is precisely because sounds not unified with thinking do not constitute language. Language is not merely pure sound but a composite containing meaning. It is such a composite because it serves as the bearer of thinking and unit with thinking to take the outcomes of thinking's reflection of the objective world—the materials of thought—as the foundation for its semantic component. Meaning is precisely the manifestation in language of the products or materials of thinking. Although it is not identical to thinking, it originates from thinking and constitutes the contentual part of linguistic elements. Human ancestors were long able to produce many sounds, yet they had no language. Only during the transition from ape to man, when labor enabled the evolving hominids to develop the capacity for abstract thinking, could language emerge—and only then could human ancestors truly evolve from mere higher primates into human beings. Pavlov stated that language is the bearer of abstract thinking, a remark that illustrates that without the abstract thinking it bears, language as the bearer could not have emerged—for a bearer exists as such precisely because there is something to be borne as its object.

On the other hand, the emergence of thinking also depends on language. While thinking certainly relies directly on the development of the human brain, it is not directly produced by language. Thinking is a function of the human brain, a product of matter—in other words, a product of the brain. Only someone like Charles Peirce would claim that "thought has no necessary connection with the human brain; it appears in the work of bees, in crystals, and in all purely physical phenomena."[1] It was only when

1 Peirce, *Collected Papers*, Volume 4, Page 551.

human ancestors developed brain functions through labor that humans acquired the ability for abstract thinking. In other words, abstract thinking developed on the basis of imaginative thinking through the evolution of the human brain. In higher animals with highly developed imaginative thinking, imagistic generalization also reaches an advanced level. Yet despite this, these animals lack abstract thinking; their cognitive processes remain confined to generalizations or associations within the domain of imaginative thinking. Human ancestors undoubtedly possessed similarly advanced imaginative thinking and even exhibited nascent forms of abstract thinking, but these remained undeveloped—mere "buds" that had not yet matured into true abstract thought. Abstract thinking only emerged as a fully realized faculty concurrently with language, when its nascent forms were actualized on the material foundation of linguistic structures.

Second, the respective characteristics of language and thinking also illustrate their inseparable connection and mutual dependence. Language serves as both a tool for human communication and the bearer or embodiment of abstract thinking. Thinking is the faculty of the human brain to reflect the objective world. Language functions as a communication tool precisely because it embodies and expresses human thinking and its outcomes; it serves as the bearer of abstract thinking precisely because it manifests thinking and its products. Thus, the essence of language—whether viewed through its communicative function or its role in embodying thought—lies in its status as the bearer of abstract thinking.

Thinking is the brain's faculty to reflect the objective world, but this faculty pertains not to imaginative thinking but to abstract thinking. As discussed earlier, the emergence of this faculty relies on language as its material shell. Hence, the characteristics of both language and thinking reveal the profound intimacy of their relationship. Why is language said to be the bearer of abstract thinking? To call language the bearer of abstract thinking is equivalent to stating that language is a necessary condition for abstract thinking to exist as such. In other words, the ability of thinking activities to qualify as abstract thinking depends on language serving as the material stimulus for such activities. Language becomes the bearer of abstract thinking precisely because it functions as the material stimulus for abstract thought processes. How can language serve as the material stimulus for abstract thinking, which operates as a neural activity of the second signal system? This is not merely because language has sound, but also because it contains meaning. Sounds without meaning are not language and cannot serve as material stimuli for abstract thinking activities. Pavlov's theory of the second signal system posits that words in language are specialized stimuli for the second signal system. Words function not only as physical stimuli with specific sound qualities, pitches, stresses, and durations but also as signals of signals—signals that possess a qualitatively distinct meaningful content. Soviet linguist Shvarts demonstrated this through experimental methods.[1] In his experiments, he paired the action of an unconditioned light stimulus (electric light) with a conditioned verbal stimulus (the word "initiative"). Over time, this established a conditioned reflex in subjects placed in darkness: when the word "initiative" was presented alone (without light), it triggered pupil constriction, just as the light had done. By contrast, when he used "neutral" words that had not been reinforced by the light stimulus, no pupil response occurred. This experimental evidence confirms that language operates as a dual-function stimulus: it combines physical acoustic properties with symbolic meaning, enabling it to serve as the material basis for abstract thinking within the second signal system. Subsequently, he replaced the word "initiative" with words of similar meaning, such as substituting "гротинка" ("path") for "дорожка" ("trail") and the Russian "дом" ("house") for the English "the house". Any word with a meaning similar to "initiative" consistently induced pupil constriction. However, when he substituted words with similar sounds but different meanings (e.g., replacing "дом" ("house") with "дым" ("smoke")), the pupil constriction initially occurred but ceased after a dozen repetitions. It should be noted that meaning is the form in which the outcomes of thinking or the materials of thinking are consolidated and expressed in linguistic elements. In other words, meaning originates from

1 See B. И. Mashiniko, *Pavlov's Doctrine of the Two Signal Systems*, Science Press, 1956, p. 40.

thinking; without thinking, meaning in language could not exist. This shows that linguistic elements rely on consolidating or expressing thought materials. Specifically, they must contain meanings representing the results of thinking activities or thought materials. Without this, so-called linguistic elements would fail to act as stimuli for the second signal system. In fact, they would cease to be linguistic elements altogether. Therefore, the existence of language as a stimulus for the second signal system is contingent upon thinking.

On the other hand, the existence of thinking as a neural activity of the second signal system also depends on the existence of language, because thinking in the context of the second signal system relies on language as its material stimulus. Neural activities in organisms vary in nature. Tropisms, sensations, perceptions, representation, and abstract thinking are all forms of neural activity, but they differ fundamentally in their characteristics. Lower animals are only capable of tropistic neural activities, or at most sensations and perceptions. Other higher animals, in addition to these, can also exhibit neural activities related to mental images. However, humans are distinct from all other animals in that they possess neural activities associated with abstract thinking. Pavlov argued that human neural activities can be divided into three levels based on the interacting mechanisms (systems) of the brain. The first-level mechanism, closest to the subcortical centers of the brain, governs the complex interactions between humans and other higher animals and their surrounding environment. Its activities are manifested as the most intricate unconditioned reflexes (instincts, appetites, passions, emotions), which are triggered only by a few unconditioned external stimuli—those that act naturally. The second mechanism is the cerebral hemispheres (excluding the analyzers that perceive linguistic stimuli). Here, a new functional principle comes into play: through temporary conditioned connections, it links with unconditioned reflexes, allowing countless other stimuli to replace unconditioned stimuli. This system serves as the bearer of sensations, perceptions, and mental images triggered by the real world. It is the sole signaling system in general animal organisms, known as the first signal system in humans. The third mechanism is an additional new signaling system and functional faculty in the frontal lobe of the human brain. Here, kinesthetic stimuli from the speech organs replace the first signaling system, thereby enabling abstraction and generalization of the first signaling system. This is the second signaling system.[1] Since the second signaling system uses stimuli from speech motor organs (i.e., linguistic elements) to replace the first signaling system, its activities essentially consist of responses to linguistic stimuli. Without language as its stimulus, this neural activity, which constitutes thinking, cannot arise. The human nervous system possesses highly developed analytical and synthetic capabilities. It can not

1 Cf. Ю. M. Pratusevich. *On the Speech Movement Analyzer and Its Role in the Cognitive Process*. In *Language, thought, will, emotion and others*, Science Press, 1956, pp. 6-7.

only generalize the images of external or internal stimuli—and the reappearance of experienced image traces triggered by these images—into mental representations, but also generalize the reappearance of experienced image traces triggered by word stimuli into concepts. As words in language replace the image stimuli in the first signaling system, human abstract thinking can perform abstract generalization independent of concrete images. However, this generalization activity requires a specific type of stimulus as the motivating factor for the activity—and this stimulus is language. Therefore, without language serving as the material stimulus for the second signaling system, thinking activities cannot exist.

Some people believe that thinking can exist independently of language because individuals can engage in silent thought without speaking or listening. This view, however, is a misunderstanding. According to Pavlov's theory, the second signal system consists of three analyzers. The most critical analyzer in the speech nervous system is the speech motor analyzer, which perceives kinesthetic impulses from the speech organs (larynx, tongue, lips, and oral muscles). It plans speech, determines the nature of speech movements, and structures the entire speech chain. In addition, there are two other analyzers for perceiving speech stimuli: the speech auditory analyzer for processing spoken language and the speech visual analyzer for processing written language. Impulses from the speech auditory analyzer and the speech visual analyzer excite various conditioned speech structures within the speech motor analyzer. Since the speech auditory and visual analyzers activate these conditioned speech structures in the speech motor analyzer, it follows that the speech motor analyzer is the primary analyzer. In fact, the movement of the speech organs activates the speech motor analyzer, which in turn triggers thinking.[1] From this perspective, we can understand why a person can think without hearing others speak: even when not listening to others, they cannot avoid making subtle movements associated with producing linguistic sounds. The crux of the matter lies in the distinction between linguistic motor actions that are outwardly expressed and those that are not. So-called "silent thinking" in fact operates on the basis of inner speech that is not externally manifested. It cannot exist without the material substrate of language, for inner speech still involves speech motor stimuli—that is, the words of language. Soviet linguist Boroysky (Боровский) demonstrated the role of inner speech in thinking through experiments: he embedded needle-like electrodes in subjects' tongue or lower lip muscles and asked them to perform mental arithmetic, such as multiplying numbers, while engaged in silent thought. The results showed that although the subjects remained silent and exhibited no obvious movements of their speech organs, there were consistent fluctuations—more or less—in their electrical potentials, which precisely matched the electrical potential changes observed during verbal articulation.[2] This

1 Cf. B. И. Mashiniko, *Pavlov's Doctrine of the Two Signal Systems*, pp. 18–20.
2 Cf. B. И. Mashiniko, *Pavlov's Doctrine of the Two Signal Systems*, p. 18.

indicates that even during silent thinking, the activity of the speech motor analyzer associated with producing linguistic sounds is required as a stimulus for thinking. Without this stimulus, silent thinking could not occur.

Third, when using language for communication or thinking, the activities of language and thinking are also interdependent. In using language, we presuppose the activity of thinking: we employ language precisely to express or embody thought. Of course, as we have discussed, language and thinking arise or exist simultaneously—but this applies to the final manifestation of abstract thinking. It should be noted that thinking is a process. When generating thoughts, we often first form imaginative thinking before developing it into abstract thinking. In this developmental process, without language as the bearer of abstract thinking, abstract thinking would remain in a latent or nascent state. For example, we often perceive a particular object in the objective world through our senses, but due to insufficient contact with it, we may not yet grasp its essential characteristics. Consequently, we cannot assign it a name (determine a word for it), and thus we have not embodied our abstract generalization of this object—yet we have already begun to engage in abstract thinking. This scenario is concretely reflected in the subjectless judgments we often make. For example, when we see an object we have never encountered before, we may perceive its shape and color but not understand what it is fundamentally. In such cases, we might make a judgment like, "Something round and red" or "This is something round and red". This judgment lacks a grammatical subject because our understanding of the object remains trapped in imaginative thinking: we have not yet abstracted its essential characteristics into a concept, assigned that concept a linguistic sign (i.e., a name), or integrated that sign into grammatical structure. This illustrates that even before we embody our abstract understanding of the object through language (as its material shell), we are already in a transitional state from imaginative to abstract thinking about it. If, during this developmental process, we observe other aspects of the object and conclude it is a yarn ball, thereby stating, "This yarn ball is round and red", our abstract thinking about the object is fully embodied. Although this abstract thinking emerges simultaneously with the linguistic term "yarn ball", the reason we utter this term is driven by the need to embody abstract thinking. If we had no intention of understanding the object or communicating our understanding, we would not use this word or make this statement. This demonstrates that we use language to embody our thinking and express our ideas, and we employ language on the premise of engaging in thinking activities. Of course, in most cases, we use subject-predicate sentences, and the thinking we aim to embody also involves forming judgments structured as subject-predicate units. When making such judgments, we always employ words and grammatical elements that already exist in the language and have been learned by us. However, in terms of the current act of embodying and expressing thought, every time we use language, we do so on the premise of embodying thinking and expressing ideas. Therefore, the specific use of language in practical contexts depends on our need to concretely embody thinking and express ideas.

On the other hand, when engaging in concrete thinking, we cannot carry out abstract thinking activities without the material substrate of language. Thinking activities are concretely manifested in the formation of judgments or inferences. Concepts serve as the basic materials of thinking activities and are the outcomes of prior thinking processes. Concrete thinking activities always involve judgments or inferential activities that combine several judgments. These judgments all utilize acquired concepts as their fundamental materials. Only subjectless judgments may partially dispense with acquired concepts in their formation. Acquired concepts can function as the basic materials for thinking precisely because language serves as their material shell—concepts are anchored in language through words, which serve as their material carriers; in this way, concepts become the semantic content encoded in linguistic terms. Even subjectless judgments are formed on the basis of linguistic materials: they either use acquired concepts (i.e., concepts consolidated in words or phrases) as predicates, or invent new words as predicates. Thus, human thinking activities are carried out on the basis of words and grammatical rules in language. Concrete thinking cannot occur without words and grammatical rules to serve as the material vessels for concepts and the connections between them. As Stalin noted: "Some people claim that thoughts arise in the human mind before they are expressed in words, that they arise without linguistic material, without a linguistic outerwear, as it were, in a 'naked' form." This view is entirely incorrect. No matter what thoughts arise in a person's mind, or when they arise, they can only be formed and exist on the basis of linguistic materials, on the basis of linguistic terms and expressions. There is no such thing as naked thought completely devoid of linguistic materials or the "natural substance" of language. "Language is the direct reality of thought" (Marx). The authenticity of thought is manifested in language. Only idealists can speak of thinking unconnected to the "natural substance" of language, or of thinking without language.[1] His exposition is the most explicit. However, some people doubt this important Marxist thesis about the relationship between language and thinking by raising the question of whether dumb people can think. They believe that since dumb people can think without speaking, this proves that thinking can occur in the human brain independent of the material basis of language. This is in fact a misunderstanding. There are various types of dumbness, and only those who are born deaf, lose their hearing, and cannot learn to speak are truly mute—that is, deaf-mutes. Nevertheless, such deaf-mutes have not lost the function of the second signal system, and through special education, their second signal system can be developed. Deaf-mutes can "understand their surrounding environment based on the images, perceptions, and concepts of external objects and their interrelationships formed through

1 Stalin, *Marxism and Problems of Linguistics*, pp. 38–39.

vision, touch, taste, and smell in their daily lives"[1], and can engage in primitive communication with each other through facial expressions and gestures. However, they cannot develop extensive abstract thinking, which is only possible on the basis of spoken language. Although deaf-mutes lose their hearing and cannot learn language because they cannot hear the speech of others in society, they do not lose the ability to use speech motor nerves or speech visual nerves. Therefore, educational approaches for deaf-mutes often involve training them to recognize words through lip movements (speech reading), imitate pronunciation to activate their speech motor pathways, and establish connections between these motor functions and speech-related visual processing. After acquiring this mode of speech, though unable to verify their language through auditory feedback, they can nevertheless employ it to express their opinions and desires. They can even learn writing, through which the systematization, generalization, and abstraction of various sensations acquired from the objective world can be carried out on the basis of written symbols—thus further expanding the possibilities of their thinking.[2] Thus, even the thinking of deaf-mutes is carried out on the material basis of language (parole motor nerves and parole visual nerves).

Fourth, the development of language depends on the development of

1 Stalin, *Marxism and Problems of Linguistics*, p. 47. Here, "idea" corresponds to "representation".
2 See B. И. Mashiniko, P*avlov's Doctrine of the Two Signal System*s, pp. 20–21.

thinking, and the development of thinking also depends on the development of language. The development of language does not merely equate to the evolution of phonetics, though phonetic changes can influence linguistic development. Language development refers to the evolution of the combination of semantic meaning and phonetics. Changes in sound alone do not signify language development, while changes in semantic meaning always do—because meaning constitutes the content of linguistic components, and content is fundamentally more important. As a general rule, content determines form. When thinking develops, language—as the tool for expressing or embodying thought—must necessarily evolve alongside it; the alternative is inconceivable. Of course, under exceptional conditions, there may be cases where form determines content, but this is not a universal law. We can find numerous facts in any language to prove that the development of many meaningful words and the emergence of new words are facilitated by the development of thinking and the formation of new concepts. After the founding of The People's Republic of China, the creation of countless new words in Modern Chinese was driven by the need for new concepts in the thinking of the entire nation, which reflected the new objective reality during the rapid social development. Examples include "Great Leap Forward", "People's Commune", "cosmic rocket", and "artificial satellite".

On the other hand, the development of thinking also relies on the development of language. Although thinking is not directly generated by language, it requires linguistic material to be embodied and consolidated. Abstract thinking emerges from figurative thinking, with transitional states in its developmental process. During these transitions, abstract thinking exists only as a germ and has not yet been fully realized—it is unstable and unformed. Only on the material basis of language can abstract thinking be embodied and solidified. Although concepts are not identical to words, or even to word meanings, concepts remain unstable and vague before the emergence of words. A concept only takes shape, manifests as a concept, and is consolidated when words emerge as its material shell. The same applies when new concepts arise from the development of thinking. When we see a flying machine in the sky, we might form the judgment: "This is a machine flying in the sky." Here, we use existing words and concepts to think. In this case, although the germ of a new concept exists, we have not yet formed a new concept. When uttering this sentence, we already recognize in our minds that this is a new object, but we cannot clearly define what it is, because "a machine flying in the sky" could refer to a kite or an airplane. Only when we hear or say the word "rocket" can we truly develop a new concept in our minds. "Rocket" is not merely a machine that flies in the sky; it is a flying machine propelled into the sky by violent explosives. In the process of learning and imparting knowledge, we always use existing words to explain new words or concepts. Without the mediation of words that solidify known concepts, we would have no way to grasp such new concepts. From this perspective, we can also say that the formation of new concepts is embodied on the basis of words. This holds even in scientific research—i.e., in the process of understanding the laws of the unknown world—where new concepts are also formed on the basis of words. For example, when a biologist studies a group of plant organisms previously unknown to science and discovers many common characteristics among them, these characteristics enable him to distinguish this group of organisms from others and reveal their essential traits. In the process of learning and imparting knowledge, we always use existing words to explain new words or concepts. Without the mediation of words that solidify known concepts, we would have no way to grasp such new concepts. From this perspective, we can also say that the formation of new concepts is embodied on the basis of words. This holds even in scientific research—i.e., in the process of understanding the laws of the unknown world—where new concepts are also formed on the basis of words. For example, when a biologist studies a group of plant organisms previously unknown to science and discovers many common characteristics among them, these characteristics enable him to distinguish this group of organisms from others and reveal their essential traits. Upon completing this research, one can assign a term (word) to designate this category of organisms, and this term will solidify the results of his research. However, this does not imply that the results obtained during the investigative process existed independently prior to the formulation of the corresponding new terminology—prior to linguistic expression. Before this point, such outcomes existed as particular aggregates of thought, grounded in our existing repertoire of words and concepts. It can be seen that before new terminology emerges, new concepts have not yet been formed or consolidated, and the results of such research still cannot exist independently of language—they merely subsist as a specific aggregate of thoughts grounded in existing words and concepts.[1] However, the formation and consolidation of new concepts depend on the emergence of new words.

Precisely because language and thinking are inseparably linked and interdependent, to understand human thinking, its laws, and developmental patterns, one must understand human language; conversely, to understand human language, its laws, and developmental patterns, one must understand human thinking.

Section 3 The Distinctions Between Language and Thinking

Despite this interdependence, it is profoundly erroneous to conflate language and thinking or treat them as identical without differentiation. Although both exist within the unified "language-thought" entity, they are not the same thing. Rather, they are two interdependent yet distinct opposites within this unity, each with its own characteristics that brook no

1 Gao Mingkai. *Language and Thought*. SDX Joint Publishing Company, 1956, pp. 41-42.

confusion. In other words, while language and thinking are unified, they constitute two distinct social phenomena. This can be illustrated from several perspectives.

First, language and thinking each have distinct functions that cannot be confused. As we know, thought is a function of the human brain, whose role is to reflect objective reality, recognize the characteristics of objective things, their internal connections, interrelations, and various laws, enabling people to transform the world accordingly. However, this function is not inherent to language. If a person has never come into contact with a particular objective thing, even if they hear others use a language they understand to describe what that thing is, they cannot grasp its characteristics—nor, in other words, can they recognize the thing without relying on other indirect experiences as references. Language serves as a tool for human communication, as well as a vehicle for embodying and conducting thought. Its functions include enabling people to engage in communicative activities—such as expressing ideas, sensations, emotions, and volitions—to achieve mutual understanding. Simultaneously, it provides a means for embodying and processing thought, empowering individuals to engage in social production, labor, and class struggle. Both language and thinking are social phenomena: they emerged from human social labor, serve social labor and life, and developed on the basis of collective activity. However, despite both being social phenomena, language and thinking differ fundamentally in their essential characteristics and functions. While they are inseparably intertwined in specific activities of communication or thought embodiment—much like a form and its shadow—they remain distinct entities. Each exercises its unique function through its own attributes: language serves as a tool for communication and thought processing, while thought functions to reflect objective things and their laws. Language acts as the carrier or embodier of thought, whereas thought is the object carried or embodied by language. A carrier or embodier and the object it carries or embodies cannot be the same thing—just as a photograph and the subject it depicts are not identical. Therefore, while language and thinking are inseparably intertwined, they remain distinct entities and two different social phenomena.

Second, the structural units of language and thinking are inconsistent, despite their mutual correspondence. Since language serves solely as the carrier or embodier of thought—and as a social phenomenon distinct from thought—it cannot maintain a one-to-one relationship with thought, just as the form of a literary work cannot have a one-to-one correspondence with its content. This is vividly reflected in the inconsistency of structural units between language and thinking. While there is an inseparable connection between language and thinking, the structural units of language do not necessarily form one-to-one associations with those of thought: different linguistic units can correspond to the same conceptual unit, and the same linguistic unit can correspond to different conceptual units. This is precisely why language contains synonymous and homophonic elements, and why different languages can have varying linguistic manifestations for the same concept. Words are the unit of linguistic building materials, while concepts are the basic material units of thinking. However, words in language do not coincide with concepts in thought, despite a certain correspondence between them. This discrepancy is evident not only in the fact that words have a sound component while concepts do not, but also in the divergence between the semantic content of words and the content of concepts. Lexical meaning not only includes non-conceptual elements such as emotive coloring, stylistic nuance, and imagistic connotation but also differs from concepts in unit scope. The same concept may be consolidated in a specific language by different words, forming semantic components of multiple lexemes. For example, the concept of "看" (kàn, to look) is encapsulated by words like "看", "瞧" (qiáo) and "视" (shì), serving as a semantic component of these terms. Across languages, the same concept often exhibits even greater variation in semantic structure. The Chinese word "姊姊" (zǐzǐ, elder sister) is rendered in English as elder sister (two words), while the English sister can denote both "姊姊" and "妹妹" (mèimèi, younger sister)—a semantic range that zǐzǐ does not cover. Grammatical categories in language correspond to logical categories in thought, but the two are not identical.[1] The linguistic realization of the same logical category also varies. For example, the logical category of "quantity" can be

1 See Gao Mingkai, *Grammar Theory*, The Commercial Press, 1960, pp. 116–123.

expressed in language through numerals, classifiers, noun "number", verb "number", adjective "number", pronoun "number", and demonstrative "number"—among which numerals, classifiers, and the "number" inflections of various parts of speech belong to different grammatical category domains. Languages also differ in how they express the logical category of "quantity". In Russian, nouns, verbs, adjectives, pronouns, and demonstratives all have "number" inflections, while in Chinese, grammatical markers of "number" apply only to person-referring words and pronouns. Chinese has classifiers like 个 (gè), 把 (bǎ), 匹 (pǐ), 尾 (wěi), 头 (tóu), which Russian lacks. Sentences in language correspond to judgments formed by thinking, but the two are not identical.[1] The same logical judgment structure can be expressed in language through different sentence types, patterns, and models. For instance, a logical judgment following only the formula "subject—copula—predicate" may be linguistically realized as sentence types such as "subject—(copula)—noun predicate", "subject—(copula)—adjective predicate", or "subject—verb predicate" to convey the same logical formula. It may also take the form of declarative, interrogative, imperative, or exclamatory sentence patterns, and manifest in various sentence models differing in structural form. The same logical subject-predicate relationships, affirmative and negative judgments, and universal and particular judgments can be expressed in language

1 See Gao Mingkai, *Grammar Theory*, The Commercial Press, 1960, pp. 233–236.

through various means—case inflections, word order, stress, pause, function words, etc.—with each language exhibiting distinct patterns. Unlike thinking, which is distinct from sensation, perception, representation, emotion, and volition, language not only embodies or expresses thought but also incidentally conveys sensation, perception, representation, emotion, and volition.[1]

Third, language is a social phenomenon with national characteristics, while thinking is a universal social phenomenon shared by all humans. As thinking functions to reflect objective laws and constitutes a fundamental capacity of the human brain, its operational capabilities and governing principles are universal to all humans—determined by both the shared objective world and the common biological structure of the human brain. Anyone without functional or pathological brain defects can think according to the same laws (i.e., logical laws), although the specific application of thinking by individuals and the ideas they acquire may have class characteristics. For this reason, logic—as the law governing thinking activities—is universal to all humans. However, the case with language is different. It is possible that a universal human language will gradually emerge after humans enters communism worldwide. However, in past and present circumstances, as humans are divided into clans, tribes, ethnic groups, and nations, language is not universal but national (in a broad sense).

1 Ibid., pp. 280–285.

As a tool for human communication, language is necessarily created by all members of a specific societal group. Developed historically within the group's unique environment, it serves as an internal means of communication. Consequently, how thought is embodied or consolidated through language is constrained by the specific communicative context. How the sound and meaning components of language are combined is established through social labor processes and specific contextual conditions. Precisely for this reason, the lexical and grammatical systems of each language, the semantic scope of each word, the phonetic structure of each word, the semantic scope of each grammatical component, and the phonetic structure of each grammatical component can all differ—even though speakers of different languages may convey the same ideas and adhere to the same logical rules in thinking. For example, we can use a logic textbook written in Russian to teach Han students logical rules, but we cannot use a Russian grammar textbook to teach them Chinese. This illustrates that language is national in character, while thinking is universal to all humans.

Fourth, language and thinking each have their own laws of development. Both are social phenomena that evolve with the development of society, yet their developmental laws differ fundamentally. Language develops in tandem with the history, communicative environment, culture, and ideology of its speakers. For example, Chinese has evolved alongside the historical trajectory, communicative contexts, cultural advancements, and intellectual developments of the Han people. The development of Modern Chinese reflects the entire socio-historical progress, communicative landscapes, cultural transformations, and ideological shifts of the Han people during the revolutionary era. In contrast, thought advances with the refinement and enhancement of human's cognitive capabilities across societies. The development of language manifests in the differentiation of its phonological, grammatical, and lexical systems as society divides. For example, Proto-Sino-Tibetan diversified into Chinese, Tibetan, Thai, and Burmese in phonetics, semantics, grammar, and vocabulary as the original Sino-Tibetan tribes split into Han, Tibetan, Tai, and Burmese ethnic groups. It also manifests in unification as societies integrate—for instance, the formation of a unified Han national language alongside the unification of the Han people. Additionally, language development involves improvements and expansions in phonetics, semantics, grammar, and vocabulary. In contrast, the development of thought is marked by enhancements in analytical and synthetic capabilities, greater abstraction, and increased precision. For example, the thinking of primitive humans was characterized by greater concreteness: most of their concepts reflected relatively specific objects in the objective world, and they lacked sophisticated analytical abilities, such as the capacity to analyze direct and indirect causal relationships between phenomena.[1] In contrast,

1 See Part II, Chapter 1, Section 4 The General Situation of Primitive Language.

modern human thinking possesses highly developed analytical and synthetic capabilities, along with highly abstract concepts and precise logical reasoning and judgment. Thus, while language and thinking mutually drive each other's development, their laws of evolution remain distinct.

Precisely because language and thinking differ in these respects, they constitute two distinct social phenomena, and it is erroneous to conflate them.

Marxist theory holds that while language and thinking are inseparably linked as social phenomena, they remain distinct in nature. This principle of their unity without identity is fundamental to understanding their relationship. Many linguists have erred in addressing linguistic issues precisely by either intentionally distorting or failing to grasp this principle: they either sever the connection between language and thinking or erroneously equate them. Some linguists of the structuralist school, particularly those of the American descriptive linguistics school, argue that language can be studied without considering its inherent meaning.[1] Their mistake lies in severing the connection between language and thinking, assuming that language can exist in isolation from thinking. This is analogous to the view of the Marrist linguists, who claimed that thought can

1 See J. B. Carroll, *A Survey of Linguistics and Related Disciplines*, Cambridge, Mass., 1950), p. 150.

exist "naked" without language—a necessary consequence of divorcing language from thinking. They argued that since language is not closely linked to thinking, thought can exist independently of language. However, such perspectives contradict objective facts and can only foster unscientific, idealist understandings of language. The Port-Royal school's so-called "philosophical grammar" conflated grammar with logic by seeking to replace grammatical rules with logical principles. This approach not only sought to eliminate grammar as an independent system but also obscured the boundaries between grammar and logic, as well as between language and thinking. Their errors exerted a harmful influence on the scientific study of language. For instance, the French linguist Ferdinand Brunot adopted the Port-Royal school's tenets in his work *Thought and Language* (Pensée et Langage).[1] Similarly, some Chinese linguists who rely on logical rules to explain grammatical phenomena have conducted research under the sway of these flawed ideas. To liberate linguistic science from such idealist distortions, it is essential to grasp the dialectical relationship between language and thinking as one of unity without identity through the lens of Marxist dialectical materialism.

1 Brunot, *La Pensee et la langue*, Paris, 1922.

Chapter 5

Langue and Parole

Section 1 The Distinction Between Langue and Parole

As the most important tool for human communication and a vehicle for abstract thinking, language is neither equivalent to the act of creating or using this tool (i.e., communicative behavior) nor to the "utterances" formed through such use. Nor is it equivalent to the logical judgments with ideological content that arise from using language in thinking. Thus, a correct understanding of language necessarily requires distinguishing between language itself, the acts of creating and using it (i.e., communicative acts), and the outcomes generated by such usage.

The language invented when creating linguistic components and the language used in speech are tools. In contrast, the acts of creating linguistic components and speaking are merely behaviors that employ linguistic faculties and are not equivalent to language itself. The sum total of linguistic components created through language-making acts—or, broadly speaking, the tools used in speech—constitutes language or "langue". Conversely, the behaviors of exercising linguistic faculties (including both creating and using language) and the utterances produced through language use are termed "parole". For example, the Chinese language commonly used by the Han people in daily life is the tool employed when they speak—that is, language. However, the actions of using linguistic faculties to create a lexical or grammatical component of Chinese, the act of speaking in Chinese by exercising linguistic faculties, and the actual utterances produced by Han speakers all constitute parole. We cannot claim that a single sentence we utter today—such as "The victories in our country's socialist construction are unprecedented"—is equivalent to the Chinese language, even though this sentence is expressed in Chinese. All members of the Han Chinese share only one common language, namely Chinese. Yet each Han individual, and indeed the entire people, engage in innumerable acts of attempting to create linguistic components and using Chinese concretely for communication and thought-expression, resulting in countless "utterances" formed through language use. Language functions as a tool for communication and thought-expression in the form of a symbolic system, owned collectively by the entire societal unit. However, the acts of creating linguistic components by any individual or group, the use of this symbolic system, and the "utterances" produced through such use are not the collectively owned tool of the societal unit. Rather, they represent individual or group-level creation, application, and outcomes of using this tool. In fact, when we speak of "Chinese", "Russian", or "Tibetan", we are referring to the symbolic systems of these languages—specifically, the sum total of their lexical and grammatical systems (including their phonological and semantic subsystems). No one would mistake the spoken words or written works of individuals (composed of Chinese lexical items and grammatical components) for the Chinese language itself; these are understood as products of using Chinese. For instance, in Chapter 45 of *Romance of the Three Kingdoms*, Zhou Yu feigns waking from a dream and asks, "Who is sleeping on the bed?" The man replies, "The commander invited Ziyi to share your bed—how could you forget?" Zhou Yu then regrets, "I rarely drink to excess, but I mishandled matters while drunk yesterday. I wonder if I said anything important?" Here, Zhou Yu's question, "I wonder if I said anything important?" is not interpreted as "What language did I speak? Was it Chinese or Tibetan?" but rather as referring to specific utterances composed of particular Chinese lexical and grammatical elements. The Speech chapter of *A New Account of the Tales of the World* records the "witty remarks" of certain individuals, not the Chinese or Xianbei languages they spoke. Although we rarely use the term "parole" in this sense today, we also do not interpret "I simply don't understand what you're saying" as "I don't know if you're speaking Chinese or Tibetan." Here, "what you're saying" refers to parole. In Chapter 46 of *Romance of the Three Kingdoms*, there is another passage: "Huang Gai lay in his tent as generals came to inquire about his condition. He did not speak, only heaved long sighs." Here, "speak" refers to the act of speaking in Chinese—no one would interpret it as "the Chinese language" or "Tibetan". When we say today, "He has stopped speaking", "speaking" also denotes the act of using language, not the language itself. In simpler terms, "speech" means speaking: it can refer to the act of speaking or the utterances produced. "speak" is the speech act, while "utterance" is the outcome or "product" of that act. Since speech acts refer to the act of speaking, and since speaking may simultaneously involve attempts to create new linguistic components (if, in addition to using existing components of the national common language, one or two new components are employed), speech acts should be understood as behaviors that utilize linguistic faculties. This includes both using linguistic faculties to create new linguistic components and to employ existing ones. When people use linguistic faculties, they combine existing linguistic components, newly created components (if any), and extra-linguistic expressive means to convey their intended thoughts. The result is utterances, or what we call "words". This demonstrates that the distinction between langue and parole is an objective reality recognized by people, even if they are not fully aware of the need to differentiate them scientifically.

In the history of linguistics, it was not until the early 19th century that the German linguist Wilhelm von Humboldt noted the need to distinguish between langue and parole. Humboldt stated: "In the strictest and most immediate sense, this definition applies to every act of living speech in daily language use. Yet, in essence and true meaning, language can also be understood as the sum total of all that is spoken. However, what is commonly called 'language'—as found in dictionaries and grammars—

contains only the individual elements produced by living speech in the form of lists of words and rules. These are often quantitatively incomplete and require new efforts to identify the characteristics generated by speech and to form a reliable conception of living speech itself...Living speech is the primary and true linguistic asset: if we seek to grasp the essence of living language, we must never forget this in the study of language. The fragmented existence of words and rules is the stiff product of the mechanical work of scientific analysis, not the natural property of language."[1] Here, Wilhelm von Humboldt argues that language is the sum total of all spoken utterances, while speech constitutes every living act of daily language use. Although Humboldt did not provide a precise analysis of the distinction between langue and parole, he already recognized the theoretical necessity of differentiating between the two.

The Russian linguist Potebnya also emphasized the distinction between parole (rek) and langue (yazyk). He argued that parole is an unbroken stream of creative speech acts that flow into a specific language understood by a community. In his view, parole is the primary form of language use and the complete, living, concrete form in which language exists creatively. The continuous change and evolution of language are realized through parole and occur for the sake of parole. He stated, "In

1 Cited in Vinogradov, *Summary of the Discussion on Stylistics Issues* (in *Selected Translations of Essays on Linguistic Style and Stylistics*, Science Press, 1960, pp. 163–164).

reality, ... there is only parole; words have meaning only in parole."[1] He also wrote, "Every occurrence of a word in parole corresponds to a single act of thinking, not multiple. In other words, each word we speak or understand in parole cannot have more than one meaning."[2] Thus, in emphasizing the distinction between langue and parole, Potebnya denied the objective existence of langue and regarded parole as paramount.

In the history of modern linguistics, it was Ferdinand de Saussure who provided a systematic theoretical explanation for the distinction between langue and parole. When analyzing the object of linguistics, he argued that human "langage" can be divided into two parts: langue and parole. Langue is a social phenomenon, while parole is an individual phenomenon. He stated, "(Langue) is a treasure trove acquired by all members of a social group through speech practice, a grammatical system that can exist in the mind of each individual—or more precisely, in the minds of many individuals within a community; for in the mind of any single individual, language is always incomplete; it is only complete among the masses."[3] He also stated: "In separating langue from parole, one simultaneously (1) distinguishes what is social from what is individual, and (2) distinguishes what is essential from what is secondary and more or less accidental. Langue is not a function of the speaker but a recorded product of individuals.

1 Potebnya, *Notes on Russian Grammar* (Russian edition), 1874, Vols. 1–2, p. 207.
2 Ibid., p. 3.
3 Ferdinand de Saussure, *Cours de linguistique générale* (French text), p. 30.

It never presupposes prior reflection, and the activity of reflection only intervenes in the classificatory operations we shall discuss... Conversely, parole is an activity of individual will and intelligence, which can be divided into (1) the combinations a speaker makes when applying grammatical rules to express personal thoughts, and (2) the psychophysical mechanisms that allow individuals to externalize these combinations."[1] Here, Ferdinand de Saussure on the one hand views langue as a social product and social phenomenon, and parole as an individual product and individual phenomenon. On the other hand, he concretely defines what he calls langue as a "grammatical system" existing in the minds of the masses, and what he calls parole as the combinations individuals make to express thoughts, along with the psychophysical mechanisms that externalize these combinations. What exactly are these combinations? Elsewhere, Saussure stated: "Langue exists in the collective form of the sum of imprints stored in each individual's mind, somewhat like a dictionary with identical copies distributed to each person for use. This form of language's existence can be expressed by the following formula:

$$1 + 1 + 1 + 1 \ldots\ldots = 1$$ (the collective model).[2]"

1 Ibid., p. 38.

2 This formula means that the sum of the linguistic systems stored in each individual's mind still equals the same linguistic system. However, the latter is the collective linguistic system, while the linguistic systems stored in each individual's mind are merely copies of this collective system.

How does parole appear in this collective? It is the sum total of what people say, including: (1) individual combinations dependent on the speaker's will; (2) the articulatory movements related to will that are necessary to realize these combinations.[1] Here, he explicitly stated that by speech he means the sum of utterances, including the linguistic combinations formed by individuals and the articulatory movements—that is, the physiological-physical mechanisms.

Ferdinand de Saussure, the most influential Western linguist of the 20th century, held a theory distinguishing between langue and parole that contains serious idealist errors. These errors are primarily manifested in: (1) opposing langue and parole on the issue of sociality; (2) excluding the material shell of language (articulation) from language itself on the question of materiality, and attributing it solely to individual speech.

As Lev Vladimirovich Sherba said, "The linguistic system and speech materials are only the distinct aspects of a certain speech activity in experimentation..."[2], "All truly individual elements that do not originate from the linguistic system or are not potentially established within it will perish forever without being able to find their own response or even be

1 Ferdinand de Saussure, *Cours de linguistique générale*, p. 38.
2 Lev Vladimirovich Sherba, *On the Three Aspects of Language Phenomena and Experimental Linguistics*, in *Bulletin of the Academy of Sciences of the USSR (Section of Social Sciences)*, 1931, No. 1, p. 115.

deeply understood"[1], "What are often regarded as individual minor differences are actually collective differences, i.e., those equally constrained by society"[2]. Ferdinand de Saussure's opposition between langue and parole in terms of sociality represents a serious misunderstanding of the two concepts. In his *The Objectivity of Language Existence*, А. И. Смирницкий (Smirnitsky) similarly criticizes Ferdinand de Saussure, stating: "Langue is a component of parole, and the most important one"[3], and "The 'extralinguistic residue' in parole includes both individual and social factors, which is not equivalent to Saussure's conception of parole as a purely individual phenomenon"[4]. Why should we not oppose langue and parole in this way? Since language is a tool for human communication, it cannot be understood as communicative behavior (actions using linguistic functions) or as a combination of speeches composed of such behaviors. Even from a practical perspective, every language user is aware that the language they have learned is not their exclusive possession but is shared by others. It exists in society in the form of spoken language with a material sound shell uttered by all individuals in the entire community. In communicative situations, they use this tool to construct what they say. Specifically, in an era when language already exists,

1 Ibid., p. 118.
2 Ibid., p. 124.
3 Smirnitsky, *The Objectivity of Language Existence*, in *Selected Translations of Linguistic Papers*, Fifth Series, Zhonghua Book Company, 1950, p. 121.
4 Ibid., p. 122.

when people communicate, they primarily use a set of vocabulary systems (including simple words, compound words, phrases that function as words in sentences, idioms, set phrases, sentence patterns, etc.) and grammatical systems commonly owned by the entire community to form their utterances. Moreover, in the process of learning a language, people are precisely learning this set of vocabulary and grammatical systems shared by the entire community. From this perspective, Ferdinand de Saussure's concrete conception of langue as "a grammatical system existing in the minds of the masses" is partially correct, because what Saussure refers to as a "grammatical system" is in fact the linguistic system[1]. The vocabulary system and grammatical system shared by all members of a particular national society constitute the langue that serves as the communicative tool of that society. Rubinstein also stated in his *On the Relationship Between Langue, Parole, and Thinking*: "By its nature, langue is national—it is the vocabulary socially processed by the people of that nation and the grammatical structure manifested as certain rules (regularities) for forming sentences with words."[2] Of course, we cannot confuse langue with parole as communicative behavior (actions using linguistic functions) and the results it produces, for communicative behavior and its outcomes are not

1 Ferdinand de Saussure once opposed the traditional linguistic approach of separating vocabulary and grammar, arguing that the linguistic system is grammar. See his *Cours de linguistique générale*, pp. 183–187.
2 С. П. Rubinstein, *On the Relationship Between Langue, Parole, and Thought*, in *Linguistics Translation Series*, 1959, No. 1, p. 44.

equivalent to the communicative tool itself. However, the question is: can we therefore conclude that langue is social and parole is individual? On this issue, Ferdinand de Saussure made a serious mistake. As Smirnitsky pointed out, in ordinary situations (except in certain cases where the use of linguistic functions involves not only the specific application of langue but also the creation of new linguistic elements, etc.), parole is people's use of langue and the "works" composed by this use. Such "works" contain linguistic elements, as they are constructed from the vocabulary of the langue and organized according to certain grammatical rules of the langue. These vocabulary elements and grammatical rules exist within parole as its constituent parts, and thus parole contains national vocabulary and grammatical components.[1] Moreover, in ordinary circumstances, since parole is the use of language as a communicative tool in communicative situations and the products formed through this use (i.e., utterances or discourses), parole itself is also a social phenomenon. This is because communication is inherently a social phenomenon, and the utterances or discourses constructed in communicative acts are precisely intended to be understood by others and can be understood by others. Furthermore, not all individual elements qualify as purely personal phenomena belonging exclusively to individuals. We cannot conclude that the individual's

1 See Smirnitsky, *The Objectivity of Language Existence*, in *Linguistics Translation Series*, Fifth Series, pp. 121–

exercise of linguistic functions or use of language is a purely personal phenomenon merely because it is an individual act. Therefore, Ferdinand de Saussure's view of parole as a completely individual phenomenon opposed to langue is an extremely erroneous perspective. Of course, from another angle, we can also say that parole contains certain individual elements. But this involves understanding the issue from a different perspective. It refers to the non-linguistic elements created and used by individuals when composing parole combinations or utterances, i.e., expressive means beyond those in the langue's vocabulary and grammatical systems—such as an individual's unique words or special grammatical components. However, this is only a partial phenomenon in parole. One cannot therefore claim that parole is a purely individual phenomenon opposed to langue as a social phenomenon. Moreover, even these non-linguistic expressive means created and used by individuals are still embryonic linguistic elements, which often develop into established linguistic components over time.

Ferdinand de Saussure's view of pronunciation as an individual speech phenomenon is another serious error. Although he regarded langue as a social phenomenon, he overlooked the material basis for the existence of this social phenomenon. He considered langue a system composed of a set of signs, but these signs were psychological. He argued that the sign (signe) is a combination of the signifier (signifiant) and the signified (signifié), where the signifier is the auditory image and the signified is the concept;

both of these combined elements are psychological phenomena.[1] He stated: "A linguistic sign does not link a thing to a name, but a concept to an auditory image (image acoustique). The latter is not the physical sound, the purely physical entity, but the psychological trace of that sound, the representation evidenced by our senses. It belongs to the realm of sensation. If we eventually call it a 'material entity', we do so only in this sense, and by contrast with the other term of the association, the generally more abstract concept... Thus, the linguistic sign is a psychological entity with two faces."[2] While Ferdinand de Saussure regarded language as a system of signs and views this system as a psychological phenomenon—albeit a collective social psychological phenomenon—he cannot avoid falling into the quagmire of idealism. Smirnitsky stated: "(He) completely severs langue from parole and from the material sounds of langue and views langue as merely a psychological phenomenon (although like any psychological phenomenon, langue exists only as a function of the brain), thus making him an idealist."[3] Smirnitsky's critique is fair. It should be noted that it is precisely the material sounds of langue that enable it to serve as a communicative tool that can be received and understood audibly in society, and it is these material sounds that give langue its materiality and objective existence. Therefore, vocalization activities cannot be regarded solely as

1 Ferdinand de Saussure, *Cours de linguistique générale*, pp. 98–100.
2 Ferdinand de Saussure, *Cours de linguistique générale*, pp. 98–99.
3 Smirnitsky, *The Objectivity of Language Existence*, in *Selected Translations of Linguistic Papers*, Fifth Series, p. 118.

individual speech acts, nor can linguistic signs be treated as purely psychological phenomena. Ferdinand de Saussure stated: "When we observe our linguistic faculty and its products, the psychological nature of our auditory impressions becomes clearly evident. We can speak to ourselves or recite a poem silently without moving our lips or tongue. For us, the words in a language are auditory impressions, and we must avoid discussing the 'phonemes' of which they are composed—this term [i.e., 'phoneme'] denotes a motor articulatory act, suitable only for describing spoken words and the actualization of internal traces in discourse. When speaking of a word's sounds and syllables, we can avoid this misunderstanding only if we remember that they refer to auditory traces."[1] His argument lacks scientific basis. Modern psychological research has demonstrated that human linguistic faculty is primarily executed by speech kinesthetic nerves, not auditory nerves.[2] Even in so-called inner speech (i.e., what Ferdinand de Saussure refers to as speaking to oneself or reciting a poem silently), speech kinesthetic nerves are still active. Here, as Smirnitsky pointed out, de Saussure confuses language with people's knowledge of language.[3] We must distinguish between the objective existence of language and its existence in the speaker's consciousness. The auditory impressions retained in the human brain are merely reflections of

1 Ferdinand de Saussure, *Cours de linguistique générale*, p. 98.
2 See Part I, Chapter 4, Section 2.
3 See Smirnitsky, *The Objectivity of Language Existence*, in *Selected Translations of Linguistic Papers*, Fifth Series.

the objectively existing language, i.e., people's knowledge of objectively existing language. Without the objective existence of language, there can be no knowledge or reflection of it, and this objective existence of language depends on its acoustic sounds—although after learning a language, we can, in certain situations, engage in internal speech activities without "uttering" words aloud. Therefore, while Ferdinand de Saussure correctly proposed the need to distinguish between langue and parole, his understanding of these concepts was incorrect.

In summary, the distinction between langue and parole is objectively real. As a communicative tool for a societal community, langue cannot be the exclusive possession of individuals; it is the common property of all members of the societal community and an objectively existing tool that people can use for communication at any time and place. Parole, however, is the exercise of linguistic functions by individuals (including the use of langue itself) and the results thereof. A societal community generally has only one language—for example, the Han ethnic group has only Chinese—but the countless individuals and groups within it produce an incalculable amount of speech. Nevertheless, langue and parole are not completely opposed; they are closely interconnected. Moreover, langue is not a psychological phenomenon: it exists objectively in society through the role of its material shell (voice).

Section 2 The Relationship Between Langue and Parole

What, then, is the relationship between langue and parole? To answer this question, we must first clarify what the concepts of "langue" and "parole" actually denote. As discussed above, "langue" refers to a system of signs (i.e., a vocabulary system, a grammatical system, and their material shell, the phonological system) that serves as a communicative tool for a societal community. This is generally accepted, though some may lack clarity on the details. However, there are differing opinions on what "parole" entails. In their essay *Does Speech Have Class Character*, Fang Guangtao and Shi Wentao proposed the view that "parole" refers solely to the expressive form of parole products. They state: "We maintain that linguistics studies only the expressive forms of parole products... Our understanding of parole (the expressive form of parole products) includes not only the material shell of parole—phonetics, the laws of word combination, and sentence patterns—but also the objective meanings of vocabulary, as these all belong to parole."[1] To understand Fang Guangtao and Shi Wentao's "expressive forms of parole products", it is necessary to clarify what constitutes a "parole product". In fact, the term "speech product"

1 Fang Guangtao and Shi Wentao, *Does Speech Have Class Character?*, in Nanjing University Forum, 1959, No. 4, p. 26.

used by Fang and Shi follows the terminology employed by Smirnitsky in his essay *The Objectivity of Language Existence*. Although in his later works Smirnitsky revised the meaning of the term "parole product" he had previously used, defining it as a "narrative"[1] with a specific composition and structure that can be repeated by different people at different times and under different conditions. A "narrative"[2] is any holistic parole segment formed for a specific purpose under specific conditions. However, in Smirnitsky's *The Objectivity of Language Existence* (on which Fang Guangtao and Shi Wentao based their arguments), the term "parole product" is used to denote "the specific outcomes generated by the use of language"[3]. In other words, it refers to the specific utterances people produce. Fang Guangtao and Shi Wentao argue that "parole" denotes only the expressive form within such parole products—in other words, the "expressive form" in what people say. As they understand it, this "expressive form" includes not only the presence of linguistic elements in parole products but also what they term the "extralinguistic residue"—such as individual speakers' pronunciation errors, vocal characteristics, inappropriate word choices, and socially recognized poetic rhythms. Furthermore, in a subsequent

1 Smirnitsky, *Language and Speech*, in *Linguistics Translation Series*, 1960, No. 2, pp. 18–19.
2 Smirnitsky, Language and Speech, p. 18. What Smirnitsky actually refers to here is "narrative". The translator's rendering of акт речи as "speech act" constitutes a misunderstanding. See Gao Mingkai, *Further Discussion on Language and Speech*, in *Chinese Language*, 1961, No. 3, p. 36.
3 See Fang Guangtao and Shi Wentao, *Does Speech Have Class Character?*, in *Nanjing University Forum*, 1959, No. 4, p. 25.

supplementary essay, Shi Wentao proposed a formula: in their view, parole is "linguistic elements + our so-called 'extralinguistic residue'= speech"[1]. In other words, linguistic elements in parole products plus individual speakers' pronunciation errors, vocal characteristics, inappropriate word choices, socially recognized poetic rhythms, and similar elements equal speech. Can we understand speech in this way? The Danish structuralist V. Bröndal formulated the following equation for parole: "parole = the act of speaking + what is said"[2]. The entry on "parole" in the Great Soviet Encyclopedia similarly defines parole as: "Parole is an activity of members of a society (tribe, ethnic group, nation), manifested as the use of language in communicative and thought processes (including oral and written forms)—this is parole activity (речь вая деятельность). At the same time, parole is the sum total of the products of this activity, i.e., linguistic materials composed of parole units (sentences)."[3] Here, the Great Soviet Encyclopedia notes that "parole" can refer both to speech activity and to the linguistic materials composed of parole units (sentences), i.e., the parole products in which linguistic elements reside. This view is in fact consistent with that of Smirnitsky and most linguists. However, Fang Guangtao and Shi Wentao argue that "parole" can only denote the "expressive form of

1 Shi Wentao, *On Langue, Parole, and Parole Products*, in *Chinese Language*, 1960, No. 4, p. 183.
2 Bröndal, *Langage et logique* (*Language and Logic*), in *Encyclopédie Française*, Vol. 1, p. 148.
3 In *Linguistics Translation Series*, 1960, No. 2, p. 17.

parole products." The formula "parole is the expressive form of parole products" appears to be an unreasonable one, akin to claiming "painting is the lines and colors of a painting" or "music is the musical notation of a composition"—formulas that are difficult to sustain. While advocating that "parole is the expressive form of parole products," Fang and Shi firmly deny that "parole" can also refer to the content of parole products. This argument, which opposes the expressive form of parole products to their content while recognizing only the former as parole, is also untenable. Why, if "parole" can refer to the expressive form of a parole product as opposed to its content, can it not also refer to the content of the parole product? The problem is clear: since a parole product is a product of speech, the entire product belongs to parole. It cannot be claimed that only the expressive form of the parole product—contrasted with its content—belongs to parole. Like any entity in the world, a parole product is composed of two inseparable and interdependent components: content and form. If "parole" can denote the expressive form of a parole product in opposition to its content, it can naturally also denote the content of the parole product. What is more, if parole is understood as the expressive form within parole products, then the very nature of a parole product becomes incomprehensible. For as everyone (including Fang Guangtao and Shi Wentao) understands, a parole product is the outcome of speech. However, the expressive form of a parole product—contrasted with its content—clearly cannot produce this outcome. We cannot possibly claim that "a parole product is the product of the expressive form of a parole product." Of course, in the history of linguistics, linguists have debated the meaning of "parole". For example, as early as the 1930s, the French linguist H. Delacroix argued for a distinction between langage, langue, parler and parole. He maintained that "parler" refers to the combinations formed by speakers when using language, while parole is the psychological mechanism that allows speakers to externalize the language system. More recently, the Soviet linguist Gernong has also stated: "The concept of 'parler' has nothing in common with the concept of 'parole'. 'Parole' is what de Saussure identified, and it is still put forward by followers of his theory on this point. 'Parole' is a psycho-physiological process, a manifestation of the activity of our 'second signal system', and an object of study in psychology and physiology." Linguists have the right to take no interest in it and remain unaware of its specific research methods. "...'parler' is the result of a speech process or many coherent speech processes. The relationship between process and result is not unique to language; it is the same everywhere. We can never understand the result from the mechanical action of the process at any time, whereas 'parler' first requires people to understand it, and this understanding is revealed through its interrelationship with the 'language system'".[1] What Delacroix and Gernong call "parler" is in fact "parole product", and their "parole" actually refers to "speech act", "speech process", or "speech activity", but

1 Delacroix, *Le langage et la pensée* (Paris, 1930), pp. 2–3.

understood from a physiological-psychological perspective. They distinguish between the two and restrict "parole" to explaining the psycho-physiological process of speaking activity. This formulation has its reasonable aspects, but it is not necessary. It is reasonable because parole acts are indeed not the same as parole products. It is unnecessary because parole products are precisely the outcomes of parole acts, and parole acts are the very actions that produce parole products—the two are inseparable. Moreover, parole products are the concrete embodiments of parole acts; some linguists even regard parole products as parole acts themselves. Prefixing both "action" and "product" with "parole" reveals the relationship between them, making it unnecessary to use different terms that obscure their inseparable connection. Furthermore, in many languages, everyday terms often denote both concepts simultaneously, and linguists have grown accustomed to this usage. Tian Ru recently has also put forward a view that "parole" refers only to "parole products"[1]. His view is precisely the opposite of that of Delacroix and Gernong. We believe that if "parole" is to refer to only one phenomenon, according to Chinese linguistic habits, it is more appropriate for it to refer to "parole activity" than "parole products". This is because in our daily language, we still say "He has stopped speaking". In this way, we treat "parole" as an "activity". However, the case of Fang

1 For example, the Chinese word "讲话" (jiǎnghuà) (a synonym for "言语" yányǔ) denotes both the act of speaking and the spoken content. The same applies to Russian речь (rech'), English speech, French parole, and German Rede.

Guangtao and Shi Wentao's "parole", which can only refer to the "expressive form of parole products", is different. This is because they do not make distinctions: since they call "linguistic elements + 'extralinguistic residues'" the expressive form of parole products, these elements naturally belong to "parole products"; since they call the content of what people say the "content of parole products", this content naturally also belongs to "parole products"; and since they call the "parler" with both content and form that people produce "parole products", such "parler" naturally also belong to "parole". However, they claim that "parole" refers only to the "expressive form of parole products", while at other times stating that parole is "speech activity"[1]—which renders their argument incoherent. The flaws in Fang Guangtao and Shi Wentao's thesis go beyond this. When explaining the expressive form of parole products, they assert: "We maintain that linguistics should study only the expressive form of parole products. ... Our understanding of parole (the expressive form of parole products) includes not only the material shell of language—phonetics, the laws of word combination, and sentence patterns—but also the objective meanings of vocabulary, as these all belong to language."[2] If they include the objective meanings of vocabulary within the expressive form of parole products, how can this expressive form not involve the content of parole products? What

1 Tian Ru, *Several Questions Concerning Language and Speech*, *Chinese Language*, 1961, No. 2, p. 10.
2 Fang Guangtao and Shi Wentao, *Does Speech Have Class Character?*, Nanjing University Forum, 1959, No. 4, p. 26.

exactly is the content of a parole product, and what is its expressive form? As discussed above, the relationship between language and thought is such that language serves as the formal component of the "language-thought" unity, while thought serves as its content. However, for language itself, its formal component is phonetic form, and its content component is meaning (meaning is not equivalent to concepts in thought). As a communicative tool and a vehicle for thought, language is used to express ideas. Unlike an axe in construction, language as a tool is more akin to bricks in construction: it is both a tool for building houses and a component of their walls. When used as tools, linguistic elements become constituent parts of the expressive form of thought—rather than merely means of expression—when organized to convey a specific idea. Linguistic elements themselves, however, are means of expressing thought, termed "expressive means". Generally speaking, the result of using language to express thought is the formation of a "parole-thought" unity, in which thought constitutes the content and parole the form. For this reason, it is widely held that the sentence, as the smallest unit of parole products, is not identical to a logical judgment but rather its expressive form; together with the logical judgment, they form a "sentence-judgment" unity. Thus, for the "parole-thought" unity, the entire parole product serves as its expressive form, which contains a complex of meanings as its content. This complex of meanings is composed precisely of the objective meanings of linguistic elements—what Fang Guangtao and Shi Wentao classify as part of the "expressive form of parole products". Of course, a parole product itself also has a content part and a form part: its content part is the complex of meanings, and its form part is the complex of sound forms among expressive means, not the things themselves like lexical components with objective meanings. Since Fang Guangtao and Shi Wentao understand the "expressive form of parole products" as including things like lexical components with objective meanings, such things cannot be the formal part of parole products but rather one of the constituent factors of the formal part of the "parole-thought" unity. This is because the meaning of a word is only one of the constituent factors of the content part of a parole product composed of linguistic elements (and sometimes extralinguistic expressive means), not the formal part of the parole product composed of linguistic elements (and sometimes extralinguistic expressive means), and thus cannot be called the expressive form of the parole product. The expressive form of a parole product should be what expresses the complex of meanings in the parole product and thus constitutes its formal part. The formal part of the "parole-thought" unity should be the parole product itself, which contains its own specific formal and content parts. However, Fang Guangtao and Shi Wentao claim that it is not a parole product but merely the expressive form of a parole product, which renders their argument incoherent. It is evident that simply combining what Fang and Shi call "linguistic elements" (sometimes with "extralinguistic residues") at random cannot constitute a parole product; these elements themselves are not parole products and therefore cannot be the expressive form of parole products.

The truth is: these elements are the means or tools for expressing parole products. In fact, they are the "linguistic elements" that people use to construct parole products, or extremely limited immature or non-standard linguistic elements (i.e., the "extralinguistic residues" mentioned by Fang and Shi). As Fang Guangtao and Shi Wentao noted, these elements belong to langue itself, not to parole products. They only come to exist within parole products and become constituent parts of them when people use these means or tools to construct parole products. This is analogous to bricks used in building a house, which subsequently exist in the house's walls as constituent parts. If parole were merely these elements, there could be no distinction between parole and language as claimed by Fang and Shi. In fact, the process of constructing a parole product is one of selecting and combining these expressive means. The result of this combination organically arranges the selected expressive means to form a parole product. During this process, the objective meanings contained in the selected expressive means (or "partial subjective meanings", i.e., the meanings contained in "extralinguistic residues") necessarily combine to form a complex of meanings, which exists as the content of the parole product. It is only under the condition of the parole product's existence that we can discuss the expressive form and content of the parole product. What Fang Guangtao and Shi Wentao call the "expressive form of parole products" is in fact a means of expression, namely "linguistic elements" and "extralinguistic" expressive means. These are clearly not parole products themselves, just as bricks are not houses. Since they are not parole products but merely expressive means existing within parole products—and since the expressive form of a parole product is not simply the presence of the formal aspects of these means—how can we claim they constitute the expressive form of parole products? By defining "linguistic elements" with objective meanings as the expressive form of parole products, Fang and Shi not only confuse the expressive form of the "parole-thought" unity (i.e., the parole product itself) with the expressive form of the parole product, but also conflate linguistic components (sometimes immature or non-standard) from the repository of expressive means or the language system with the expressive forms of parole products—generated through the selection and combination of these components, which are distinct from language itself. In summary, "parole" can refer to any entity within the scope of "parole", including both "parole acts" and "parole products"—even though distinctions exist between these concepts.

In this framework, what is the relationship between langue and parole? Langue serves as the tool employed in "parole" activities and constitutes the aggregate of expressive means that appear as constituent parts in all parole products. Parole encompasses both the use of language and the outcomes generated by that use. Langue is a repository of expressive means from which parole activities draw materials to construct parole products; parole, conversely, is the selective deployment of these stored materials, integrating them as its components. In concrete communicative situations, langue is activated through parole acts, and the resulting parole products are predominantly formed by combining lexical items according to grammatical rules. Thus, parole products inherently incorporate linguistic elements. We may say that langue and parole are not absolutely isolated: langue exists in speech, though not the entire linguistic system resides in each unit of a parole product—only varying degrees of partial linguistic components exist in each unit, while the entire linguistic system resides in the sum of all parole products by all members of society. Nor is speech, as Fang Guangtao and Shi Wentao conceive it, merely a specialized form of langue. A parole product is a distinct entity from langue: even if the expressive means employed by units of parole products (sentences) formed through speech acts are all drawn from the linguistic repository, the product itself is no longer langue. This is because it is not a haphazard accumulation of linguistic elements but an organic combination of linguistic components (and sometimes extralinguistic expressive elements), thereby forming a complex of meanings distinct from the objective meanings of vocabulary contained in linguistic elements—i.e., the representation of ideological content in speech. This complex of meanings constitutes the content of a parole product; without this content, no parole product can exist. Langue certainly has its own content and form: the content of langue is the system formed by the aggregated meanings of its components, while the form of langue is the system formed by the aggregated phonetic forms of its components. However, the content of a parole product is its complex of meanings (the meaning of an entire sentence or passage), and the form of a parole product is the complex of phonetic forms among linguistic components and "extralinguistic residues". From this perspective, Shi Wentao's problematic view posits that langue and parole embody a generality-specificity relationship, with parole characterized as a "specific form of language"[1]. The relationship between the general and the specific is such that the general inheres in the specific, and the specific represents the manifestation of the general in concrete individuals. While language does inhere in parole products through its constituent elements being scattered across all parole products, it does not inhere in individual speech products. As a system, langue never exists in its entirety within any single parole product. Only a portion of the expressive means in parole products constitutes the concrete manifestation of linguistic components, and it is only this portion that stands in a general-specific relationship to the linguistic components of langue. If langue and parole were in a general-specific relationship, there would be no scientific need to distinguish between them, since general phenomena are abstractions of similar specific phenomena and exist concretely within each individual specific instance of the same category. Although specific entities have their unique characteristics, they cannot lack general features or fail to possess the same

1 Shi Wentao, *On Language, Speech, and Speech Works*, *Chinese Language*, No. 4, 1960, p. 183.

essential traits. Shi Wentao's argument is untenable because he both asserts the scientific necessity of distinguishing between langue and parole and defines parole as merely a "specific form of langue". If langue and parole require scientific differentiation, their distinction must lie in fundamental characteristics, not in a general-specific dichotomy or in the presence of accidental, individual "extralinguistic residues". Langue and parole do not embody a general-specific relationship because langue is not abstracted from parole—what is abstracted from parole is parole in general sense (i.e., the "parole" under discussion here), while langue in general sense can only be abstracted from specific languages (e.g., Chinese, Russian, etc.). The truth is: only individual linguistic components are abstracted from variants of expressive means existing in parole. Parole differs from langue precisely because it is not a mere manifestation of linguistic components but rather the selective use of linguistic and non-linguistic expressive means, as well as their combination in parole products. This selection and this combination itself are already extra-linguistic phenomena. And precisely because it is extra-linguistic, it possesses essential characteristics distinct from those of language.

The relationship between langue and parole is also evident in how parole products provide the raw material for the components of the langue system. In reality, langue consists of an aggregate of linguistic components abstracted from the universal elements of expressive means present in all parole products of societal members. Once aggregated, these components form a self-contained system with distinct characteristics. This system then serves as a tool for individuals or groups to communicate (or engage in thinking). For this reason, although langue and parole products are distinct, they are inextricably linked: parole acts as the "vanguard" in the formation and development of langue. It is unimaginable that langue was collectively created by all members of society in an instant; rather, each linguistic component is first proposed by an individual as an innovation to meet social needs, then gradually gains societal validation and integrates into the language system. When exercising their linguistic faculty, humans can create new linguistic components. While such innovations initially emerge as "proposals", it is undeniable that any linguistic innovation arises from the gradual exercise of this faculty. When a "proposal" is first introduced, it exists in an individual's parole; only after other members of society gradually "endorse" this proposal through repeated use in communication does it become abstracted as a component of the language. Language itself evolves through this continuous process of abstraction and aggregation to meet societal needs—a process by which primitive humans first created language. The same mechanism drives the emergence of new components in existing languages: individuals or groups, adapting to social needs and following internal linguistic laws, propose innovative "proposals" that first appear in individual parole as elements of expressive means. These schemes are then generalized into language through gradual societal "endorsement" and repeated use. Thus, while we reject the idealist view that individuals create language single-handedly, we do not deny the role of individuals in language creation. However, in the process of creating and developing language, the "proposals" put forward by individuals are always extremely limited; relative to the entire language system, such individual proposals are scarce. For individuals, existing language invariably functions as a communication and thinking tool independent of individual will, through which the parole of individuals or groups is constructed. Moreover, not all "proposals" put forward by individuals succeed. When they run counter to social needs or the internal laws of language development, individual proposals prove futile. A linguistic element can only become part of langue through societal "endorsement" and repeated social use; thus, langue is a social creation, not an individual one. However, individuals play a role in formulating "proposals" for new linguistic components, and this act of exercising linguistic faculty is not entirely a personal phenomenon. In fact, the creative "proposals" formulated through individual linguistic acts exist as expressive means within parole products. In its immature stage, such a scheme is one of the expressive means in parole products and falls under the category of "extralinguistic residues"; once mature, it becomes a linguistic component functioning as an expressive means in parole products.

Section 3 The Universal Character of Langue and the Class Character of Parole

Since langue and parole are essentially distinct, where do their key characteristics lie? The critical distinction between langue and parole lies in the fact that langue is national while parole is class-based. Langue serves as a communicative tool for the entire nation: it is not only created by the whole people but also commonly used by all. It serves all classes in class-based societies impartially. As components of the linguistic sign system, both linguistic elements and lexical components lack class character and instead embody national character.

Since parole encompasses both the act of exercising linguistic faculty and the "products" formed by such acts, it is not necessarily as universal as langue. In reality, parole lacks universality and instead possesses class character—a distinction that can be clarified through two dimensions: parole acts and parole products. Here, "parole acts" refer not to the physical movements of parole organs but to the social activity of exercising linguistic faculty, primarily manifested in the concrete use of language. While parole acts certainly rely on physiological activity as a material basis (like all social behaviors), they are fundamentally social acts, not mere physiological processes, because communicative behavior is a social practice, not a biological function. The physical movements of organs carry no class character, but the conscious exercise of linguistic faculty does. In this world of innumerable things, however diverse they may be and regardless of whether they inherently possess class character, the conscious utilization of these things by individuals in class societies is imbued with class character—for human class identity is manifested in both thought and action. Natural phenomena themselves are presumably classless, yet the conscious employment of natural elements (e.g., stones) by soldiers fighting against the U.S. imperialist aggressors to strike the enemy carried distinct class character. Although langue itself is classless, the conscious exercise of linguistic faculty—including the use of langue—represents social behavior that reflects human class identity, and such behavior inherently bears class character.

Although langue serves as a communicative tool accessible to all members of society and a treasure trove of expressive means (lexical and grammatical systems) adoptable by the entire community, the act of using langue involves selection: people choose lexical and grammatical components suitable for their purposes. This selection carries class character, as choices can be made for class interests. Of course, the selected linguistic components themselves remain classless—just as the stones on Triangle Hill used to strike enemies retain no class character— but the act of organizing these components into parole products within specific contexts is a class-laden choice.

The class character of parole products is primarily manifested in the complex of meanings that represent their ideological content. Since thought cannot exist independently of language—instead forming a unity of "langue-thought". Parole acts inherently combine linguistic and conceptual elements into a "parole-idea" complex. The ideological content represented within this complex becomes the substance of the parole product, reflecting the speaker's class-based consciousness. Although individual linguistic components lack class character, their arrangement and the resulting ideological content carry class bias. While the formal composition of parole products (i.e., the combination of linguistic or extralinguistic expressive means) remains class-neutral, the class character of a parole product derives from its content, not its form. Thus, even if the formal elements are neutral, we cannot deny the class character inherent in parole products when they express class-based ideologies. Here, "class character" refers to the essential trait of parole products when expressing class-bound thoughts; it does not imply that every utterance necessarily exhibits such character. Just as when people say artistic works have class character, they refer to the essential trait that artistic works must reflect the ideology a writer intends to express—not that every artistic work necessarily has it (e.g., Qi Baishi's paintings of shrimp may not carry class character)—so too with speech products: some of their smallest units (sentences) may not reveal their class-determined nature in the absence of specific conditions. This fact does not prove that parole products lack class character or only "may" possess it. Moreover, sentences are merely the smallest units of parole products, often functioning as components of larger discourses (paragraphs or whole texts) rather than independent units. Therefore, to examine whether parole products have class character, one should analyze entire discourses or texts, not isolated sentences—for sentences are only occasionally independent units; in most cases, they serve as constituent elements of larger, normatively functioning parole units.

Does the expressive apparatus of parole products have class character? The expressive means of parole products are primarily the manifestations of linguistic components in speech, which certainly lack class character. However, the "extralinguistic" expressive means in parole products can possess class character. When using class dialects to construct parole products, apart from the expressive means borrowed from the national common language (which are classless), the unique expressive tools of class dialects embedded in parole products carry class character. On another level, linguistic components are not equivalent to language itself. In certain historical contexts or stages of social development, different classes may select specific linguistic components for expressive purposes—or even create "extralinguistic" means—to form a specialized system of expressive tools tailored to class-divided communicative scenarios. This constitutes a stylistic system of expressive means with class character, though such stylistic systems are generally classless. No one would deny that the expressive system of the Eight-Legged Essay, not its individual components (e.g., linguistic elements), bears class character.

It is an evident fact that langue is classless while parole is class-bound. However, some who acknowledge langue's lack of class character argue that parole, like langue, is also classless—for example, Fang Guangtao, Shi

Wentao, Li Zhenlin, and Dong Dawu. The sole argument Fang and Shi use to deny parole's class character is their claim that parole consists merely of parole products or expressive forms of parole. The flaws in this argument have already been discussed above. Moreover, parole products are objective entities that serve as expressive forms of thought, possessing their own form and content (distinct from the objective existence of thought itself). What Fang and Shi call "expressive forms of parole products"—linguistic components like lexis with objective meanings—inevitably interrelate in parole products to form chains of meaning complexes. These complexes, which are neither identical to thoughts nor mere linguistic meanings, constitute the objective existence of parole product content and are the "direct reality" of class-bound thought.

Li Zhenlin and Dong Dawu also argued that parole lacks class character, their reasoning rooted in a denial of the qualitative distinction between langue and parole. They claim: "Humans use langue according to communicative principles, and langue can only exist and develop through human communicative or linguistic activities; thus, langue and linguistic activities are inseparably intertwined."[1] From this, they conclude: "It is clearly inappropriate to call linguistic activities 'parole activities' while regarding them as two essentially different social phenomena from langue."

1 Li Zhenlin and Dong Dawu, *On Several Questions Concerning Langue and "Parole"*, *Academic Monthly*, 1961, No. 1, p. 50.

Does this "inseparability thesis" prove that there is no qualitative distinction between langue and parole? No one denies the inseparable connection between langue and parole, language and thought, communication and its tools, or between toolmakers and tools themselves. But does the fact that two things are inseparably linked mean they lack qualitative differences? Human consciousness is a product of the human brain; without the brain, there can be no consciousness—yet the two are inseparably connected. Can we therefore claim that the brain and consciousness have no qualitative distinction? Production and production tools are inseparably linked: tools are created for production, and apart from production, tools would not exist. Yet production is a social phenomenon, while tools can be natural objects—surely there is a qualitative difference between them? Language is indeed inseparable from its use: it was created by human society for communication and cannot exist independent of human creation and application. But does this inseparability prove that langue and parole (what Li and Dong call "the use of language") cannot have a qualitative distinction? Language is merely "the most important means of communication for human" (Lenin's words). Beyond language, people have other communicative tools, such as gestures and semaphore. One can use semaphore to express the same ideas they would convey through language to engage in communication. If the mere inseparable link between communication and its tools proves that communication and its tools cannot be qualitatively different, then not only would there be no qualitative distinction between the communicative act of expressing ideas and semaphore, but even language and semaphore would be indistinguishable in essence. The fact is clear: although the language with national character as a communicative tool is inseparably linked to class-bound ideology, language itself is merely a vehicle for expressing thoughts, not a direct counterpart to thought. Who can tell us what specific ideology Chinese directly corresponds to? Chinese can express any thought of any person who uses it, but it does not directly correspond to any specific individual user or any particular ideology. Langue and parole differ not only in their social nature but also in their structures. For example, langue structure is governed by the principle of associativity, while parole structure follows the principle of linearity. The structural units of langue are linguistic components such as lexemes and tagmemes, whereas the structural units of parole are sentences, discourses, and the like. After asserting that langue and parole represent a relationship between the general and the particular[1], Li and Dong go on to claim: "There is another argument about the class character of the use of langue, which is merely another way of asserting the class character of parole. People may ask: When it is said that 'using langue' has class character, does this refer to the class character of the user's stance and viewpoint? Or does it mean that langue itself becomes class-bound when

1 Li Zhenlin and Dong Dawu, *On Several Questions Concerning Langue and "Parole"*, *Academic Monthly*, 1961, No. 1, p. 53. We have already commented on this point when discussing Shi Wentao's arguments above, so we will not elaborate further here.

used? If it is the former, there is no problem. … If it is the latter, then there is an issue."[1] Despite the inconsistency in their argument (earlier claiming no qualitative distinction between langue and its use), their obvious intent is to prove that parole lacks class character. The class character of langue use refers to the class-based stance and viewpoint of the user, not to langue itself becoming class-bound through use. This is because "using langue" denotes human social behavior, which is determined by one's stance and viewpoint. Whether langue becomes class-bound after being used is entirely separate from the question of whether langue use has class character—and thus outside the scope of this discussion. Li and Dong sought to prove their argument that "parole has no class character" by criticizing others, but their critique missed the mark, as it lacked convincing reasoning and misunderstood their opponents' views. They claim: "There is a perspective that holds langue is classless, but 'parole' has class character. At the same time, this perspective also argues that the relationship between langue and 'parole' is one of generality and particularity..."[2] This is inconsistent with the facts. We maintain that langue is classless and parole is class-bound, but we not only reject the idea that langue and parole are related as "generality and particularity"—we also argue that precisely because they are not in such a relationship, they have qualitative differences. Therefore, Li and Dong's

1 Li Zhenlin and Dong Dawu, *On Several Questions Concerning Langue and "Parole"*, *Academic Monthly*, 1961, No. 1, p. 56.
2 Ibid., p. 55.

reasoning—"since all 'parole' is without exception class-bound, this class character is both a special attribute of 'parole' and a universal attribute that can be subsumed under the general. Thus, the only conclusion is that langue also has class character"[1]—falls apart. They further claim that those who argue parole has class character believe "langue becomes class-bound when used", but this portrayal is also inconsistent with the facts, as we do not contend that langue acquires class character through use. The issue lies in the two meanings of "parole" (parole activity and parole products): unlike langue, both forms of parole possess class character, yet neither is identical to langue nor derived from it. Langue does not become class-bound or transform into parole when used; only individual linguistic components from the langue system exist within specific parole units as part of their expressive means. Li and Dong advance a third criticism: "There is another view that langue is an internal component of 'parole', such that 'parole' is broader in scope. Therefore, according to this theory, the relationship between langue and 'parole' is one of whole and part. Following general logical reasoning, the conclusion should similarly be that langue has class character—for it is impossible for a whole to have class character while its parts do not."[2] Yet this critique also falls flat. Does the claim that "langue exists within parole" necessarily mean parole is the whole and langue the

1 Ibid., p. 56.
2 Li Zhenlin and Dong Dawu, *On Several Questions Concerning Langue and "Parole"*, *Academic Monthly*, 1961.

part? Can such a conclusion be drawn through "general logical reasoning"? Minerals exist in mountains—does that make minerals the part and mountains the whole? When we say langue exists in parole, we mean it exists in the sum total of all parole acts, not in each individual parole unit. Only certain linguistic components exist within each individual parole unit; there is no "whole-part relationship" between them. Suppose we grant, for the sake of argument, that langue and parole stand in a part-whole relationship: does "general logical reasoning" then oblige us to conclude that if speech has class character, langue must share it? Consider the intestines as part of the human body: if humans have class character, does it logically follow that the intestines must as well? The whole-part relationship is not the same as the general-particular relationship. The general is the essential aspect of the particular; thus, while they differ, they cannot be qualitatively distinct. The whole-part relationship differs in kind: the characteristics of the whole and its constituent parts can exhibit qualitative disparities. Li and Dong further attempt to argue that "the basic content and 'essential' characteristics of the 'objective' social phenomenon of 'parole' in fact partly belong to what is inherent in language itself, and partly to the realm of social culture ('parole products')"[1], in order to deny the objective existence of parole and thereby its class-based characteristics.

1 Li Zhenlin and Dong Dawu, *On Several Questions Concerning Langue and "Parole"*, *Academic Monthly*, 1961, vol. 1, p. 56.

This line of reasoning contradicts the concrete facts of the countless phenomena in the universe. For example, a radio is composed partly of glass tubes and partly of wood, to name just a few components. Glass tubes belong to minerals, and wood to plants—but does this mean radios have no qualitative difference from minerals? Or that radios do not exist? Parole is certainly a composite entity that embodies ideological content, consisting of linguistic elements and non-linguistic means of expression. Its linguistic elements naturally belong to langue, and the ideological content expressed by its semantic composites naturally belongs to social culture. But does this allow us to claim that parole does not exist? Or that parole has no qualitative difference from language or even social culture? Parole certainly incorporates representations of ideological content as part of social culture, but is parole therefore identical to social culture? The existence of speech products is a palpable reality, as evidenced by the numerous Chinese-language dissertations around us—each explicitly conveying specific ideological content. These essays are concrete entities composed of linguistic elements (and even non-linguistic expressive tools), forming semantic wholes that embody ideological meaning and exist objectively. Li and Dong's attempt to deny speech's existence—and with it, its inherent class character—thus collapses in the face of observable fact.

Section 4 The Practical Significance of the Distinction Between Langue and Parole

The distinction between langue and parole is not only a factual reality but also carries significant practical implications. This is precisely why we emphasize their differences. Drawing a clear line between langue and parole holds major practical significance in at least the following areas:

First, this distinction enables us to correctly understand langue and thus treat it appropriately. Langue is a universal tool for communication, aiding people in embodying or expressing thought. This may seem like a universally accepted principle. But without distinguishing between language and speech, one cannot truly grasp its meaning. Many confuse the "utterances" from people's mouths with langue itself. If that were the case, the principle that langue is a universal communicative tool and an instrument for human thought would be incomprehensible. If the "words spoken" were the communicative tool, what then would constitute the act of communication? And what of its content? If no distinction is made between the act of communication, its content, and the communicative tool, can we then distinguish between the act of production, its content, and the means of production? Many conflate thought with language—this is true of American behavioral psychologists, for example, who argue that judgments in thought are equivalent to sentences (units of speech products). If that were the case, why would children with the faculty of thought need to learn language to aid in thinking? What distinction would there be between thinking and the tool that aids thinking? Between ideas and the tool for expressing them? If one fails to understand that language is merely a tool to assist thinking and express ideas—distinct from thought itself and from ideas—how can any difference be drawn between language and thought or ideas? Why then would we need to master language to aid our thinking and express our ideas? Why learn language to understand the vast knowledge generated by others' thinking? All these questions would be unanswerable. The distinction between langue and parole also helps us grasp the principle that language has no class character. Many struggle to accept that langue is classless precisely because they fail to understand the difference between langue and parole. One of the reasons the Marr School argued that langue has class character is precisely their failure to grasp the distinction between langue and parole. Since everyone's act of speaking has class character, and since the "utterances" from everyone's mouth also have class character, and since "speaking" and the "utterances" produced are not distinguished from langue itself, it followed naturally that they concluded langue has class character and could not comprehend the principle that langue is classless. By distinguishing between langue and parole, we clearly understand that langue does not refer to the act of creating linguistic elements, using language, or the words composed through language use. Instead, it is a system of signs shared by all members of a society—a system that all members can use and master. It exists in society even when individuals are not using it. People from one class can use it, and people from another class can also use it. The lexical components of this system directly correspond only to concepts without class character, not to judgments composed of concepts. The grammatical components of this system directly correspond only to logical relationships without class character, not to ideologies with class character. Therefore, langue has no class character. As a concrete application of language functions—primarily as the specific use of language and the outcomes derived from such use—parole naturally has class character. However, it is not langue itself but parole, and thus we cannot infer that langue has class character on this basis. By the same logic, we can understand various characteristics of language, such as its social nature, universality, symbolic function, and gradual evolution—all of which derive from the distinctions between langue and parole (as a tool for communication, not the act of communication; as a tool for thinking, not thinking itself; as a means of expression, not the ideas expressed). With this correct understanding, we can properly engage with langue. For example, we will not mistakenly believe langue has class character and reject the linguistic legacy left by past societies, but instead study language through its lexical and grammatical systems.

Second, this distinction helps us clearly define the object of study in linguistics. Every science has its specific research object, and linguistics is no exception. Generally speaking, linguistics studies langue. However, if what exactly constitutes langue remains unclear, the discipline's research object becomes ambiguous. While arguing that speech has no class character, Fang Guangtao and Shi Wentao emphasize that “parole” must be understood solely as the expressive form of speech products, claiming that only this can clarify linguistics’ research object—otherwise, the interpretation of “parole” as “parole products” would obscure it.[1] Their intention is good, but their worry is unfounded. The distinction between langue and parole precisely allows us to define linguistics’ research object clearly. Understanding “parole” as both “parole acts” and “parole products” does not have the opposite effect. By distinguishing between langue and parole, we can identify what exactly constitutes the langue that is the object of linguistic study, and thus direct our research toward this target. Even when studying the close connections between language and other phenomena, we can still distinguish clear boundaries and the true relationships between langue and these phenomena. Since langue is a system of signs (distinct from parole) serving as a universal communicative tool—the sum of a lexical system and a grammatical system—the object of linguistic study should be the lexical and grammatical systems (along with their phonetic systems as material shells and semantic systems as content elements) of each langue existing in various societal units, as well as variations of these systems, and even the variants of these systems manifested in parole by their members. As Smirnitsky noted, “langue must

1 Fang Guangtao and Shi Wentao, *Does Speech Have Class Character?* Nanjing University Forum, 1959, vol. 4, p. 26.

be studied in speech, and research must be based on the richest possible collection of parole products"[1]. From such materials, we select the true objects of study: linguistic elements (including former speech elements that have become linguistic elements in the course of development, such as idiomatic sentences that have become members of the language's lexical system and are used as words). Without studying langue through speech materials, linguistic research would lack a solid foundation and remain ungrounded. However, when studying such materials, the linguist's aim is clearly to analyze and synthesize their linguistic elements, not their semantic composites—though linguists must also examine the relationship between semantic composites (i.e., the embodiment of ideological content in speech) and means of expression. In short, by distinguishing between langue and parole, we can clarify that the true or direct object of linguistic study is the sum of linguistic elements in parole products and the lexical and grammatical systems they form. Moreover, "langue draws nourishment and supplementation from parole and develops through elements created in parole (from individual words and word forms to entire sentences)"[2]. Linguists also study individual expressive means in speech products that can influence language development, systems of individual expressive devices, special systems of expressive means formed through language use

1 Smirnitsky, *The Objectivity of Language's Existence*, in *Selected Translations of Linguistic Papers*, Fifth Series, p. 126.
2 Smirnitsky, *The Objectivity of Language's Existence*, in *Selected Translations of Linguistic Papers*, Fifth Series, p. 129.

in specific communicative contexts, and variants diverged from language in other respects.[1] Fang Guangtao and Shi Wentao feared that understanding "parole" as "parole products" would obscure linguistics' research object, but this worry is unwarranted. By grasping the correct relationship between langue and parole, the object of linguistic study becomes clear: Linguists recognize that semantic composites of ideas in parole products are extralinguistic, and thus do not treat them as the primary object of study. Instead, their focus naturally includes expressive means in parole products—whether these are existing linguistic elements or individual expressions that may evolve into linguistic components. On the contrary, treating "parole" as merely the expressive means of parole products—thereby effectively eliminating the distinction between langue and parole—would instead create intellectual complacency. This confusion leads to the flawed assumption that no distinction between them matters, as they are wrongly seen as indistinguishable. Recognizing the distinction and relationship between langue and parole, one can appreciate the overlap between them: linguistic elements exist within parole, and parole relies on linguistic components for composition. This interplay draws scholars' attention to questions of how to organize parole using linguistic elements, immature linguistic elements (i.e., expressive means not yet generally accepted), and even other extralinguistic expressive means akin to langue,

1 See Gao Mingkai, *On Langue and Parole*, *Chinese Language*, 1960, vol. 2, pp. 71–81.

such as discourse structure. While such research is not purely linguistic, it can form a linguistic border science—parole linguistics. Although langue itself has no class character, its use exhibits distinct class characteristics, as different classes (which are "far from indifferent" to langue[1]) employ it for their own purposes. Thus, they select lexical and grammatical components from the linguistic system's repository that serve their interests and construct parole products beneficial to and serving their class in ways aligned with their needs. Although the use of langue pertains to the realm of parole, and while the expressive means in parole products generally consist of linguistic elements in parole and their modes of combination, linguists must study the laws governing people's use of these elements and combinations. They must also employ a class-analytical perspective to examine the role of class in language use. The issue of writing style emphasized by Chairman Mao is, on the one hand, a political and ideological matter, and on the other, a question of how class influences language use. The emergence of certain disciplines within linguistics is also linked to how language is used. Traditional rhetoric, in fact, constitutes the study of speech linguistics: it focuses on how to effectively and skillfully organize speech products using the lexical and grammatical components of language, rather than merely studying the language's lexical and grammatical systems in isolation. Even the so-called practical linguistics

1 See J. V. Stalin, *Marxism and Questions of Linguistics*, p. 10.

emerging in modern linguistics—such as statistical linguistics, machine translation studies, and electronic communication studies—focuses on the practical use of langue, examining how people organize parole products or translate parole products composed of different linguistic elements. In other words, these fields also arose from inquiries into how langue is used and how parole products are structured. Moreover, the rise of modern linguistic stylistics is a direct outcome of parole theory.[1] The systems of stylistic devices that language differentiates into within specific communicative contexts to adapt to particular communicative purposes are precisely the objects of study for modern linguistic stylistics. While these stylistic systems arise from the use of langue in specialized communicative scenarios and purposes (thus belonging to the realm of parole), they also constitute unique combinations of linguistic elements and variants of langue in parole. As such, they equally fall within the scope of parole linguistics. It is precisely under the impetus of parole theory that research on literary parole—one of these stylistic systems—has advanced. Therefore, the distinction between langue and parole and the establishment of parole theory represent profoundly significant issues in modern linguistics, with substantial practical implications.

1 See Gao Mingkai, *The Content and Tasks of Linguistic Stylistics*, in *Linguistic Essays (Linguistics Series)*, Shanghai Educational Publishing House, 1960, Fourth Volume, pp. 174–178.

Chapter 6

Language Variants

Section 1 What Is "Dialect"?

The universality of language is absolute, but as societal units undergo internal differentiation with social development, the common language of a universal societal unit may relatively diverge into various variants, known as "dialects".

The term "dialect" generally refers to regional linguistic forms, i.e., so-called "local speech". However, the meaning of "regional linguistic forms" has evolved over time. In ancient China, the term "dialect" already existed. Yang Xiong 扬雄 of the Han Dynasty authored *Fangyan Shiyi Bieguo Fangyan* 《辅轩使者绝代语释别国方言》 (abbreviated as *Fangyan*), which used this term. In his *Preface to Fangyan* 《方言序》, Guo Pu 郭璞 wrote: "It is said that Fangyan was compiled by imperial messengers who roamed the states to collect diverse languages. Wherever carts traveled and human feet trod, all were recorded in official documents." The"dialects" mentioned at the time did not necessarily refer to regional variants of the same language—they were not necessarily "all ancient and elegant alternative terms" (Yang Xiong, *Fangyan*, Volume 1)—but rather the languages of "various states" or "unconventional speech of distant regions" and "archaic terms of past dynasties" (Guo Pu, *Preface to Fangyan*). At that time, the term "dialect" referred to "regional distinct languages" (from Guo Pu's *Preface to Erya*《尔雅序》), regardless of whether these "regional distinct languages" were variants diverged from the same language. Yang Xiong noted in his book: "喧 (xuān), 唏 (xī), 灼 (zhuó), 怛 (dá) all mean 'pain'. Endless sobbing is called 恒 (gěng); grief without tears is called 唏 (xī). Regionally, in Chu dialect, grief is expressed as 唏 (xī); in the outlying areas of Yan and along the Lishui River in Korea, children's unceasing crying is called 恒 (gěng)." This statement raises doubts about whether the dialects recorded by Yang Xiong were merely regional variants of Ancient Chinese, and whether the "language of a certain region" mentioned therein referred to vocabulary components like trade jargon. However, since most other states in ancient times denoted fiefdoms under the feudal dynasty, the records by ancient "imperial messengers" were mostly regional variants of Ancient Chinese—particularly so in Yang Xiong's Fangyan. Gradually, the term "dialect" came to denote regional variants of the same language. In this sense, a "local linguistic form", such as what we call the Kaifeng dialect, refers to the variant of Chinese spoken in the Kaifeng region. The term "dialect" is rendered as диалект in Russian, dialecte in French, dialect in English, and Dialekt in German. These words all derive from the Greek dialektos, which originally denoted regional linguistic forms. Consequently, most Russians and other Europeans understand terms like диалект to mean "regional linguistic forms". Initially, the meaning of "regional linguistic forms" was vague, but with the development of historical-comparative methods, it came to refer specifically to regional variants of the same language—a shift parallel to the evolution of "dialect" in Chinese. For this reason, when translating European linguistic works, we have long used "dialect" to render Russian диалект, French dialecte, English dialect, and German Dialekt. However, as scholars have deepened their understanding of dialects' essential characteristics, the term's meaning has evolved in modern linguistics. What is commonly referred to as "dialect" ("regional speech") is fundamentally a social phenomenon rather than a geographic one, though its formation is indeed tied to geographic factors.

Thus, modern linguistics no longer interprets "dialect" merely as "regional linguistic forms". More importantly, it understands dialects as differentiations that arise from a language's development alongside societal change. The Greek dialectos is formed with the root *di-*, which carries meanings such as "two", "divide into two", and "differentiate from one into two". Dialectos came to denote "regional linguistic forms" precisely because it refers to branches diverging from a language. Ancient European language scholars only observed geographic differentiations in language, hence their interpretation of these terms as merely "regional linguistic forms"—just as Ancient Chinese scholars, who observed "distinct languages in different regions", interpreted "dialect" as "local speech". Even historical-comparative linguists, by focusing solely on regional variants of a single language, failed to fully grasp how social conditions influence dialect formation.

Today, with the development of linguistic science, many linguists—particularly Soviet linguists—no longer interpret "dialect" merely as "regional linguistic forms". Instead, they understand it as linguistic differentiation: the result of a language diverging alongside social differentiation. Defined as "linguistic differentiation", "dialect" thus refers not only to regional divergences but to all forms of linguistic differentiation, including regional ones. This has expanded the term's scope. A look at the works of Stalin and other Soviet linguists reveals that the term диалект (corresponding to Chinese "方言") in their writings can denote both "regional dialects" and "sociolects". Stalin used both диалекты местные (or территориальны) and классовые диалекты in his works, which translate as "regional dialects" (or "territorial dialects") and "class dialects", respectively. In his Russian textbook *Introduction to Linguistics*, in the section *Language and Dialects* (языки диалекты), Chikobava uses terms such as диалекты территориальные ("territorial dialects"), социальные диалекты ("sociolects"), and классовые диалекты ("class dialects").[1] The same applies to A. A. Reformatsky (A. A. Реформатский).[2] In their French work *A Compendium of Modern French Lexicology*, N. N. Lopanikova and

1 Chikobava, *Introduction to Linguistics* (Введение в языкознание), Part I, Moscow, 1952, pp. 61–67.
2 Reformatsky, *Introduction to Linguistics* (Введение в языкознание), Moscow, 1955.

N. A. Movchovitch even adopted similar French terms: dialectes locaux ("regional dialects") and dialectes sociaux ("sociolects").[1] Precisely because "dialect" is understood as "linguistic differentiation", Soviet scholars often classify dialects. For example, in his *Introduction to Literary Studies*, T. П. Abramovich (Т. П. Абрамович) categorizes dialectal vocabulary—based on dialectal characteristics and nature—into three types: provincial dialect vocabulary (i.e., "regional dialect" vocabulary), argot vocabulary, and trade jargon vocabulary.[2] In this context, the term "dialect" (диалект, dialecte, dialect, Dialekt) as used in modern linguistics no longer refers merely to the everyday understanding of "regional linguistic forms", but to linguistic differentiation itself.

Some argue that terms like Russian диалект or French dialecte—in short, these words in European languages—can encompass this meaning, while Chinese "dialect" cannot, as in Chinese usage, "dialect" exclusively refers to "local speech". This may seem plausible, but it is not the case. Historically, the Chinese term "dialect" did not originally denote "local speech" as a regional variant of a single language; only later did it evolve into its current common understanding. Similarly, the corresponding terms in European languages (диалект, dialecte, etc.) did not originally signify

1 Lopanikova, N. N., & Movchovitch, N. A. *Précis de Lexicologie du Français Moderne*. Moscow, 1958, pp. 126–134.
2 Abramovich, T. П. *Introduction to Literary Studies* (Введение в литературоведение). Moscow, 1953, p. 61.

linguistic differentiation. They acquired the meaning of "linguistic differentiation" in linguistics only after modern linguistic developments led to new understandings of "dialect". To adapt to new advancements in linguistics, the meanings of terminology have been revised in the past, and there seems to be no reason they cannot be revised now. Just as Soviet scholars modified the meaning of the Russian term, there is no justification for us to cling to outdated conventions without question. Of course, due to habit, when we use the term "dialect" alone and context permits, it can still refer to "local speech". However, when it comes to scientific understanding, it is necessary to define "dialect" as "linguistic differentiation". Chikobava stated in his *Introduction to Linguistics*: "A language spoken over a large area is divided into various dialects or local varieties... this is the 'territorial dialect'."[1] This statement reflects a scenario where what is scientifically termed "territorial dialects" (or "regional dialects") is commonly referred to as "dialect" in everyday usage. Thus, in daily life, we commonly refer to "territorial dialects" as simply "dialects". Even in scientific writing, we may use "dialect" to mean "regional dialects" when context permits. However, this practical flexibility does not alter the theoretical understanding: in modern linguistics, "dialect" specifically denotes linguistic differentiation.

"Linguistic differentiation" in fact refers to "linguistic variants"—that is, variants diverged from the national common language. We call it

1 Chikobava, *Introduction to Linguistics* (Russian edition), Volume I, p. 61.

linguistic differentiation because although it is not a language in the full sense (not a language shared by all members of society), it shares certain characteristics with the national language: it serves as a type of communicative tool, a system of expressive means, and a symbolic system used for communication. This symbolic system is derived from the national common language, with some of its components directly originating from it. Due to various factors, societal units may, during their development, internally divide into diverse groups and communicative contexts. Consequently, the national common language may also differentiate into various variants. All these variants utilize a symbolic system primarily derived from the national common language as tools for communication and thinking.

Section 2 Types of Language Variants

Although there are numerous language variants diverged from the national common language, they can be broadly categorized into three types: regional variants of language; social variants of language; speech variants of language.

What is commonly called "dialect" refers to the regional variants of a language. These qualify as language variants because they each possess a symbolic system, serve as tools for communication and thinking, and originate from the national common language. Due to historical social conditions, societal units may evolve into semi-independent regional communities during their development. Within these regional societies, people interact frequently, but communication with members of other societal units outside the region diminishes. As a result, changes in the scope of communication—combined with unique social developments within regional societies—drive the differentiation of language into specialized symbolic systems. These systems are adapted to the specific environments of regional communities and function as their tools for communication and thought. However, these symbolic systems originate from the national common language: many of their components are directly inherited from it, and even when changes occur, they develop on the foundation of the national language. In most cases, inherited components differ only in pronunciation, which is why the primary defining feature of regional dialects lies in so-called "regional accents". This is because changes in pronunciation are not changes to linguistic components themselves but rather changes to the material shell of those components—that is, differences in phonetics. As long as the semantic units of words or linguistic components with "regional accents" as their material shell remain unchanged, they remain integral components of the national common language—having undergone only superficial ("material shell") changes rather than qualitative transformations. Of course, components of the national common language can also undergo qualitative changes in regional dialects, with the degree of change depending on the extent of differentiation. Regional dialects may also generate new lexical elements or even new grammatical components, but these new lexical and grammatical elements are integrated with inherited lexical and grammatical components from the national common language to form a unified system. Precisely because this system emerges from the gradual transformation of the national common language's original system—through changes in "material shell", occasional qualitative changes in individual elements, and the addition of new components—it qualifies as a variant of the national common language's symbolic system, i.e., a variant of the national common language.

A regional dialect is a linguistic variant of the national common language in a local society. It serves as a tool for communication and thinking for all members of the local society, embodying "universality" within that society: it is developed and used collectively by all members, regardless of gender, age, class, or occupation. Additionally, it is classless, as it emerges from the collective development and shared use of all members of the local society. Just as a "language" refers to a symbolic system collectively created and used by a national society, a regional dialect refers to a symbolic system developed and used by a local society—though it is merely a variant diverged from the national common language's symbolic system. The lexical elements within this symbolic system directly correspond to the classless basic material concepts in thinking, and its grammatical components align with the classless logical rules in thinking, hence their lack of class character. However, the use of a regional dialect and the speech of individuals or groups within the local society formed by this use do exhibit class character. This is because they represent the application of the regional dialect by members of a specific class within the local society, as well as the products of combining linguistic components to express complex meanings (where ideology is manifested in the interplay of linguistic elements). Such products are essentially speech works, though their means of expression consist primarily of components of the regional dialect as a linguistic variant.

A national society may also be divided into social groups due to differences in the social status of its members. Such social groups are commonly referred to as "communities". With this social group differentiation, patterns of communication change. Members of each community not only interact with members of other communities within the national society but also engage in internal communication within their own group. This internal communication within a community has its own unique characteristics. As a result, language, which functions as a communication tool, may differentiate into variants specific to that community. These variants are called "social group variants of language", or "community dialects". For example, the specialized languages used by members of different professions (e.g., industry-specific jargon).

Specialized languages like trade jargon are termed linguistic variants because they too possess a symbolic system and serve as tools for communication and thinking; they also represent differentiations from the national common language's symbolic system. Due to the qualitative difference between the division of a national society into social groups and its division into regional societies, the structures of community dialects differ from those of regional dialects. Members of a social group not only communicate within their own community but also interact with members of other groups in the national society. As a result, community dialects are less likely to develop phonetic variations ("regional accents") akin to those in regional dialects. The unique communicative need of community dialects lies in expressing terms related to the group's specific interests, leading to their primary characteristics: the creation of new lexical components exclusive to the community or the modification of lexical components from the national common language. In other words, the vast majority of the components in a community dialect's symbolic system are drawn from the national common language's symbolic system, with only a portion consisting of modified components from the national language and another portion being newly created. In reality, a community dialect's symbolic system is composed of these modified national language components, newly created components, and the original components of the national common language—thus, it too is a variant of the national common language. Some argue that community dialects consist only of scattered lexical elements and do not form a system. This view is incorrect. Just as a regional dialect may contain only some new lexical or grammatical components, yet we do not define it solely by these new elements but rather as a combination of these elements and the original components of the national common language, we should similarly regard a community dialect as a synthesis of its newly created lexical components, modified lexical components, and the original components of the national common language's symbolic system. Because language as a symbolic system features systematic relationships among its component parts, regional dialects and community dialects as linguistic variants are no exception. Although community dialects may include only some newly created symbols, their use requires coordination with the original lexical components of the national common language. The newly created lexical elements and the original lexical components of the national language mutually constrain and influence each other, and they must conform to the grammatical rules of the national common language. In fact, community dialects themselves form an organically interconnected symbolic system. It is just that most of the lexical components and nearly all grammatical components in this system are derived from the national common language. This is precisely why they qualify as variants of the national common language.

Social group dialects lack universality because they are always used by specific social groups composed of a subset of members within a national society—or even within semi-independent, semi-universal regional societies. When no regional dialects exist, social group dialects function as direct variants of the national common language. When regional dialects are present, social group dialects are mostly variants of regional dialects—that is, indirect variants of the national common language. Social group dialects also differ from regional dialects in terms of class character. Regional dialects are used collectively by all members of a semi-universal social unit, regardless of gender, age, class, or occupation. In contrast, social group dialects are used by specific subgroups within national or semi-national societies. As tools of communication, social group dialects constitute a symbolic system and a system of expressive means. Their lexical components directly correspond to classless concepts in thinking, and their grammatical components align with classless logical rules in thought. However, this entire system of symbols and expressive means is chosen, generated, modified, or created by a specific subset of individuals within the national society. As a result, it may exhibit class character. The crux lies in the type of social group dialect it is. Whether occupational languages (as part of social group dialects) exhibit class character depends on the occupational context. In class societies, certain occupations may belong to a specific class. If so, such occupational languages carry class character because their symbolic and expressive systems are selected, modified, or created by individuals engaged in these class-specific occupations—and are shaped to serve the interests of that class, even though many of their components are shared with the national common language.

Social group dialects, as tools for communication and thinking, refer to the symbolic systems and expressive frameworks collectively produced and used by the social group—not to the speech of individual members or their utterances laden with complex meanings. Speech falls within the realm of parole (individual language use) and is not a linguistic variant.

Within a national society, the specific communicative contexts in which language is used can lead to the differentiation of linguistic variants in speech—that is, in the practical application of language. Such variants are termed "speech dialects". As previously discussed, speech refers to the communicative behavior of individuals or groups, encompassing their concrete use of linguistic functions and the outcomes of that use. Typically, these outcomes are speech works. In such works, we can identify not only linguistic components but also individual or group innovations in vocabulary, grammar, or phonetics; erroneous or subjective usage; and differences in speech content. However, beyond these "extralinguistic residues", we may also observe another outcome of language use: the formation of fixed expressive systems by individuals or groups that deviate from the standardized symbolic systems of language—though not everyone or every group necessarily develops such systems, nor do they emerge in all contexts. While constructing parole works, individuals primarily use existing linguistic components. However, they may also select from these components and incorporate personally or group-created elements not yet socially recognized to form their own parole works. This process can give rise to fixed systems of expressive means unique to individuals or groups—tools of communication and thought created and used by them. These systems qualify as linguistic variants: variations emerging from language use in speech. In his *Critical Study of de Saussure's Cours Générale*, Rogér proposed the need to distinguish between "collective language" (Kollektiv Sprache) and "individual language" (Individualsprache). He termed the national linguistic system "collective language" and an individual's system of expressive means "individual language"[1]. The claim of "individual language" is fundamentally flawed because language serves as a universal tool for societal communication; an individual's system of expressive means cannot legitimately be termed a "language". Rogér compounded this error by positing that an individual's expressive system (his "individual language") constitutes the basic unit of language when defining linguistic units[2]. In reality, what he describes as "individual language" is merely a system of expressive means that emerges from an individual's use of language. Following R. A. Hall's terminology, this system may be called an "idiolect"[3]. However, Hall's critical limitation is his exclusive focus on "idiolects", as he fails to recognize that they represent only one type of speech dialect and overlooks the existence of other speech dialects. Just as "regional dialects" are geographical variants of a language, "idiolects" are variants arising from individual speech. Like regional dialects, an "idiolect" is a system of expressive means composed of both components of the

1 Rogér, *Kritischer Versuch über de Saussure's Cours générale* (*Critical Study of de Saussure's Cours Générale*), ZRPHI, xi, pp. 161–217.
2 Ibid.
3 Hall, *Idiolect and Linguistic Superege*, *Studia Linguistica*, No. 5, pp. 21–27.

national common language and elements unique to the individual. This system precisely constitutes the systemic means of an individual's speech style, and in itself becomes one of the individual's tools for communication and for conducting thinking. As Smirnitsky noted, "Because speech is not only a tool for communication but also the process of applying this tool."[1] Language is undoubtedly a tool for communication, but this tool can be used by anyone in a society and is created by all members of that society. In addition to adopting elements of the national common language, idiolect also contains elements of extra-linguistic expressive means created and uniquely used by the individual. However, the emergence of idiolect is the result of an individual's specific application of language functions, so it represents a variation of language in individual speech. Idiolect can emerge because an individual's use of language always occurs in specific communicative contexts, for specific communicative purposes—including the purpose of expressing personal individuality. During the process of language use, the recurrence of communicative purposes and environments facilitates the formation of such a system. However, the specific application of language is not merely an individual matter. Not only can any individual in a society use language, but also combinations of certain individuals within that society can engage in collective speech activities—such as the

1 Smirnitsky, *The Objectivity of Language Existence*, in *Linguistics Translation Series* (Vol. 5), p. 120.

creation of collective declarations or collective speech works (e.g., literary and artistic works). Therefore, speech dialects are not necessarily the "idiolects" defined by Hall; they can also be systems of collective speech style techniques. Whether it is an individual speech dialect or a collective speech dialect formed by the language system under the determination of communicative purposes and contexts in speech, such speech dialects are in fact systems of speech style techniques. In other words, they are systems of expressive means formed in linguistic contexts and speech activities that are suitable for specific communicative purposes and environments. Because the specific communicative contexts and purposes in language use determine the emergence of speech style technique systems, what is formed is not only individual style technique systems or collective style technique systems, but also potentially systems of style techniques shared by an entire society—such as those of scientific treatises, literary and artistic works, or editorial comments. Although systems of style techniques shared by society can be commonly used by all members, they are employed only in specific communicative scenarios and for specific purposes—for example, the style technique system of editorial comments is used only when writing editorials. Whether individual, collective, or societal, all these style technique systems are variants of language in speech. We may as well call it "discurslect". A "discurslect" is a variant of language, as it constitutes a system of expressive means composed of elements of the national common language (or modifications thereof), plus special elements created to specifically adapt to certain communicative purposes and contexts.

A discurslect also serves as a tool for communication and a means to manifest thought, rather than being the verbal expressions constructed by individuals or certain groups when using it. While it belongs to speech, it also pertains to language. As a result of speech use, it is categorized under speech. However, as a variant of language, it also falls within the realm of language. Precisely because it belongs to language, we understand it as a variant of language.

Since the regional variants, social variants, and speech variants of a language are all linguistic variants, they all fall within the scope of linguistics research.

Part Two

The Origin and Development of Language

Chapter 1

The Origin of Language

Section 1 The Nature of the Problem of Language Origin

As a symbol system and human's most important tool for communication, as well as a tool for embodying abstract thinking, how did language emerge and develop in human society? Like other phenomena, language has its own origin and developmental history. Understanding the origin and historical development of language is a prerequisite for a correct and in-depth comprehension of language. Therefore, after discussing the social essence of language and its internal structure, we must further explore how language originated and how it has evolved.

When approaching the problem of language origin, it is first essential to distinguish between the origin of the general linguistic activity of human and the origin of specific languages. The origin of general human linguistic activity refers to how humans created language during their historical development, how they began to speak, and how they started using the most important tool for communication and embodying thought. This issue belongs not only to linguistics but also to general human history. The origin of specific languages, by contrast, refers to the process by which a particular language came into being. While this is a question within linguistics, its study necessarily involves connecting with the history of the people who use that language. It is necessary for us to understand how humans (not specific linguistic communities) initially created this communicative and thought-embodied tool characterized by a symbolic system of phonetic-semantic combinations, without asserting which specific language—such as Chinese or Russian—this symbolic system represents. This is the question of the origin of general linguistic activity of human, not the origin of specific languages. Of course, to understand this question, we must also refer to the general patterns of specific languages and cannot answer it without any linguistic knowledge. However, the exploration of this question requires, in addition to linguistic knowledge, the foundation of human cultural history, anthropology, general psychology, the history of cognitive development, and social history. Therefore, this research pertains to both linguistics and general human history. In his *Treatise on Language*, Vendryes argued that the question of the origin of language as specific languages should be distinguished from the origin of linguistic activity. He stated, "For a hundred years, those describing the origin of linguistic activity have only drawn erroneous conclusions, fundamentally because they approach the issue from a linguistic perspective, as if the origin of linguistic activity and the origin of language were the same thing."[1] He

1 Vendryes, *Treatise on Language*, Paris, 1921, p. 6.

further maintained that linguists study the languages people speak or write; while they can trace a language's history, no matter how far back they trace the oldest records, they can only study languages that have already evolved. The even more ancient conditions remain unknown, so reconstructing the state of a primitive language based on existing languages is futile. In his view, the oldest languages we know—so-called "parent languages"—are not primitive languages. Neither are the languages of "savage" people primitive, nor can the state of children's language illustrate the conditions of primitive language. It is asserted that the question of the origin of linguistic activity lies outside the scope of linguistics and is linked to the problem of the origin of human or human society.[1] While he correctly distinguished between these two problems of different natures, his exclusion of this problem from the domain of linguistics represents a metaphysical approach to problem-solving. All things in the universe are interconnected; thus, not only the study of the origin of linguistic activity but also the study of the origin of specific languages must involve exploring phenomena beyond language, particularly the history of the peoples who use those languages. Therefore, whether to conduct research solely on the internal structure of language cannot be regarded as the criterion for distinguishing between these two questions. The crux of the matter is that specific languages are the manifestations of general human linguistic

1 Ibid., pp. 6–8.

activity within particular social units, while so-called general human linguistic activity cannot be separated from the use of specific languages. In fact, the question of how humans began to speak is closely intertwined with how they began to speak specific languages. Just as biologists study both the origin of a particular organism and the origin of life in general, linguists must investigate both the origin of specific languages and the origin of general human linguistic activity. However, due to differences in focus, the question of the origin of general human linguistic activity may, in the absence of sufficient documentation, refrain from probing the specific internal structure of such a language. Since linguistic activity is a form of human social activity, it becomes one of the subjects of study in human social history—and no answers can be derived without examining human social history. Therefore, it is both a question of linguistics and of human social history.

However, the question of the origin of specific languages is a different matter. Each specific language is used by a particular social unit, and its origin is not directly linked to general human social history. Moreover, each such language has its specific internal structure, and the origin of the language cannot be explained without an account of the history of this specific structure. Therefore, while it is also connected to social units, the starting point is the origin of linguistic structure. For example, Chinese, used by the Han people, was created by them during their historical development and differs in origin from the Russian language. Chinese evolved from Sino-Tibetan languages. Its origin is on the one hand the result of social differentiation among the ancient peoples speaking Proto-Sino-Tibetan, and on the other hand the result of certain internal structural changes in Proto-Sino-Tibetan. Without understanding the historical development of this internal structure, it is impossible to grasp the origin of Chinese. This shows that the question of the origin of general human linguistic activity and the origin of specific languages (such as Chinese) are two issues of different natures, and it is erroneous to confuse them. Some mistaken linguistic theories of 19th-century historical comparative linguists precisely arose from this confusion. For example, when Schleicher asserted that Proto-Indo-European was an organic inflectional language, Turkic was agglutinative, and Chinese was isolating, he believed that the isolating language represented the oldest or most primitive state of human language. In reality, the characteristics of specific languages relate only to each language's history and its own origin, not to the origin of general human linguistic activity. We cannot use the origin of a specific language to explain the origin of general human linguistic activity. The reason Chinese is an isolating language is that it evolved from Proto-Sino-Tibetan with isolating features, which has nothing to do with the primitivity of general human linguistic activity. Of course, with sufficient documentation, we may be able to identify the structural features of human's original language, but this cannot be explained by the primitive state of any specific language. Therefore, it is necessary to distinguish between the origin of general human linguistic activity and the origin of specific languages.

The question of the origin of general human linguistic activity comprises two sub-questions. First, under what conditions did general human linguistic activity arise? Second, from what did this linguistic activity develop? In recent discussions of the origin of general human linguistic activity, scholars often conflate these two issues. For example, when criticizing individualistic theories of language origin, Chikobava stated: "The interjection theory holds that the earliest words were cries, which escaped involuntarily (due to pain or to express terror, joy, etc.). These cries were supposed to have paved the way for the creation of other words. This theory fails to consider that cries cannot be regarded as words, because they are not names of the feelings (emotions) they express; they are direct manifestations of feelings. The distance from such cries to words denoting specific objects remains considerable."[1] This is not the place to debate whether the interjection theory is correct, but Chikobava's use of the argument that "cries cannot be regarded as words... the distance from such cries to words denoting specific objects remains considerable" to prove that language did not originate from interjections is insufficient. This is because the original elements that developed into language should not have been words in the first place—just as humans evolved from apes, but apes were not humans to begin with. If these original elements were already words,

1 Chikobava, *Introduction to Linguistics*, Part I, Volume I, p. 117.

we could not discuss from what words evolved. Chikobava failed to identify the flaw in his argument because he conflated the question of the conditions under which language formed with the question of what language evolved from. In his view, "explaining the origin of language means revealing the conditions under which language could have sprouted, i.e., the conditions under which humans were able to begin speaking."[1] It is undeniable that explaining the origin of language requires revealing the conditions under which language could have sprouted, but this is not the only question in explaining language origin. When explaining human origins, is it unnecessary or impossible to discuss whether humans evolved from apes, apart from clarifying that humans formed under labor conditions? In his *Introduction to Language Science*, Budagov, when criticizing the bow-wow theory, argued that the theory treats language as a natural phenomenon rather than a social phenomenon[2]. He also shared the same flaw as Chikobava. In reality, whether language originated from onomatopoeia is unrelated to whether language is a natural phenomenon, just as whether humans are social animals is unrelated to whether they evolved from apes in nature. The bow-wow theory certainly has its errors, but the issue does not lie in whether it views language as a natural phenomenon, for what this question demands is merely an answer to what preceded language, not what

1 Ibid., p. 114.
2 Budagov, *Introduction to Language Science*, Moscow, 1958, p. 336.

language itself is. The question of the origin of general human language is analogous to that of human origins: when answering it, we must of course reveal the conditions under which this linguistic activity formed, just as we explain that humans formed under conditions of labor. But this does not mean we cannot discuss whether linguistic activity evolved from interjections, onomatopoeia, or other activities under certain conditions—just as we debate whether humans evolved from apes under labor conditions. Therefore, whether linguistic activity evolved from interjections or onomatopoeia is a separate question from the conditions under which it arose. We cannot determine the correctness of answers to the latter question based on whether people have answered the former one. What conditions caused interjections or onomatopoeia to become language is one matter; whether language evolved from interjections or onomatopoeia is another. We cannot conclude that language could not have evolved from interjections or onomatopoeia merely because they lack the function of expressing abstract thinking, do not serve as communicative tools for coordinating labor, and are not social phenomena. This is just as we cannot argue that humans could not have evolved from apes merely because apes lack abstract thinking and the ability to create labor tools.

Section 2 The Role of Labor in the Origin of Language

The problem of the origin of specific languages falls within the research scope of individual linguistics. Chinese linguistics studies the history of the Chinese language and thus its origin; Russian linguistics studies the history of the Russian language and thus its origin. Since this work does not aim to explore the current state and history of individual languages, our goal is to establish a general theory of language. We will discuss the origin of general human linguistic activity, which is what we mean by the "problem of language origin" in this context.

As noted above, the question of the origin of general human linguistic activity in fact comprises two main sub-questions. Let us first address the first of these questions: what conditions propelled the emergence of general human linguistic activity—in other words, under what circumstances did humans begin to speak?

Scholars have advanced various hypotheses regarding the origin of general human linguistic activity. In ancient times, Hebrews, Egyptians, and Indians all had mythological legends about this question. Greek philosophers also debated it, putting forward differing views on the origin of general human linguistic activity through the arguments of "by nature" and "by convention" (or "by regulation", "by agreement", "by custom"). The former held that people named things according to their essence and based on true knowledge of their nature, while the latter maintained that people named things merely according to custom, mutual agreement, or self-established rules or regulations. Plato was a representative of the former doctrine, while Aristotle subscribed to the latter. The Romans, inheriting Greek thought, revisited the Greek debates under the banner of nominalism and realism, while medieval Christians, relying on the Hebrew Bible, believed that language was a gift from God to human—even asserting that the original human language was Hebrew. It was not until the 17th and 18th centuries, with Leibniz's critique of the theory that Hebrew was the primitive human language, that people gradually broke free from the theological understanding of the origin of general human linguistic activity. Ancient explanations of the origin of general human linguistic activity were clearly aimed at addressing philosophical and theological questions, with only a tiny portion attempting to account for it based on linguistic facts. Plato was a representative of the former doctrine, while Aristotle subscribed to the latter. The Romans, inheriting Greek thought, revisited the Greek debates under the banner of nominalism and realism, while medieval Christians, relying on the Hebrew *Bible*, believed that language was a gift from God to human—even asserting that the original human language was Hebrew. It was not until the 17th and 18th centuries, with Leibniz's critique of the theory that Hebrew was the primitive human language, that people gradually broke free from the theological understanding of the origin of general human linguistic activity. Ancient explanations of the origin of general human linguistic activity were clearly aimed at addressing philosophical and theological questions, with only a tiny portion attempting to account for it based on linguistic facts. In his dialogue *Cratylus*, Plato advanced the argument that general human linguistic activity originated from onomatopoeia.[1] He explained the so-called "primitive names" in Greek—words that could not be linked to other words to explain the origin of derived or compound words—by claiming that each letter imitated a specific quality of things. He stated, "Clearly, a name is a vocal imitation of the thing it denotes; the name-giver always imitates the thing he names with sound," and gave examples such as the Greek letter rho (ρ) symbolizing motion, since pronouncing r requires tongue vibration (e.g., ρεζυ [flow], ῥοη[river], ζρόμος [vibration]); the Greek letter lambda (λ) signifying soft and smooth things (e.g., λεζοε [smooth], λιπαρός [oily]). The Roman-era writer Augustine held a similar view, arguing that the soft sound of the Latin word mel (honey) conveyed its sweetness, while the sound of acer (iron) reflected its hardness. After the 17th and 18th centuries, scholars put forward more opinions on the origin of general human language activities. Leibniz was the first to distinguish between the origin of general human language activities and the origin of individual specific languages. He called the former the origin of the "primitive language" and the latter the origin of the "derived language". He believed that the primitive language was created based on the principle of onomatopoeia, while derived languages were developed based on the principle of symbols in more cases.[2] Smith (A.

1 In this dialogue, Plato expresses his views through the conversations between Socrates, Cratylus, and Hermogenes. The opinions of Socrates mentioned in the dialogue are actually Plato's own.
2 See his posthumous work *Nouveaux essais sur l'entendement humain* (*New Essays*

Smith) and Stewart (Dugald Stewart) believed that the ancestors of human beings lived a mute life for a period, and the only means of communication were body postures and facial expressions. When the number of concepts increased and they could no longer be pointed out with fingers, language was born. People felt the need to create artificial symbols, and through mutual agreement, the meanings of these symbols were determined. Smith believed that verbs were the first to be created because things could be pointed at or imitated with hands, but actions could not.[1] Stewart believed that nouns were the first to be created because verbs could be supplemented by gestures.[2] Jean-Jacques Rousseau also once believed that language was initially established through careful consideration and mutual agreement among humans, and this kind of agreement, like the "social contract" of social institutions, served as the foundation of social order.[3] De Brasses,[4] Maupertius, and others also advocated the "social contract theory", arguing that language emerged from the need for human communication but also claiming that it originated from "social conventions." Condillac, a member of the Encyclopedia School, believed that the original source of human

on Human Understanding), 1704.

1 See his works *Essay on the Origin of Language* and the appendix to *Treatise on Moral Sentiments*.

2 See his *Complete Works*, Volume III, Page 27.

3 See his posthumous work *Essai sur l'origine des langues* (*Essay on the Origin of Languages*).

4 See his work *Traité de la formation mécanique des langues et des principes physiques de l'étymologie* (*Treatise on the Mechanical Formation of Languages and the Physical Principles of Etymology*).

language was the various cries emitted by emotional impulses, accompanied by various gestures. Later, these cries evolved into sounds designating various objects and thus became language.[1] Johann Gottfried Herder, however, argued that language was not truly "created" by humans through elaborate planning, but rather arose from their inner essence. The reason why humans have language is like a woman being pregnant: when the time is ripe, the baby will naturally be born. Although humans are inferior to other animals in physical strength and the accuracy of instincts, they have a broader range of attention. The entire human state of mind forms an unanalyzable whole, and humans can select one feeling from the countless sensations that strike the depths of their hearts and transform it into a word. For example, a sheep can give people many sensations, but the one that most strongly strikes the human heart is the sheep's bleating. Later, humans would remember that the sheep is the animal that makes a "baa-baa" sound, so the "baa-baa" sound became the name for a sheep.[2] Some 19th-century scholars attempted to replace the onomatopoeic theory with the echoic theory or the reflex theory, with Stendhal and Potebnya being representatives of this school. They attempted to explain the connection between sound and meaning through the commonality of emotional responses caused by the laws of sound concepts, perception, association,

1 See his work *Essai sur l'origine des connaissances humaines* (*Essay on the Origin of Human Knowledge*).
2 See his work *Abhandlung über die Ursprung der Sprache* (*Treatise on the Origin of Language*), 1772.

and apperception, and linked the creation of language to figurative thinking, arguing that primitive linguistic activities originated from the analysis of reflexive cries of emotion. Some scholars, such as Windelband and Whitney, argue that there is no fundamental difference in principle between the postures of the vocal organs that produce sound and other expressive gestures. This is also reflected in their repeated attempts to identify the necessary conditions for the further development of natural cries from the life forms of primitive humans. Darwin sought to link the shouts emitted by humans in times of alarm to the instinct of preserving the species. He compared it to the mating songs of birds and beasts. L. Noiré proposed the theory that linguistic activity originated from labor or work, attempting to prove that it stems from involuntary cries "accompanying" the labor process.[1] Bühler, citing the habit of primitive peoples engaging in collective labor under rhythmic cries, further sought to demonstrate that "accompanying" cries could indeed be emitted during specific phases of physical labor.[2]

O. Jespersen, in his *Language: Its Nature, Development and Origin*, categorized theories about the origin of linguistic activity into four doctrines: (1) The Bow-Wow Theory (or Onomatopoeic Theory). According to this doctrine, lower animals can utter cries, and humans created language by

1 See his work *Der Ursprung der Sprache* (*The Origin of Language*), 1877.
2 See his work *Arbeit und Rhythmus* (*Work and Rhythm*), 1896.

imitating these animal sounds. "Bow-wow" represents the vocalizations of lower animals, hence the name. Of course, humans imitated not only animal cries but also the vocalizations of other humans and even sounds from inanimate objects, which is why it is also called the Onomatopoeic Theory. (2) The Pooh-Pooh Theory (or Interjectional Theory). This doctrine posits that linguistic activity originated from human cries of pain or other sensory experiences. When humans are driven by emotional impulses, they emit "pooh-pooh" sounds, which later evolved into language, hence the name "Pooh-Pooh Theory". (3) The Ding-Dong Theory (or Sound-Image Theory). This doctrine asserts that there is a mysterious harmony between sound and meaning: all things in nature possess unique sounds, akin to various bells striking human perception, and language arises from the instinctive impression of these sounds. As things "strike" human senses like bells, this theory is termed the "Ding-Dong Theory". (4) The Yo-He-Ho Theory (or Labor-Chant Theory). According to this doctrine, during labor, human muscle activity produces gasping sounds like "yo-he-ho" as byproducts of physical exertion. These sounds later came to denote specific labor movements, serving as names for various tasks.[1] Jespersen also proposed his own theory, arguing that linguistic activity originated from emotional expression. Citing examples such as the musicality of primitive languages

1 Jespersen, *Language, Its Nature, Development and Origin*, London, 1922, pp. 413–416.

and the singing prowess of ancient peoples, he posited that humans, akin to birds and beasts uttering cries for entertainment, created language by singing to express emotions in pursuit of pleasure or love. He stated: "Long before people could articulate their thoughts, they sang their feelings. Of course, we cannot imagine that 'singing' here refers entirely to the kind performed in modern concert halls. When we say linguistic activity originated in song, we merely mean that our relatively monotonous spoken language and our highly developed vocal music emerged from primordial vocalizations that contained more musical elements and fewer linguistic components. These vocalizations, akin to bird songs, the roars of many animals, or the crying and babbling of infants, were exclamatory rather than communicative... We first approach linguistic activity when the communicative nature surpasses the exclamatory, and when sounds are produced with the purpose of 'telling' others about something—just as a mother bird warns her chicks of great danger."[1] A.S. Diamond, in his History and Origin of Language, also categorized theories about the origin of language into the Bow-Wow Theory, Pooh-Pooh Theory, Ding-Dong Theory, Yo-He-Ho Theory, Gesture Theory, Mouth-Gesture Theory, Entertainment Theory, and Strike Theory. He proposed his own view and revised the Strike Theory, arguing that language originated from the cries of primitive humans demanding help with actions like breaking, cutting,

1 Ibid., pp. 436–437.

smashing, killing, or destroying during labor.[1]

Whether it is the various theories summarized by Jespersen and Diamond, other theories they did not mention (such as the "social contract theory"), or the theories they themselves proposed, they all indiscriminately discuss what linguistic activity originated from and the conditions for its emergence. Most of them answer the question of "what language originated from", with only some opinions addressing the conditions for linguistic activity's emergence. Claims that linguistic activity originated from onomatopoeia, interjections or emotional cries, labor-related gasps, or singing all respond to the question of origins. We will set these aside for now. By contrast, assertions that linguistic activity arose from social conventions, individual emotional impulses, communication needs, the need to name labor movements, entertainment needs, or the need for assistance address the conditions of its emergence. It should be added that Marr once offered a unique explanation for this question: he argued that the emergence of spoken language was determined by the need of sorcerers to communicate with deities.

1 Diamond, *The History and Origin of Language*, London, 1959, pp. 6–8, 259–275. The "mouth-gesture theory" described by Diamond refers to the doctrine of A.S. Paget, according to which language originated from gestural symbols—initially hand gestures, later replaced by oral gestures as the mouth imitated hand movements to become symbols for things. The "strike theory" mentioned by Diamond refers to the doctrine proposed by Murray in his posthumous work, which posits that primitive language used gestures and different tones to indicate actions, with these actions denoted by monosyllabic sounds representing different types of strikes.

Needless to say, these theories fail to accurately clarify the conditions under which human linguistic activity in general arose. As Aleksandr Reformatsky noted, the "social contract theory" of Rousseau and others cannot explain the conditions for the emergence of linguistic activity; although they recognized the relationship between linguistic activity and social life, they could not elucidate under what conditions language actually arose, since people who had not yet created language obviously could not engage in "negotiations" or hold meetings to discuss plans for inventing it.[1] Moreover, Rousseau's claim that early language was emotional and that later cultural language represented a degradation is entirely unfounded. Expressing emotions requires no "contract", nor is emotional expression a condition for language production—animals have long been able to express emotions, as have newborn infants, yet neither animals nor newborns possess language. If humans had only created language to express emotions, they would fundamentally not have created it at all, for they already possessed tools to convey feelings. The emergence of language activities is certainly related to the need for communication, but this need alone could not have generated language. In our daily life experiences, we can find numerous examples of needs that failed to lead to the creation of something to meet them. Moreover, although other animals lack language, they are not without communicative activities. Labor naturally played a decisive role in

1 Aleksandr Reformatsky, *Introduction to Linguistics*, p. 351.

the origin of language, but the theories put forward by Noël (suggesting language arose from gasping sounds accompanying labor) and Diamant (arguing it stemmed from the need to request help for striking) clearly cannot fully explain the conditions for language's emergence. In Noël's view, language was merely the result of gasping sounds produced by muscular movements during labor. If this were the case, gregarious animals capable of making such gasping sounds would have equally created language, yet this is not the reality. Moreover, labor is accompanied by activities of other parts of the human body, such as the hands and feet. Why did these activities not develop into language? In Diamant's view, language was created during labor solely for the purpose of requesting help with actions like breaking, cutting, smashing, killing, and destroying. However, the labor process involves not only such actions but also the need to understand objective things and exchange various ideas about carrying out labor. The needs for entertainment or the pursuit of love proposed by Jespersen are even less explanatory. Primitive poetry clearly had practical purposes and was not necessarily for entertainment. Under the pressure of nature's power, primitive humans (or birds and beasts) could not pursue entertainment like a leisurely scholar such as Jespersen; the pursuit of love by birds and beasts is an instinctive activity, and the ancestors of humans were no exception in this regard. If this condition alone were sufficient to prompt the emergence of language activities, animals would have developed language long ago. As for Marr's claim that the need for sorcerers to communicate with gods drove language creation, it is nothing but nonsense. Leaving aside the fact that gods fundamentally do not exist, even if primitive humans superstitiously believed in their existence, this so-called "need" could not have spurred the invention of language. After all, not everyone in primitive times was a sorcerer, yet language was used by all. Moreover, archaeological evidence—such as the excavation of the Egyptian pyramids—shows that the incantations used by ancient priests were merely variants of the language spoken by ordinary people. Marr fails to explain how the language of the people, upon which these sorcerers' "language" supposedly relied, was actually created in the first place.

Although Noël and Diamant once mentioned the relationship between the emergence of language activities and labor, they failed to explain the role of labor in human's creation of language. It was the Marxist classical writer Engels who provided a profound scientific explanation of the conditions for human language creation. In his famous work *The Part Played by Labor in the Transition from Ape to Man*, Engels elaborates on the process by which human language activities arose, particularly clarifying the role of labor in this process. Engels argued that hundreds of thousands of years ago, human ancestors lived in a tropical region, possibly on a continent now submerged beneath the Indian Ocean[1], with human

1 Engels, F. 1953. *The Part Played by Labor in the Transition from Ape to Man*. People's Publishing House. (p. 1)

origins dating to the end of the Tertiary Period[1]. Human ancestors were originally four-footed apes. These apes, which had originally lived in trees but later moved to the ground, were covered in hair, lacked abstract thinking and language, and could only emit monotonous cries. These anthropoid apes "undoubtedly passed through hundreds of thousands of years before evolving from tree-dwelling ape communities into human society—a period that represents but a second in the history of the Earth, yet an eternity in human existence."[2] With the emergence of human society, humans began to speak. "What, then, is the characteristic distinction between ape communities and human society? It is 'labor'." Engels pointed out that labor not only transformed human ancestors into humans but also gave rise to language activities. After these apes migrated from trees to the ground, they gradually established the habit of walking upright, freeing their front limbs entirely to evolve into hands. When human ancestors learned to walk upright, the decisive first step in the transformation from ape to human was completed, for the hands became free. They could be used to fend off enemies, perform many of the simplest labor movements, and learn to make simple tools—initially of stone. This, of course, required passing through many geological periods.[3] "Labor began with the making of tools."[4] This

1 Ibid.
2 Ibid., p. 8.
3 Engels, F. 1953. *The Part Played by Labor in the Transition from Ape to Man*. People's Publishing House. (pp. 1–8)
4 Ibid., p. 10.

is also specific to human labor, for "no ape's hand has ever made even the crudest stone knife."[1] As this labor of human ancestors became regularized, they not only began their transition to human but also developed the possibility and need to create language. Engels said, "Language arose from and alongside labor... Among animals, even highly developed ones, there is little that needs to be communicated, and what little there is can be conveyed without articulate language. In a state of nature, no animal feels that being unable to speak or understand human language is a defect... Those who are close to such animals cannot but admit that these animals often now feel the lack of the power of speech. Unfortunately, their vocal organs have become so specialized in a definite direction that this lack cannot be remedied in any case."[2] Why do humans differ from these animals? Because labor gave human ancestors both the need and the possibility to create language.

Why was there a need to create language? Humans did not create language for no reason, still less to "communicate" with gods. Humans created language because labor gave them the need to do so. Marx and Engels stated, "Language, like consciousness, arose from need, from the urgent need to communicate with others."[3] What kind of communication is this? Animals also communicate, but their communication does not prompt

1 Ibid., p. 3.
2 Ibid., p. 6.
3 Marx, K., & Engels, F. 1961. *The German Ideology*. People's Publishing House. (p. 24)

them to create language, because animal communication is not communication in the context of labor, whereas human communication is. Engels explained, "The development of labor necessarily helped all members of society to unite more closely, as it increased the occasions for mutual aid and joint collaboration... these forming humans had reached the stage where they had something to say to one another."[1] The emergence of language is not purely a physiological adaptation to external conditions, nor is it merely a special function of the human body. It was created by humans during labor to meet the need for exchanging ideas, sharing experiences, and in a word, communicating with one another for common collaboration. On the one hand, labor made it necessary for people to communicate with each other in joint efforts; on the other hand, it enabled them to engage in thinking, form ideas, and use these ideas to communicate and exchange opinions, so that labor could achieve better results. Therefore, labor determined the need to create language.

However, need alone cannot create language. Labor not only determined the need to create language but also the possibility of creating it. As we have stated, human language serves as a communication tool and bearer of abstract thinking, functioning as an organic unity of sound and meaning. Therefore, language emergence requires both the ability for

1 Engels, F. 1953. *The Part Played by Labor in the Transition from Ape to Man*. People's Publishing House. (pp. 5–6)

abstract thinking and the capacity for articulate speech, so that the outcomes of abstract thinking can become the semantic elements in language structures, and the sounds produced by the motor nerves of speech can become phonetic elements. How did human ancestors gradually develop the ability for abstract thinking and articulate speech? This was once again driven by labor. Engels tells us that the decisive first step in the transformation from ape to human was the learning of upright walking by anthropoid apes. Upright walking freed the hands of anthropoid apes and enabled them to gradually improve through labor. Stalin stated that if primitive humans had not walked upright, "they could not have freely used their lungs and vocal cords, and therefore could not have spoken, a situation that would have fundamentally hindered the development of human consciousness."[1] Walking upright not only allowed human ancestors to observe the surrounding world more easily but also enabled them to interact with various objects in the physical world, thereby developing their consciousness. Engels said, "The most essential and closest foundation of human thinking is precisely the changes in nature brought about by humans themselves, not nature alone; human intelligence develops in accordance with how humans learn to alter nature."[2] Transforming nature is labor. It can be seen that labor has developed human thinking. Engels also said,

1 Stalin, J. 1953. *Collected Works of Stalin* (Vol. 1). People's Publishing House. (p. 288)
2 Engels, F. 1955. *Dialectics of Nature*. People's Publishing House. (p. 192)

"With the development of the hand, with labor, man began to dominate nature, and this domination expanded man's horizon with each new advance. They continuously discovered new and previously unknown properties in natural objects."[1] Human consciousness has been enriched in the process of the development of production. The ability of human abstract thinking—first to form extremely simple concepts of the surrounding world and then to establish more complex concepts—has grown with labor. The development of primitive human thinking began with labor. Humans needed to master, through active behavior, the things in the external world that were most significant to them, so as to satisfy their needs. Marx said, "Through the repetition of this process, the property of these things that enables them to 'satisfy needs' is impressed upon their minds, and men, like beasts, learn to 'theoretically' distinguish the external objects that can satisfy their needs from all other external objects."[2] The essential difference between the human brain and the ape brain lies in the human brain's ability to engage in language activities and abstract thinking. However, without labor having developed human thinking to the point of possessing abstract thinking ability, language—as the carrier of abstract thinking—could not have emerged. Labor also promoted the development of the human brain and vocal organs. Engels said, "First labor, then

1 Ibid., p. 140.
2 Marx, K. 1963. Critique of A. Wagner's T*extbook of Political Economy*. In *Collected Works of Marx and Engels* (Vol. 19, pp. 398–399). People's Publishing House.

language alongside it, became the primary driving forces. Under their influence, the ape's brain gradually transformed into the human brain; while the latter is quite similar to the former, it far surpasses the former in terms of size and degree of perfection. In parallel with the further development of the brain, its closest tools—the sensory organs—also became more developed." Simultaneously with the gradual development of language, there must have been a corresponding improvement in auditory perception. Similarly, the development of the brain must have been accompanied by the refinement of all sensory organs in any case.[1] The upright walking facilitated by labor enabled human ancestors to produce a variety of different sounds more easily, and "the organs of the mouth gradually learned to emit a succession of articulate syllables." It can be seen that labor also gave human ancestors the possibility of using various articulate syllables for speech. In summary, labor determined the preconditions for creating language, making its creation possible, as it promoted the emergence of human abstract thinking and the perfection of human vocal organs, thus enabling the birth of language as a combination of sound and meaning. It was under the conditions of labor and driven by labor that humans created language. This is the only correct understanding of the question of under what conditions human general language activities arose.

1 Engels, F. *Dialectics of Nature*, p. 140.

Section 3 What Did Language Develop From?

Human labor provided both the need and the possibility for the creation of language, but from what did language develop? Just as writing emerged under the conditions created by the needs of human social labor and developed from drawings, language also arose under the conditions of human social labor's needs and creation, and it may have had a predecessor.

What was the predecessor of language? Scholars discussing the origin of language have proposed many theories about language's predecessor. The onomatopoeia theory, exclamation theory, and others mentioned above all address this question. The onomatopoeia theory holds that language originated from primitive humans' imitation of objective sounds, with human's earliest language developing from this activity of mimicking sounds in the environment. The exclamation theory posits that language arose from interjections, with primitive language evolving from spontaneous emotional cries. Some linguists have specified more concretely that language originated from animal calls, singing, or gestures and body movements. What attitude should we take toward these theories?

First, we maintain that language could not have originated from so-called "gestural language" or body language. The gestural theory, proposed by some Western linguists, has been a popular doctrine for nearly fifty years.

The German psychologist Wilhelm Winter elaborated on the theory of gestural language in several of his works. In *Ethnic Psychology*, he argued that human language developed from expressive body postures, which constituted a primitive form of body language. He categorized body gestures into two types: imitative and indicative. Humans could use their hands to indicate or imitate objects in the objective world. Winter believed that human hands and arms were initially organs for seizing and dominating objects, a function differing from similar animal actions only in degree, not in essence. The original function of hands and arms gradually evolved into an important action—gesturing, which is essentially an "airified" version of seizing, with its role being to indicate. Winter believed this developmental process can also be observed in children's lives: children similarly use their hands to grasp distant objects, later evolving this action into pointing to things. Winter further argued that gestures are fundamentally equivalent to sounds—both gestures and sounds are "expressive movements" (Ausdrucks Bewegungen)—and that in terms of their functions, gestures convey concepts while sounds initially only express sensations, with sounds expressing concepts occurring later.[1] Thus, Winter not only claimed that language originated from body language or gestural language but also that gestural language preceded spoken language. The Russian linguist Овсянико-Куликовский also advocated the theory that human language

1 Winter, W. *Volkpsychologie*, Vol. 1.

originated from gestural language, asserting that humans relied solely on gestures for communication for tens of thousands of years before spoken language emerged.[1] Marr held similar views. According to Marr, primitive humans had no spoken language; their language was merely "gestural", with so-called gestural language serving as a tool for communication for a long period. He claimed that spoken language had existed for only 50,000 to 500,000 years, while gestural language persisted for 1.5 million years.[2] He further argued that gestural language enabled people to express their thoughts and traverse several long periods of material culture. Marr maintained, "The language of the hands not only made it possible for humans to express their thoughts and visualized concepts, communicate with all members of the group, but also served as a tool for communication between humans and other tribes as well as within the tribe, enabling the development of their concepts...."[3] Marr even argued that gestural language was more "natural" than spoken language because it was more directly linked to the core of thought. Most human language, particularly in its primitive stages, may have emerged completely spontaneously from sensory impressions, then been imprinted as "physical habits", with these habits becoming reflexes directly linked to phenomena in the corresponding living environment. This gave it social meaning and content. Marr stated,

1 See Итоги Науки (*Summary of Sciences*), X, 1914, p. 270.
2 Marr, N. *Selected Works* (Russian Edition), Vol. 2, p. 202.
3 Ibid., pp. 89–90.

"The long-term dominance of gestural language—tens or hundreds of thousands of years—was the wellspring of thought and its functions. In this regard, if the role of gestural language was technical, then everything in the ideological realm was subordinate to society, and ultimately to the economic structure of that time. The emergence of this economic structure, if not due to man-made production tools, was at least due to the artificial utilization of natural materials."[1] In Marr's view, gestural language played a significant role. The hand was the sole production tool in ancient times, and it also created human reason and thought. Human hands could perform various tasks, while the upper limbs of apes could only carry out limited movements and extremely restricted labor. The hand created human and its entire culture. Its role was not only as a tool for labor but also as an important means of "exchanging ideas" in primitive times. Primitive humans had no spoken language; their language was merely gestural. In his opinion, spoken language emerged later, and its mission had a mysterious nature. "The initially used spoken language could not but have a magical quality, and its individual words could not but be regarded as mysterious things. People cherished them and kept them secret, not allowing others to know, just as people still do not reveal the mysterious hunter's language today."[2] This language belonged solely to the shamans. Its singular purpose

1 Marr, N. *Selected Works* (Russian Edition), Vol. 2, pp. 89–90.
2 Ibid., p. 129.

was to serve as a means of communication between the shamans and their totems. The primitive spoken language inherently possessed a mystical quality. Marr, while emphasizing that earlier gestural language had created human "rationality", paradoxically argued that primitive human thought was also imbued with mysticism and operated on a pre-logical level. Marr stated: "At that time, humans engaged in pre-logical thinking, devoid of abstract concepts and relying solely on visualized representations—the interconnections of which remain alien to our modern sensibilities."[1] He further claimed that early humans "were incapable of reasoning" and could only "perceive the world mythically". Marr's theory of gestural language is fundamentally erroneous. This is evident not only in his disregard for the communicative function of spoken language (which he reduced to a mere tool for interaction between shamans and totems), not only in his insistence on prioritizing gestural language as primary while relegating spoken language to a secondary role—but also in his paradoxical claim that gestural language served as the instrument for human's creation of "rationality" and culture, a medium for "exchanging thoughts", whereas spoken language was framed merely as a vehicle for mythopoeic perception. Yet once we recognize that spoken language, as previously established, emerged simultaneously with labor, that it carries the burden of human abstract thought, and that it remains the most vital medium of communication,

1 Stalin, J. *Marxism and Problems of Linguistics*, p. 46.

Marr's errors become glaringly apparent. Stalin stated: "Spoken or written language has always been the sole and fully developed means of communication in human society. History knows no human community, no matter how primitive, that existed without its own spoken language. Ethnography is unaware of any backward tribe... lacking its own spoken language. Throughout human history, spoken language has been one of the decisive forces that helped people distinguish themselves from the animal kingdom, form societies, develop their thinking, organize social production, wage successful struggles against natural forces, and achieve the progress we witness today." These words deliver a powerful refutation of Marr's theory prioritizing gestural language. As Marx and Engels emphasized: "The production of ideas, conceptions, and consciousness is at first directly interwoven with the material activity and material intercourse of men—the language of real life."[1] To regard spoken language merely as a tool for mythopoeic perception fundamentally contradicts Marxist principles. It is evident that human language could not have originated from gestures. Undoubtedly, the hand has played a significant role in the cultural history of human, but gestures themselves could never have evolved into language. While other animals—though incapable of bipedal locomotion—can also employ certain bodily movements for communication, humans convey

1 Marx, K., & Engels, F. *The German Ideology*. People's Publishing House, 1961, p. 19.

meaning not only through hand gestures but also through eye movements and other physical expressions. The crux of the matter lies in whether these primitive bodily gestures constituted language itself or whether language somehow developed from them. If language could have evolved from hand gestures, then logically it could just as well have emerged from any other bodily movement—why should hands alone have been the exclusive precursor to language? All phenomena certainly have their origins, but these origins must adhere to historical continuity. Before the invention of writing systems, humans employed physical objects such as message sticks, knotted cords, and wampum beads to convey thoughts in place of language. However, these objects—message sticks, knotted cords, and wampum beads—never evolved into writing. What developed into writing were primitive pictorial representations. Why did these objects fail to transform into writing while primitive drawings succeeded? The reason lies in the absence of historical continuity between these physical markers and true writing. Writing emerged when humans began using tools to etch linear symbols onto surfaces as linguistic representations. In contrast, message sticks, knotted cords, and wampum beads employed entirely different methods of symbolic communication—they did not involve the inscription of linear marks as language substitutes. Although pictorial representations still exist today, they are a parallel phenomenon to writing—both having evolved from primitive drawings. Writing can be considered the descendant of primitive pictures precisely because, like its predecessor, it exists through the act of etching linear markings onto surfaces, inheriting this fundamental characteristic from early pictorial forms. Of course, humans have continued to employ physical objects to convey meaning. For instance, in the regional opera Cilang Zhou, the character Zhang Da, before sacrificing himself for his country, leaves a letter to Chen Biniang containing a lock of hair she had given him at their parting. Here, the hair serves as a physical substitute for language, expressing Zhang Da's longing. Yet such objects cannot be regarded as successors to primitive pictures nor as writing, for they lack historical continuity with these systems. The same principle applies to language. Before creating language, humans did use some gestures or other body movements for certain communication, but language could not have developed from gestures, as there is no historical continuity between gestures (or so-called gestural language) and spoken language. Spoken language uses sounds produced by the mouth for communication, whereas gestures are different—they rely on hand movements for signaling. Although the two share certain commonalities (both aid communication), things with the same function do not necessarily have historical continuity or identity. Whether historical continuity exists depends on the intrinsic structure of the things themselves, not their functions. For example, both sulfur and wood can start fires, but sulfur is a mineral and wood is a plant—they are fundamentally different. There is no historical continuity between language and gestures, nor do they share structural similarities in their intrinsic makeup. Therefore, language could not have originated from gestures.

Does language, then, originate from sound imitation? Scholars have ascribed different meanings to this concept of imitation. Herder's notion of sound imitation refers to the mimicking of sounds produced by objective phenomena—such as his example of imitating a sheep's bleat. In contrast, Plato and Augustine conceived of sound imitation as using phonetic characteristics to simulate features of objective things. For instance, the trilled quality of the [r] sound, produced by the tongue's vibration, mirrors the flowing (or rippling) nature of rivers—hence Greek employed rhoē to represent it. Modern British linguist Paget, however, defines sound imitation as using articulatory gestures to simulate objective features. For example, the velar and rounded sounds [ku], [gu], or [nu] appear across many languages as roots denoting objects with "concave", "hollow", "spherical", or "elongated" qualities (the latter due to the lips' forward protrusion during articulation). [1] Although the contents of these onomatopoeia theories differ, they share a common premise: the origin of language lies in primitive humans imitating the sounds or specific characteristics of objective things through vocal sounds or certain aspects of their vocal capabilities. Undoubtedly, onomatopoeic elements do exist in human languages. Sapir once opposed the theory of language originating from onomatopoeia by arguing that the languages of the Athabaskan Tribes

1 Bagert, J. *The Evolution of Language Function*. In *Psychologie du Langage*, p. 97.

in the Mackenzie River Valley of the Americas lack onomatopoeic words.[1] Sapir's criticism of onomatopoeia theories is superficial. The languages of primitive peoples (such as the Athabaskan Tribes) are not as devoid of onomatopoeia as Sapir claimed, for by the definitions of onomatopoeia understood by Plato, Augustine, and Baggott, any language contains numerous onomatopoeic words. Moreover, since animals possess the instinct to imitate natural sounds, human ancestors could not have been an exception. The crux of the matter is whether language originated from the onomatopoeic activities of human ancestors. We argue that some linguistic elements clearly originate from onomatopoeia, but these constitute only a minimal portion of language, not its main component, and onomatopoeia does not necessarily serve communicative purposes. However, from the perspective of linguistic structural features, a subset of onomatopoeia with communicative functions may have contributed to the origin of certain language components. Although such onomatopoeia does not function as a communicative tool for abstract thinking, it represents a primitive form of communication using sound materials to express specific sensations, emotions, or intentions. This type of onomatopoeia is neither the kind described by Plato nor by Baggott, for their notions of onomatopoeia are clearly groundless. It refers specifically to the imitation of sounds produced

1 Sapir, E. 1939. *Language: An Introduction to the Study of Speech*. New York, pp. 5–6.

by objective phenomena. Even in modern times, human still struggles to fully comprehend the supposed sound-imitative relationship between “r” and ῥοή [roe]. Our primitive ancestors certainly could not have consciously created such sound-symbolic words. Any imitative characteristics these words possess are purely coincidental.

Some linguists propose that language originated from animal-like vocalizations. They argue that human ancestors, akin to other animals, possessed an instinct to vocalize, uttering sounds of distress or joy during painful or pleasurable experiences, much like other creatures. These sounds were supposedly the precursors to language, though claiming no fundamental distinction between human language and the calls of mountain birds or forest beasts is misleading. Undoubtedly, human ancestors did emit cries of sorrow or joy, similar to wild animals. But could such cries have evolved into language? It is crucial to recognize that these were purely instinctive utterances, not necessarily serving a communicative purpose—even in its most primitive form. We must differentiate these cries from interjections: the latter aim to convey emotions and thus fulfill a basic communicative function. However, human ancestors also produced specific communicative calls, such as danger warnings, which were not mere emotional outbursts. While interjections express feelings, they do not communicate environmental information. Communicative calls might have contributed to some linguistic elements, but only marginally; language could not have originated exclusively from such vocalizations. The interjection theory and the expressive theory are closely linked. Scholars advocating these theories argue that human language originated from sounds of joy, anger, sorrow, and pleasure emitted during emotional impulses. The expressive theory goes further, claiming that such emotional sounds formed the poetic language of early humans. Thinkers like Rousseau, Herder, von Humboldt, and Stendhal have all held this view. Undoubtedly, human ancestors had sounds to express emotions, and primitive societies did have rich poetry. But did language originate from interjections or emotional sounds? From the perspective of historical continuity, since interjections and emotional expressions served a rudimentary communicative function and used sound as a medium, they may have contributed to language's historical origins. The crux is that interjections and expressions alone could not have produced human language, as human ancestors also engaged in non-emotional communicative activities using sound or other means.

None of these theories proposed by scholars can adequately explain what language developed from, although the onomatopoeia theory, the cry theory, the interjection theory, and the expressive theory do glimpse partial truths. Of course, we cannot agree with Forstlikov's critique of these theories, which argues that human language is fundamentally opposed to animal sounds: language is primarily a tool for exchanging ideas and mutual understanding. Therefore, the fundamental distinction between human language and animal sounds lies in the fact that language, by its origin and development, is conditioned by social factors, while animal sounds are the result of physiological adaptation to the environment. Consequently, it is fundamentally erroneous to directly explain the origin of primitive humans' articulated language through the pre-human animal sounds.[1] For as we stated above, the question of what language originated from must be distinguished from the question of under what conditions language formed. These theories do not necessarily claim that onomatopoeia, cries, interjections, or emotional expressions themselves are language; some merely argue that language as a social phenomenon developed from these activities—just as humans evolved from non-social apes. However, these theories still fail to address the issue comprehensively, as they only touch on one aspect of the problem without taking a holistic view.

The reason these theories address part of the problem but fail to grasp it comprehensively is that they do not explain why certain onomatopoeia, cries, interjections, or emotional expressions became components of language. We know that language is the second signal system, which clearly evolved from the first signal system. As a signaling system, the first signal system likely had communicative functions, though this communication did not use the products of abstract thinking as its material. The first signal system operates within the realm of imagistic thinking: it uses sensory

1 Forstlikov. 1952. *Marx, Engels, Lenin, Stalin on the Relationship Between Language and Thinking*. *Learning Translation* Series, August Issue, pp. 40–41.

images as signals and expresses only imagistic thoughts. Of course, such communication is primitive and fundamentally different in nature from linguistic communication. Nevertheless, it remains a form of communication, as it elicits specific sensations among members of the same species—for example, a certain birdcall triggers other birds to fly away, as the call makes them sense impending danger. Of course, the communicative functions of the first and second signal systems differ qualitatively. However, the issue is not whether they share qualitative identity, but rather whether they share a common historical origin. Humans and apes also differ qualitatively and do not share qualitative identity, yet humans evolved from apes, meaning the two have a common historical origin. The second signal system was not bestowed by God nor did it emerge out of nothing; it arose from the highly developed first signal system and evolved on the basis of the first signal system, which uses images as stimuli. In other words, it represents a "leap" from the first signal system. Nevertheless, due to their historical continuity or identity, they still share certain common characteristics—both are signaling systems.

The first signal system of human ancestors encompassed a wide range of stimuli, as any mental image formed by the senses—such as visual or tactile perceptions—could serve as a stimulus for it. Language clearly did not evolve from the entirety of the first signal system. As the second signal system, language relies on verbal kinesthetic or auditory stimuli as its material basis while being inherently linked to abstract thinking, with the conceptual meanings representing the core content of these stimuli. Since language uses verbal movements or auditory signals that embody abstract meanings as its material stimuli, it must have evolved from the communicative, sound-based portion of the first signal system. Certain onomatopoeic elements are sources of linguistic components precisely because they were originally part of the first signal system: sound-based stimuli with communicative functions. Some cries are the source of certain linguistic components, as they were originally part of the first signal system—sound-based stimuli with communicative functions. Similarly, some emotional outbursts or expressive vocalizations are sources of linguistic elements, as they too were once sound-based, communicative components of the first signal system. Moreover, since verbal activity is fundamentally communicative, only the communicative elements within onomatopoeic, crying, interjectional, or expressive activities could have evolved into language. The imagistic communicative activities of human ancestors used not only sound as stimuli but also other means, such as gestures. However, gestures could not develop into language because they do not rely on sound as stimuli. With the emergence of abstract thinking, original imagistic thoughts were indeed generalized into abstract concepts. Meanwhile, the sound stimuli of language—as the carrier of abstract thinking—are linked to all other senses. Stimuli received by various sensory organs (not just sound) could be associated with sound stimuli, but these stimuli themselves did not become linguistic stimuli. After the emergence of human language, not only did non-vocal stimuli of the first signal system persist, but not all sounds were subsumed into the second signal system—sounds could still operate as stimuli for imagistic thinking. However, just as the continued existence of paintings does not invalidate the origin of writing from paintings, the persistence of communicative, sound-based stimuli in the first signal system does not undermine the thesis that language originated from a specific subset of sound-based, communicative first-signal-system elements.

In summary, language originated from a subset of the first signal system that used sound as stimuli and had communicative functions. Driven by the conditions of labor, language evolved from this sound-based, communicative portion of the first signal system.

Section 4 The General Situation of Primitive Language

What was the general state of human linguistic activity in primitive times, i.e., during the era when apes were just transforming into humans? Although linguistic knowledge cannot tell us which specific language was human's original language, or its concrete phonetic and semantic elements, or its lexical and grammatical components, we can infer the general situation and formation process of primitive human linguistic activity based on the developmental history of human society and anthropological materials. Since language is the carrier of abstract thinking and a second signal system using word sounds as material stimuli, the study of the development process of primitive humans' speech organs and thinking can help us understand the general state and formation of primitive human linguistic activity. Bunak once stated: "Using these materials, modern anthropology can quite closely reconstruct the structural characteristics of ancient people's speech organs. When these characteristics are compared with the sound signals of anthropoid apes and archaeological facts, it becomes possible to outline the early developmental stages of speech functions."[1]

Since language emerged as a second signal system—the carrier of abstract thinking—from a subset of the first signal system that used sound as stimuli and had communicative functions, understanding the formation of general human linguistic activity requires understanding the developmental processes of primitive humans' vocalization and thinking. Sound is something all animals can produce; anthropoid apes can even emit more than thirty different sounds related to daily life. Higher anthropoid apes are human ancestors. The number of these life-related sounds gradually increased with the variety of activities in food procurement, while also expanding the scope of various mental representations. In this way, the

1 Bunak. 1951. *The Origin of Speech from the Perspective of Anthropological Data*. In *The Origin of Man and Ancient Human Distribution* (Russian Edition). Academy of Sciences of the Soviet Union. pp. 206.

pre-linguistic stage transitioned to the eve of linguistic activity. During this phase, basic prosody formed, followed by basic concepts that could be memorized regardless of the organism's state. Bunak stated: "After sound images became a necessary factor within a certain range of mental representations, these sound images acquired a basic core of meaning. This core could link different representations and reproduce the most complex combinations of our secondary impressions—in other words, concepts were formed." Therefore, concepts can be voluntarily reproduced in consciousness, or reproduced in consciousness without any close connection to specific contexts in any situation.[1] Driven by labor, general human linguistic activity emerged during the period when primitive humans consciously manufactured stone tools like stone flakes and stone cores. Labor demands spurred the development of intelligence through the use of external objects, which was tied to the urgent need to employ wooden sticks and stones in specific ways. This cognitive development inevitably gave rise to general concepts and basic vocabulary. Tool-making and tool-use established the cognitive significance of these concepts, while collective life stabilized their meanings and fueled the advancement of linguistic activity. As labor practices evolved, vocalizations multiplied, vocabulary expanded, and basic concepts grew more complex. Single-word utterances

1 Bunak. 1951. *The Origin of Speech from the Perspective of Anthropological Data*. In *The Origin of Man and Ancient Human Distribution* (Russian Edition). Academy of Sciences of the Soviet Union. pp. 271.

were supplanted by continuous sentences with distinguishable grammatical components, leading to the formation of syllabic language.

Primitive humans did not invent a specific language overnight. Words were created incrementally: initially, an individual in the group developed a word prototype, which the collective then solidified through usage. Grammatical rules were also forged step by step, with individuals first drafting rule prototypes, followed by communal stabilization through practice. During this phase, proto-humans engaged only in general linguistic activity—namely, speech—not yet language. They did not truly acquire a language (i.e., a specific linguistic system) until they amassed collectively established words and grammatical rules to form a system of basic vocabulary and grammatical structure. A specific language did not formally emerge until even the simplest vocabulary and grammatical systems took shape. However, when human ancestors completed their transition from apes to humans and acquired fully formed language, this language was a specific system with basic vocabulary and grammatical structure—even though anthropological and linguistic research cannot identify which language it was. Stalin noted: “It is reasonable to infer that the foundations of modern languages were established in the distant era preceding the slave society. At that time, language was simple, basic vocabulary was sparse, yet it possessed a grammatical structure—primitive as it was, it was nonetheless a grammatical structure."[1]

Since language is the carrier of abstract thinking and a second signal system, it develops alongside the evolution of human thought. When primitive humans first began to use language, their thinking was naturally less refined than that of modern humans, and their language exhibited simplicity and primitivity. Not only was their basic vocabulary meager and their linguistic structure simple, but the concepts expressed by their words were also elementary. The language of primitive humans consisted mostly of words designating concrete objects. Many words that later evolved to denote qualities originally referred to specific things. For example, the ancient Iranian word *suxra* ("red") has a root *suk* meaning "fire, burning".[2] In Russian, many color names are derived from the names of specific objects with those colors: розовый ("pink") from роза ("rose"), фиолетовый ("violet") from фиалка ("violet flower"), пурпурный ("red") from пурпур ("red robe"), and малиновый ("raspberry red") from малина ("raspberry").[3] During that period, humans had not yet achieved a high level of abstract ability, and the languages of primitive societies reveal traces of the concreteness and mystery of the thinking reflected in early

1 Stalin, J. V. *Marxism and Problems of Linguistics*. p. 24.
2 Cf. В. И. Abayev, *On the Principles of Etymological Dictionaries*, *Problems of Linguistics* (Russian edition), 1952, No. 5, p. 60.
3 Cf. A. Г. Spirkin, *The Formation of Abstract Thinking in the Early Stages of Human Development*, in *Speech, Thought, Will, Emotion, and Others*. Science Press, 1956, p. 51.

human language. For example, Thurnwald noted that when South Island residents wanted to announce the arrival of five people, they never said "five people have come". Instead, they would say something like, "a man with a big nose, an old man, a child, a pale man, and a very small child have come."[1] Nansen observed that the Eskimo had no names for numbers larger than five; they counted on their fingers: 5 was "one hand", 6 was "the first finger of the left hand", 7 the second finger, and so on up to 10. Twenty was "one person", and 100 was "five people". Lafargue stated: "In the languages of many savages, the first five numbers are named after fingers. Only after the development of sustained intellectual activity did the numbers of civilized humans gradually shed all forms resembling specific objects, allowing the mind to focus solely on the contours of conditional symbols."[2] History also demonstrates that numeral names in many languages are derived from the names of real-world objects. For example, in New Guinean languages, 5 means "one hand", and 10 means "crocodile" (referring to the ten tracks a crocodile leaves on a riverbank). The Latin word calculus ("to calculate") originally meant "stone", as the Romans used stones as practical counting units. In Melanesian languages, a buru denotes ten coconuts, bola ten fish, a koro one hundred coconuts, and selavo one thousand coconuts. They all indicated quantities by the numbers of concrete objects, so their

1 Cf. R. Thurnwald, *Psychologie des primitiven Menschen* (*Psychology of Primitive Man*), in *Handbuch der Vergleichenden Psychologie* (*Handbook of Comparative Psychology*), vol. 1, pp. 273–274.
2 *Collected Works of Lafargue* (Russian edition), 1931, Volume 3, p. 54.

thinking still retained the characteristic concreteness of primitive human thought. It was also natural for the thinking reflected in primitive human language to possess a mystical quality. At that time, people had limited knowledge and could not fully comprehend reality correctly, which explains why ancient humans were prone to religious superstitions.

However, the simplicity of primitive human language and the concreteness and mystery of the thinking it reflects do not imply that early humans lacked abstract thought. The French scholar Lévy-Bruhl, in his *La Mentalité Primitive* (*Primitive Mentality)*, described the entirety of primitive thinking as something severed from the laws of the objective world—"something that cannot be tested by our experience, i.e., the conclusions that observation can draw from the objective connections between phenomena", and seemingly "something filled with mystical self-experience". Lévy-Bruhl even posited that the very real world in which primitives lived was itself a mysterious entity. He further argued that experience equates to mental activity, and that self-enclosed societies differ essentially from their collective experiences, such that "a society of a certain type, with its own specific institutions and morality, inevitably has its own distinct way of thinking". Thus, he divided societies into "advanced" and "backward", and categorized thinking into types: low-level prelogical thinking and high-level logical thinking. He classified the thinking of primitive societies as low-level prelogical, arguing that such societies could not distinguish between direct and indirect causes, thus lacking the central element of logical thinking—the concept of causality. In this way, Lévy-Bruhl denied the commonality in logical laws between the thinking of culturally backward and advanced nations, concluding that they could never relate to each other under any circumstances, as each possessed a unique logic of thought and a language resistant to translation. In Lévy-Bruhl's view, translating the language of "inferior races" into that of "superior races" was tantamount to a crime, as he believed these races were fundamentally incapable of understanding one another. This doctrine is steeped in bourgeois ideology that despises and slanders culturally marginalized peoples. From a scientific perspective, we do not deny the evolution of language and thought. Equating primitive human language and thought with those of modern humans while claiming no development occurred runs counter to historical materialism and empirical evidence. However, it is profoundly mistaken to characterize primitive human language and thought as reflections of prelogical thinking and its language. From their very inception, humans have been logical thinking beings, endowed with abstract thought and its vehicle—language. While primitive human language does reflect the concreteness and mystery of primitive thought, the concreteness of thought does not imply that such thought was non-abstract or non-logical.

It is true that primitive human language predominantly reflected concrete objects, but this reflection of concrete things was already conceptual. Today, we still use names for specific objects like "table", "shark", "mulberry", and "wheat"—do these names not express concepts?

When ordinary people oppose the concrete to the abstract, they are making a relative comparison. Grammar books distinguish between "concrete nouns" and "abstract nouns", but these terms only indicate the relativity of abstractness; they do not imply that concrete names do not denote abstract concepts. All names are the products of abstract thinking and possess abstractness, differing only in degree. Gongsun Long's paradox "A white horse is not a horse" illustrates the following concept: "White horse" is a more specific concept, while "horse" is more abstract in comparison to "white horse", hence the two concepts differ. Although the concept of "white horse" is not identical to that of "horse", both are still concepts. Primitive human thought certainly had relative concreteness, and their language contained many words designating specific objects, but these words were already concepts generalized through abstract thinking. The difference is only that primitive humans could not further generalize the concepts designating specific objects into higher so-called "more abstract" concepts. As Marx put it: "Since the process of thinking itself is generated by specific conditions and is a natural process, the thinking that can truly understand things can only be homogeneous, differing only in degree due to differences in the maturity of development, particularly the maturity of the thinking organs."[1] It can be seen that the difference between the

1 Marx, *Letters to Kugelmann*. The translation can be found in Cen Qixiang's *Outlines of the History of Linguistics*, published by Science Press in 1958.

thinking of primitive humans, as reflected in their language, and that of modern humans is only a difference in the degree of abstraction, not a qualitative difference, nor a difference between prelogical and logical thinking.

We do not deny that the thinking reflected in primitive human language has a mysterious quality. However, this mysterious quality is not sufficient to prove that primitive human thinking was pre-logical or non-abstract. Mystery originates from incorrect reflection or unfounded fantasy. Due to their meager knowledge and lack of experience, primitive humans could not correctly reflect objective things and often constructed myths with abstruse fantasies, so their thinking was mysterious. However, under the practical demands of labor, they were not entirely unable to correctly reflect objective things, especially certain specific ones. It was only that their understanding of the various relationships between things could not always be scientifically explained and instead led to mysterious and superstitious conclusions. Such conclusions concern the fruits of thought and have nothing to do with the logic of thinking.

Today, in the era of modern scientific development, we still cannot correctly interpret all objective phenomena. However, we do not regard modern human thinking as pre-logical. Why, then, should we attribute the incorrect and mysterious thoughts of primitive humans to pre-logical thinking? It should be noted that in human cognitive activities, logical thinking (i.e., abstract thinking) is always intertwined with figurative thinking. Humans can not only generalize figurative thinking (including fantastical imagery) into concepts but also connect concepts back to figurative representations. Lenin stated: "Human wisdom's engagement with individual objects—its representation of them (= concepts)—is not a simple, direct, mirror-like process. Instead, it is complex, dualistic, circuitous, and prone to detaching fantasy from reality. Moreover, it can subtly transform abstract concepts and ideas into fantasies (ultimately culminating in deities). Even in the simplest generalizations, such as the fundamental concept of a 'table', there is an element of fantasy. Conversely, it would be absurd to deny the role of fantasy even in the most exact sciences (cf. Pisarev's distinction between 'productive' and 'empty' fantasies)."[1] Here, Lenin not only clarifies that concept formation arises from representing individual objects—thus demonstrating that primitive humans' relatively concrete thinking was not non-conceptual or pre-logical—but also highlights that even the most ethereal fantasies (e.g., deities) do not negate abstract thinking, as such fantasies may emerge from transformed abstract concepts. Therefore, the mysterious qualities reflected in primitive languages do not imply that primitive thinking was pre-logical.

The development of human thinking does have stages, but these stages

1 Lenin, *Excerpts from Aristotle's Metaphysics*, in *Philosophical Notebooks*, 1956, p. 339.

are all within the scope of logical thinking, differing only in degree rather than in quality. Compared with modern thinking, the thinking embodied in primitive human language does exhibit relative concreteness and mystery. However, these characteristics are insufficient to prove that the thinking carried by primitive human language is pre-logical. The reactionary essence of the Lévy-Bruhl school lies in their exploitation of this fact of thinking development, distorting it to claim through their misrepresented stage theory of thinking development that the thinking of primitive humans, and even of early human societies in historical periods (i.e., the thinking of certain backward ethnic groups today), is pre-logical and low-level, attempting to degrade the thinking of primitive humans, early historical societies, or modern backward ethnic groups to the developmental level of ordinary animals and thus defame them. This is a natural outpouring of bourgeois ideology. Regrettably, after criticizing Lévy-Bruhl's racist views, Spirkin made such assertions as:[1] "In the early stages when thinking had not yet reached the abstract stage, numbers had not been separated from the objects of calculation, and numbers were inseparably linked with the objects of calculation."[2] "The historical path of thinking's development from primitive concrete forms to abstract forms is clearly reflected in the entire history of language and the history of individual words." Here, Spirkin argued that early human thinking had not yet reached the stage of abstract thinking, and that the history of language demonstrates this failure to attain

1 A. Г. Spirkin, *The Formation of Abstract Thinking in the Early Stages of Human Development*, in *Speech, Thought, Will, Emotion and Others*, p. 46.
2 Ibid., p. 47.

abstract thinking in early humans. His argument clearly undermines the claim that language is the carrier of abstract thinking, and instead inadvertently supports Lévy-Bruhl's erroneous view that early human thinking was pre-logical. This is because non-abstract thinking is inherently equated with pre-logical thinking. Spirkin's contradiction arises from his failure to grasp the stage-based nature of abstraction and the principle that abstract thinking is intertwined with figurative thinking. It is a fact that primitive numerical concepts were concrete—early humans always linked numbers to the quantity of specific objects. However, this does not prove such concreteness was non-abstract. For example, when we say "one hand" to signify the number five today, does this mean our thinking is pre-logical or non-abstract? The crux lies in the fact that however concretely we describe "a man with a big nose," the concept of "one" is still embedded within it. Representing specific objects does not inherently equate to non-abstract thinking—today, myriads of our concepts denote concrete things. Linking numerical concepts with specific objects only demonstrates the relative concreteness of such concepts, not that they had not reached the stage of conceptualization. Countless concepts in our modern language exhibit the same characteristic. When we say primitive human thinking was concrete, it merely means they lacked higher-stage abstraction and that primitive languages lacked words for more general abstract concepts denoting advanced generalizations—it does not mean they were incapable of abstract thinking or forming concepts. Therefore, while we agree with Spirkin's distinction between early and later stages of thinking development, we cannot accept his argument that primitive human thinking had not reached the stage of abstract thinking.

Chapter 2

The Development of Language

Section 1 Language Development and Qualitative Changes in Language

Ever since primitive humans created language with basic vocabulary and grammatical structures during labor, language has continuously evolved. A comparison between primitive languages and those of today immediately reveals the striking nature of this development. Languages in primitive times, including those from the ancient period before the slave era, were "unsophisticated, with a meager basic vocabulary," and their grammatical structures were "highly primitive". Take Modern Chinese as an example: its rich lexical system and precise grammatical structure are nothing short of astonishing. When comparing Ancient Chinese with Modern Chinese, we find that many words in Modern Chinese did not exist in ancient times, such as "火车" (huǒchē, train), "摩托车" (mótuōchē, motorcycle), "电影" (diànyǐng, film), "概念" (gàiniàn, concept), "前提" (qiántí, premise), "演绎" (yǎn yì, deduction), "邮政" (yóu zhèng, postal service), "邮船" (yóu chuán, mail steamer), "巡洋舰" (xún yáng jiàn, cruiser), "潜水艇" (qián shuǐ tǐng, submarine), "飞机" (fēi jī, airplane), "照相机" (zhào xiàng jī, camera), "打字机" (dǎ zì jī, typewriter), "国际" (guó jì, international), “护照” (hù zhào, passport), “身份证” (shēn fèn zhèng, ID card), “入场券” (rù chǎng quàn, admission ticket), “预算” (yù suàn, budget), “决算” (jué suàn, final account), “赤字” (chì zì, deficit), “现实” (xiàn shí, reality), “直觉” (zhí jué, intuition), “错觉” (cuò jué, illusion), “引渡” (yǐn dù, extradition), “见习” (jiàn xí, probation), “座谈” (zuò tán, panel discussion), “笔名” (bǐ míng, pen name), “联系” (lián xì, connection), “有机” (yǒu jī, organic), “无机” (wú jī, inorganic), “本能” (běn néng, instinct), “综合” (zōng hé, synthesis), “分析” (fēn xī, analysis), “形态” (xíng tài, form), “卡车” (kǎ chē, truck), “汽车” (qì chē, automobile), “啤酒” (pí jiǔ, beer), “沙发” (shā fā, sofa), “拖拉机” (tuō lā jī, tractor), “芭蕾舞” (bā lěi wǔ, ballet), “青年舞” (qīng nián wǔ, youth dance), “交响乐” (jiāo xiǎng yuè, symphony), “管弦乐” (guǎn xián yuè, orchestral music), “话剧” (huà jù, modern drama), etc. Conversely, certain words from Ancient Chinese have vanished in Modern Chinese, such as “丹弓” (dān gōng, cinnabar bow), “素赠” (sù zèng, plain gift), “狭输” (xiá shū, narrow cart), “封豨” (fēng xī, mythical wild boar), “地维” (dì wéi, earth’s framework), “魅” (mèi, evil spirit), “大弩” (dà nǔ, large crossbow), “斗机” (dǒu jī, ladle mechanism), “组” (zǔ, silk ribbon), “敷贲” (fū bēn, splendid attire), etc. Modern Chinese also contains grammatical elements absent in Ancient Chinese, such as “们” (men, plural suffix in “我们” wǒ men, we), “俩” (liǎ, in “夫妻俩” fū qī liǎ, husband and wife), “由于” (yóu yú, because of), “到底” (dào dǐ, after all), “一切” (yī qiè, all). Meanwhile, certain grammatical particles from Ancient Chinese, such as “矣” (yǐ, past tense marker), “夫”

(fú, modal particle), “孔” (kǒng, very), “浸” (jìn, gradually), “焉” (yān, there), “咸” (xián, all), “鼎” (dǐng, greatly), “雅” (yǎ, elegantly), “甫” (fǔ, just), “窃” (qiè, humbly), “缘” (yuán, because), “盖” (gài, probably), have ceased to be used in Modern Chinese. Even when comparing the Chinese language during the May Fourth Movement era with today’s Chinese, we can observe obvious differences. Words such as “劳动日” (láodòngrì, workday), “生产队” (shēngchǎnduì, production team), “变工队” (biàngōngduì, labor exchange team), “服务站” (fúwùzhàn, service station), “多面手” (duōmiànshǒu, versatile person), “红旗单位” (hóngqí dānwèi, red flag unit), “宇宙空间” (yǔzhòu kōngjiān, cosmic space), “星际旅行” (xīngjì lǚxíng, interstellar travel), “人造卫星” (rénzào wèixīng, artificial satellite), “雷达” (léidá, radar), “电视” (diànshì, television), “原子能” (yuánzǐnéng, atomic energy), “导弹” (dǎodàn, missile), “可的松” (kědísōng, cortisone), “半导体” (bàndǎotǐ, semiconductor)... and structures like “不难看出” (bù nán kànchū, it is not hard to see), “应当指出” (yīngdāng zhǐchū, it should be pointed out), “作为…… 的” (zuòwéi...de, as a...of)... did not exist in May Fourth era Chinese. Conversely, words from that period such as “二房东” (èrfángdōng, sublessor), “老爷” (lǎoye, master), “少爷” (shàoye, young master), “小姐” (xiǎojie, young lady), “茶房” (cháfáng, waiter), “听差” (tīngchāi, manservant), “伙计” (huǒji, shop assistant), “戏子” (xìzi, actor/actress)... have gradually fallen out of use. Like all other things, language is constantly evolving.

The development of language is manifested both in the evolution of existing linguistic components and in the emergence of new ones and the demise of old ones. For example, in Ancient Chinese, "田" (tián) and "畋" (tián) were different written forms of the same word, while both referred to both "hunting" and "farming". The *Book of Documents* 《书经》 contains both "今尔尚尔宅，畋尔田" (jīn ěr shàng ěr zhái, tián ěr tián, "Now you still occupy your homes and till your fields") and "畋于洛之表" (tián yú Luò zhī biǎo, "Hunting on the outskirts of the Luo River"), where the first "畋" denotes "farming" and the second denotes "hunting". While it is well-known that "田" means "farming", it actually also referred to "hunting" in Ancient Chinese—for instance, in the *Book of Songs·Zheng Wind*, "叔于田" (shū yú tián, "Uncle goes hunting"), the character "田" specifically means "hunting". Initially, the primary lexical semantic feature of this word was "hunting", but later, with changes in its lexical meaning, it diverged into two words. The original word with "hunting" as its primary semantic feature later took both "hunting" and "plowing" as equal primary semantic features, thus splitting into two distinct terms. Another example is the Ancient Chinese word "金" (jīn), which originally denoted "copper", later came to mean "metal", and eventually took "gold" as its primary lexical semantic feature and "metal" as its secondary feature. The evolution of these Ancient Chinese words through history exemplifies one aspect of language development. However, the development of language refers not only to the evolution of existing linguistic components but also to the emergence of new components and the disappearance of old ones. Language is a system composed of many constituent elements. When the original components of this system change, it means that a part of the system has undergone transformation. The addition of new components also expands and alters the scope of the system, while the disappearance of old components changes its overall character. However, since the disappearance of old components does not necessarily mean new ones must fill their place, nor does the emergence of new components necessarily mean they are intended to replace old ones, the general situation is often one of coexistence between old and new. Therefore, the development of language is reflected in the gradual expansion and increasing precision of the entire system.

The development of language and qualitative changes in language are two distinct concepts. Language development includes qualitative changes, but qualitative changes do not necessarily encompass all aspects of language development. This is because language development can manifest in quantitative and qualitative growth, while qualitative changes specifically refer to developmental shifts in the essence of language. Since the founding of the People's Republic of China, with the vigorous development of Chinese society, Modern Chinese has also evolved rapidly. However, this does not mean that Chinese has undergone a qualitative change during this historical period, nor does it imply that the Chinese language after 1949 is fundamentally different in its essential characteristics from what it was before. Language is an integrated system, and qualitative changes in individual components of the system do not necessarily signify a qualitative change in the entire system. A qualitative change in the language system occurs only when the essential components that define its characteristics undergo transformation. As previously mentioned, the essence of a language's characteristics lies in its basic vocabulary and grammatical structure. Therefore, qualitative changes in language can only be discussed when fundamental shifts occur in these two core elements. This is because the basic vocabulary and grammatical structure of a language themselves form a subsystem (an internal system within the overall language system). Changes—even qualitative changes—in individual components of basic vocabulary or grammatical structure do not necessarily signify a qualitative shift in the essential characteristics of the language. Therefore, when examining the question of qualitative changes in language development, we must distinguish between qualitative changes in linguistic components (or linguistic elements) and qualitative changes in the language itself. The former refers to qualitative shifts in individual components (e.g., a single word or grammatical element), while the latter denotes a fundamental transformation of the entire language system.[1] Some argue that Chinese underwent a qualitative change from the pre-1949 era to the post-1949 period, precisely because they fail to grasp this distinction. In

1 See Gao Mingkai, *Issues of Historicalism in Chinese Language Research*, in *Linguistic Studies*, Third Series, pp. 152–155.

reality, while Chinese has indeed undergone significant changes and development during this period, these represent quantitative changes, not qualitative ones. This is because, despite the countless lexical differences including even those in individual components of basic vocabulary or grammatical structure between pre- and post-1949 Chinese, changes in general vocabulary alone do not constitute qualitative linguistic change. Nor do qualitative changes in individual basic vocabulary items or grammatical elements necessarily indicate a systemic transformation of the basic vocabulary or grammatical structure subsystems.

Section 2 Internal and External Causes of Language Development

The development of language is an observable fact, but the question of what causes this development has been a subject of debate among scholars. Needless to say, scholars relying on the metaphysical methodologies of mechanical materialism or idealism hold various views on this issue, and even those attempting to base their theories on Marxist dialectical materialism have not yet reached a consensus. Many opinions have been put forward regarding this question: some argue that a fundamental cause for language development should be identified, while others insist that there are multiple different causes. Scholars have also proposed theories to explain language development. The Anatomical View, represented by the theories of H. Ortel, posits that language development arises from changes in the anatomical structure of the speech organs.[1] According to this theory, certain tribes with customs such as lip-cutting or tooth-filing influenced linguistic changes, which continued even after the customs themselves ceased. The Geographical View, represented by the theories of H. Meyer-Benfey and H. Collitz, attributes language development to the impact of geographical or climatic conditions on phonetic characteristics. For example, this theory claims that consonant shifts in languages primarily occur in mountainous regions—such as the consonant changes in High German, which originated in the Alpine regions of southern Germany, diminished gradually as they spread beyond the mountains through Franconia, and faded away on the northern German plains.[2] The so-called Psychological View, which encompasses various theories, offers another perspective on language development. Linguists represented by the historical-comparative linguist Jacob Grimm argued that language development stems from national psychology. When explaining the consonant shifts in Germanic languages, Grimm claimed that these changes were the result of the Germanic people's progressive urge for freedom, a manifestation of their courage and pride during tribal migrations.[3] When calm was restored, these sounds persisted as evidence of the noble, amiable, and modest character of the Gothic, Saxon, and Scandinavian tribes that

1 See H. Ortel, *Lectures on the Study of Language*, New York, 1961.
2 For Meyer-Benfey's theory, see *Zeitschrift für deutsches Altertum*, 1901, p. 45. For Collitz's theory, see *American Journal of Philology*, 39, 1918, p. 413.
3 See Grimm, *Geschichte der deutschen Sprache*, 4th ed., Leipzig, 1880, p. 306.

underwent the first consonant shift, while the fierce High German tribes experienced the second consonant shift. Wilhelm Winter[1] proposed another psychological perspective, arguing that the consonant shifts in Germanic languages arose from the indigenous population's submission to warlike immigrants, the formation of new state structures, the complication of daily life, and the resulting rapid speech. The historical-comparative linguist Hermann Paul, however, maintained that language development primarily stems from psychological analogy. Additionally, scholars like William Dwight Whitney[2] and Charles Bally[3] argued that language development results from the drive to conserve the effort of the speech organs, while Ludwig Sütterlin[4] countered that it arises from the urge to strengthen the force of speech. Vilhelm Thomsen[5] contended that language development is driven by frequency of use, with frequently used linguistic components undergoing drastic changes. After acknowledging that the above factors all play a role in language development, Otto Jespersen proposed a new factor: language as play. Citing numerous examples of argot (secret languages), he argued that these developed under the influence of linguistic play.[6] Some linguists have also emphasized the role of children's language acquisition in language development. For example, Henry Sweet argued, "If each

1 See Winter, *Language*, p. 424.
2 See Whitney, *Language and the Study of Language*, London, 1868, p. 280.
3 See Bally, *Linguistique générale et linguistique française*, Paris, 1944, p. 595.
4 See Sütterlin, *Werden und Wesen der Sprache*, Leipzig, 1913, p. 33.
5 See *Samlede Afhandlinger*, ii, 1920, p. 417.
6 See Jespersen, *Language—Its Nature, Development and Origin*, pp. 289–310.

generation of children could learn language perfectly, there would be no linguistic change: English children would continue to speak a language as ancient as Anglo-Saxon, and languages like French and Italian would not exist. Linguistic change arises from minor errors that, over generations, completely transform the character of a language."[1] E. Herzog went so far as to claim that even if children correctly learn adult language, generational linguistic changes can still occur due to the process of children acquiring speech. According to Herzog, even if children perfectly mimic adult language, their smaller oral cavities cannot produce sounds that give adults the same auditory impression. To correctly imitate adult speech, children use different positions of their speech organs. After forming such habits, when they grow up and their oral cavities expand, their pronunciation habits from childhood persist. The larger oral cavity causes them to produce sounds different from those they learned in infancy when using the same speech organ positions. This process, repeated generation after generation, drives linguistic change. Herzog even created a chart to illustrate his point:[2]

1 See Sweet, *The Practical Study of Language*, London, 1899.
2 See Herzog, *Streitfragen der romanischen Philologie*, Vol. 1, 1904, p. 57.

Pronunciation movements (corresponding to) sound impressions

Generation	Young	Old
First generation	1	1
	1	2
Second generation	2	2
	2	3
Third generation	3	3
	3	4

Some linguists have proposed the so-called "sociological perspective" on language development. For example, Meillet believed that the development of language is determined by social development. He stated that, in terms of structure, language is both continuous and discontinuous. All utterances are composed of sentences, and sentences are made up of words. Some sentence components are phrases formed by several words. Words are independent components because in different sentences, they can be replaced by other words. Similarly, auxiliary words and grammatical forms can also vary and be interchanged. However, many words and grammatical forms can be interrelated, forming aggregates or "families". This demonstrates that words, despite being characterized by discontinuity, can also form associated groupings. Language activities among individuals are conducted through specific sentences. Speech is a particular phenomenon. Yet, for speech to be comprehensible, the speech-community using the language must speak in a consistent manner, as they share a common language. Language reveals itself only through various specific instances of speech, and speech is feasible only when a language exists.[1] Meillet also believed that there are three types of continuity and discontinuity in language structure. The first type of continuity is the interconnection among the components of a sentence, while the first type of discontinuity is the independent existence of words as sentence components. The second type of continuity is the aggregation among independent words, and the second type of discontinuity is the independent words that do not form aggregates. The third type of continuity is the existence of the entire language as a general social institution, and the third type of discontinuity is the manifestation of language in various particular instances of speech. Since all continuity is composed of discontinuous elements, language is thus subject to rapid and profound changes. The fundamental condition for such changes is the discontinuity of language tradition.[2] When people do not replace the language, children need to learn to understand what others in society say and how to use the language each time. However, they do not

1 See Meillet, *Le Développement des Langues*, in *Linguistique Historique et Linguistique Générale*, Second Series, pp. 70–71.
2 Ibid., pp. 71–73.

master the entire language all at once. What they hear each time are only particular sentences, and they learn the language by comparing these sentences. The situation is the same when people replace the language. In this case, adults will become bilingual for a certain period. When children learn the language, some discontinuities may arise due to individual characteristics.[1] At every moment, only a minority of people are learning the language. If a linguistic society's language reaches a state of equilibrium and its structure is harmonious, it will not change, and individual idiosyncrasies will not become generalized. However, human history is marked by countless events. The circumstances of communities are constantly changing, and these changes erode part or even all of the language's stability. As a result, this discontinuity triggers linguistic change. However, such change does not necessarily produce direct or inevitable alterations in the language's structure, as it can occur through the adoption of another language. In the case of adopting another language, individuals with high intellectual and social standing can learn it very accurately, while those from culturally less developed groups that replace their language may struggle to master it correctly. Through a bilingual phase, the previously used language tends to recede, and the newly adopted language becomes the general medium of communication.[2] Regardless of how minor the

1 See Meillet, *Le Développement des Langues*, in *Linguistique Historique et Linguistique Générale*, Second Volume, pp. 74–75.
2 Ibid., pp. 76–77.

discontinuity may be—whether it is the intergenerational transmission of language or language replacement—those causing the change must understand each other and consciously continue to use a particular language. From this perspective, there is a continuity of language. Thus, what is perceived as a single identical language at one moment can eventually be perceived as many different languages. This leads to linguistic differentiation, language convergence, and the emergence of substrata. Meillet argued that languages can diverge or unify in response to social environments, with linguistic differentiation arising from various factors. Child language acquisition and adult language use can both trigger linguistic changes. Regional dispersion then gives these changes a local character, leading to the formation of dialects. However, such changes are constrained by social contexts, as they must be reproduced by contemporaneous social groups within the same region. Social group differentiation also drives linguistic divergence. For example, different classes may develop distinct linguistic features, while gender differences can likewise shape language variation. Even religious or recreational groups may generate specialized linguistic forms, known as "special languages" (or idiolects).[1] On the other hand, small speech communities using different languages may not resist the influence of larger groups, leading to

1 See Meillet, *Différenciation et Unification dans Les Langues,* in *Linguistique Historique et Linguistique Générale*, First Volume, Paris, 1926, pp. 110–116.

linguistic unification through conquest—a common historical phenomenon. Yet linguistic unity does not necessarily require military conquest or political dominance. Meillet emphasized the role of culture, arguing that for a language to become universal, it must be a culturally superior one—and with this condition alone, the language can achieve universalization. The political, economic, and religious conditions determining language universalization are complex and diverse, yet all require cultural superiority as their foundation. Linguistic unification is the counteraction to linguistic differentiation: when differentiation renders mutual understanding impossible among groups, a new unification becomes necessary.[1] Meillet's theory encapsulates the "sociological perspective" on language development held by scholars such as G. I. Ascoli, H. Schuchardt, and J. Schmidt, including their theories of substrata, language convergence, and the "wave theory".

It is not difficult to see that the so-called theories of these scholars are untenable or incomplete. Changes in the structure of the speech organs clearly cannot explain language development. Physiologists have not discovered any significant differences in the speech organs of different ethnic groups, yet the same language can develop into different languages among different peoples. If we consider minor differences in speech organs, there is another fact that contradicts this theory: each person's speech organs

1 Ibid., pp. 127–129.

may have unique characteristics, yet individuals within the same ethnic group do not have different languages or phoneme systems. The "geographical perspective" also fails to solve the problem. Collitz argued that the consonant shifts in High German originated in mountainous areas, but facts show that such shifts also occurred on plains; conversely, in other mountainous regions (e.g., the Italian-speaking populations in the Alps), no such shifts took place. It is also futile to invoke "national psychology" to explain the causes of language development. If the change of stop consonants to fricatives (p, t, k > f, θ, x) in Germanic languages is said to reflect national pride, how should we explain the simultaneous change of voiced stops to voiceless stops in the same Germanic languages? The change of stop consonants to fricatives represents a shift from "hard" sounds to "soft" sounds, while the change of voiced stops to voiceless stops is a shift from "soft" sounds to "hard" sounds. Does this mean the Germanic people felt both pride and its absence at the same time? This is clearly contradictory. Rapid speech is a common phenomenon in daily life. If the Germanic tribes spoke faster due to more complex lives during their migration, their descendants today should speak even faster (given that modern life is far more complex). Why then did the Germanic consonant shifts occur only during the tribal migration period and within limited regions? If language development were driven by the urge to conserve effort, languages would become increasingly simple—and the ultimate conservation of effort would be silence. Why then do languages produce new components and words with more syllables than before (e.g., the massive increase in disyllabic words in Modern Chinese)? If language development were driven by the urge to strengthen expressive force, why do phenomena like syllable reduction and morphological simplification occur (e.g., the shift from synthetic to analytic structures from Ancient Indo-European to modern European languages)? Analogical change, while playing a role in language development, is not its fundamental cause. Phonological changes in language, such as the palatalization from Middle Chinese to Modern Chinese, were by no means triggered by analogy. Linguistic elements used frequently should be the most stable—which is proven by basic vocabulary—making the explanation of language development through frequency of use contradictory to many facts. If, as Jespersen argued, play is the cause of language development and argot emerges from the purpose of linguistic play, then language would become a "toy" rather than a tool for communication. In reality, the emergence of new linguistic elements is rarely related to so-called play, let alone dependent on it. The theory that language development stems from children's language acquisition is also problematic. This theory essentially applies the "analogical theory" to children. Proponents argue that children extensively employ analogical reasoning during language acquisition, a process that induces significant linguistic changes. We have already stated that analogy is not the primary cause of language development. Even if we assume analogy were the primary cause, we still could not confirm that children's language acquisition is the basis for language development. Language learning is not exclusive to children—adults also continuously learn elements of language they have not yet mastered. In the learning process, both children and adults undergo the same procedures. If the analogical reasoning used by children in language acquisition were the sole or fundamental cause of language development, the analogy used by adults in language learning should also be the sole or fundamental cause. Why should children be privileged over adults in this regard? No wonder Sweet himself later felt his theory was inconsistent, admitting in his subsequent works: "(Children's imitation) is in most cases actually perfect... so the main causes of sound change must be sought elsewhere."[1] The claim that language development stems from habits formed by children's smaller oral cavities in each generation, which persist into adulthood, is even more absurd. Children across generations are not all the same age; from a societal perspective, there are always children and adults who were once children. Why then doesn't language change constantly, but only supposedly between generations? Although children's and adults' oral cavities differ in size, there is no difference in the shape of their resonators. Moreover, strictly speaking, everyone's oral cavity is slightly different, yet identical articulatory methods produce sounds with the same timbre despite these minor differences. If slight oral variations alone caused linguistic

1 Sweet, *The History of Language*, London, 1900, p. 19.

differences, no two people would speak the same language—not just children. Clearly, this theory is untenable. The so-called "sociological perspective" likewise fails to explain the fundamental causes of language development. On this point, we will defer further discussion to a later section. In any case, these theories are either untenable or unable to fully account for the phenomenon. This does not mean, of course, that the factors they cite as causes of language development play no role whatsoever. For example, the physiology of the speech organs clearly influences linguistic change to some extent, as do geographical environment or climate. Factors such as national psychological traits, rapid speech, the drive for articulatory economy, emphasis on tone, analogical processes, child language acquisition, linguistic play, and cultural development all contribute to varying degrees. However, these are either partial, indirect, or secondary causes—not the fundamental drivers of language development. As such, these theories are all one-sided.

Since these theories fail to explain the fundamental causes of language development, how should we approach this problem? As with studying the causes of any phenomenon's development, we must first distinguish between external and internal factors. There may be many causes for language development, but the most important is its internal logic, not external factors—though the latter certainly play a role, and sometimes a significant one. Chairman Mao stated: "In contrast to the metaphysical view of the universe, the materialist dialectical view holds that development should be studied from the interior of things and from their relationships with other things. That is, the development of things is seen as the inevitable self-movement within things, with the movement of each thing interconnected and interacting with the movements of surrounding things. The fundamental cause of development does not lie outside things but within them, in their internal contradictions. Everything contains such contradictions, which give rise to its movement and development. This internal contradiction is the fundamental cause of development, while the interconnections and interactions between one thing and another are secondary causes."[1] The divergence between our perspective and that of certain scholars lies precisely in the question of external versus internal causes. The factors cited by the scholars discussed above as causes of language development are not entirely baseless, but they represent only partial and one-sided explanations. This is because they all identify causes external to language itself, rather than internal factors. These align precisely with what Chairman Mao described as "the interconnections and interactions between one thing and another", which constitute "secondary causes of development"—not the "fundamental cause of development" rooted in "the internal contradictions of things" that drive "the movement and development of things from within". Therefore, to understand why

1 *Selected Works of Mao Zedong*, Beijing, 1st Edition, March 1952, Volume 2, pp. 767–768.

languages develop, we must first seek their internal causes: namely, the internal contradictions that propel linguistic change.

The distinction between internal and external causes of language development appears to be universally acknowledged by those seeking to understand the drivers of language change through the lens of dialectical materialism. However, when applying this principle to explain the actual mechanisms of language development, scholars hold divergent views. In his paper *On the Internal and External Causes of Language Development*[1], Ji Yongyou summarizes current disagreements in applying Chairman Mao's principle, categorizing them into three perspectives:

(1) All linguistic changes and developments are driven by social progress, with societal development serving as the fundamental cause of language evolution.

(2) The primary contradiction in language development is the tension between langue and parole. The evolution of this contradiction constitutes the internal cause of language development, while social development acts as an external condition (i.e., an external cause).

(3) The fundamental contradiction of language development lies in the internal conflicts within its structural components (morphology, vocabulary,

1 Cf. Ji Yongyou, *On the Internal and External Causes of Language Development*, in *Chinese Language* (《中国语文》), 1961, No. 1, p. 1.

phonology), with social development functioning as an external cause.

Faced with these three perspectives, what stance should we adopt?

No one can deny the significant role that social development plays in language evolution. But does this mean that social development is the internal cause of language change? Those who argue that social development is the internal cause of language development contend that, since language is a social phenomenon created and used by human society, and since it emerges with the birth of society, evolves with societal growth, and declines with societal collapse, language must be an intrinsic part of society—or society an intrinsic part of language—making social development the fundamental cause or internal driver of linguistic change. They claim: "Because language remains social throughout its developmental stages, societal evolution is its primary factor," and "Clearly, for language as the essence of society, the internal cause or basis for its changes can only be social development..."[1] As Ji Yongyou pointed out, this perspective represents a determinist view of external causes[2] and embodies mechanical materialism. First, it is essential to clarify that language is only a social phenomenon, not society itself. Marx stated: "The sum total of these relations of production constitutes the economic structure

1 Tang Qiyun, *Critiquing Erroneous Theories on Language Development in Chinese Linguistics*, *Chinese Language* (《中国语文》), 1959, No. 2, p. 60.
2 See Ji Yongyou, *On the Internal and External Causes of Language Development*, *Chinese Language* (《中国语文》), 1961, No. 1, p. 1.

of society, the real foundation on which arises a legal and political superstructure and to which correspond definite forms of social consciousness. The mode of production of material life conditions the general process of social, political, and intellectual life."[1] When measured against Marx's definition of society, language is clearly not society itself, for language is not a form of production relations; it is merely a tool of communication for social groups. Of course, social phenomena may be constituent elements of society, but not all social phenomena are integral components of society. Language was indeed created by society—it emerged with the birth of society, evolves with societal development, and declines with societal collapse. However, not everything that emerges, develops, and declines alongside society is necessarily society itself. Human emerged with the birth of society; from the outset, humans have been social animals, and every individual human exists and develops in conjunction with societal existence and progress. Yet, although we say every individual is a social animal, we cannot thereby conclude that individuals are society. It is true that language exists within society, but not everything that exists within society is society itself. The billions of cultural products created by human all exist within society, and apart from society, they would lose their existence. However, we cannot thereby conclude that these things are society. Therefore, it is inappropriate to use the close

1 Marx, *Wage Labour and Capital*, Sanlian Bookstore, 1953, pp. 21–22.

correlation between the emergence, development, and decline of language and those of society to prove that language is society or an internal component of social structure. Language has indeed always belonged to society, but what belongs to society is not necessarily society itself or its constituent elements. There are two types of things that belong to society: (1) Elements composing society: Society cannot exist without these elements; (2) Things created and possessed by society to serve its survival: Society cannot exist without these either, but their relationship to society is not that of component parts to a whole. For example, production tools are created and possessed by society—human society could not exist without them—but they are not constituent elements of society. The relationship between language and society is of the latter type. Language is created and possessed by society; society could not exist without it. However, we cannot therefore claim that language is a constituent element of society. When we say language is "within society", we mean it cannot exist apart from society—it is embedded in society, created and sustained by it, not that it is a structural component or member of society. Since language is not a constituent element of society, it cannot be construed as an internal factor of social structure, nor can society be regarded as an internal factor of linguistic structure. In other words, from the perspective of structural internal elements, language exists outside society, just as society exists outside language—like the countless things created by society, such as the "Peaceful" train created by the Chinese people, which do not belong to the internal components of social structure. Not only does language emerge with the birth of society, develop with societal growth, and decline with societal collapse, but conversely, society would also be conditioned by language's existence, evolution, and disappearance. Yet we do not thereby claim that society is an internal component of linguistic structure. Therefore, although language is a social phenomenon, we cannot treat society as an internal element of linguistic structure; we can only assert that language possesses sociality and has an inseparable, intimate connection with society.

Some argue that because language cannot exist without being created and used by society, society must be an internal component of language—and that societal dynamics, as the driving force behind language development, constitute its internal cause. This view is flawed. Consider the innumerable things that cannot exist apart from society, far beyond mere language. If we were to conclude that society is the internal cause propelling language development solely because language is created and used by society, then by the same logic, society would also be the "internal component" of the billions of objects it has created and employed—such as production tools, writing instruments (brushes, ink, paper, inkstones), and furniture (tables, chairs, beds). On this reasoning, societal development and decline would also be the internal causes for the "development" (e.g., the decay of a table) of these objects. This is a claim contrary to common sense. The crux of the issue lies in the fact that objects created by society still have their own internal structures—hence why brushes, ink, paper, and inkstones, though all socially created and used, remain distinct from one another. For these objects, their internal structures do not include society as a constituent element. While society and these objects are inseparably linked, society remains external to them. The relationship between society and these objects is one of creator to created, user to used—not one of opposing internal elements constituting the objects themselves. There is a bond of flesh and blood between father and son. No son can exist without a father, but this does not mean the father is "within" the son. The father remains an independent entity, and the son's development depends primarily on his own nature, not the father's. Similarly, anthropoid apes use natural sticks and stones to obtain food, yet this does not make them "internal components" of the sticks or stones. If we argue that society is internal to language merely because language's existence depends on society, we would equally have to concede that human's existence depends on nature, therefore nature is internal to humans; and that society's existence depends on nature, so nature is internal to society. Society certainly plays a significant role in driving language development, just as oxygen is vital for a child's growth into adulthood. But this does not mean society is the internal cause of language development—any more than we would call oxygen the internal cause of human growth. When we say, "Language develops alongside society", this very formulation implies that society is not the internal cause of linguistic development. The internal cause lies in a thing's own internal contradictions, not in what it "follows". For example, to say someone's thoughts develop alongside society does not mean society is the internal cause of their ideological growth; the internal cause is their own intellectual struggles, not society—even though society profoundly influences it. Chairman Mao clearly distinguished between internal and external causes: "The fundamental cause of development does not lie outside things but within them, in their internal contradictions." ...This internal contradiction within things is the fundamental cause of their development, while the interconnections and interactions between one thing and another are secondary causes of development.[1] To regard the mutual connections and influences between society and language as the internal cause of language development is likely a misunderstanding.

That the development of other social phenomena cannot be construed as the internal cause of language development is even more self-evident. Language is undoubtedly a social phenomenon, sharing common traits with other social phenomena: it serves society, is interconnected with them in varying degrees, and mutually influences and constrains them. However, this does not mean there are no distinctions between language and other social phenomena, nor does it imply that other social phenomena are internal to language. As Stalin noted: "Language possesses what is common to all social phenomena—including both the base and the superstructure—

1 *Selected Works of Mao Zedong*, Beijing, 1st Edition, March 1952, Volume 2, pp. 767 - 768.

namely, that it serves society... But this commonality is limited to this alone. Beyond that, profound differences begin to emerge among social phenomena." Specific social phenomena outside language certainly influence linguistic development. Yet precisely because they are not language itself, we cannot assert that these phenomena are internal to language or that their development constitutes the internal cause of language change. It must be understood that despite the infinite diversity of things in the universe, they ultimately share a common ground as existents. Social phenomena share not only the characteristic of sociality but also the universal trait of being "things" in the cosmos, akin to natural phenomena in this fundamental aspect. If we were to conclude that other social phenomena are internal to language merely because they share certain similarities with language, we would equally have to admit that natural phenomena are also internal to language, as they too share similarities with language in some respects. By this logic, we would have to regard the development of any natural entity influencing language—such as geographical changes affecting linguistic evolution—as an internal cause of language development. This would ultimately lead us to view all phenomena in the universe as internal to language, and all cosmic developments as internal causes of linguistic change—for language inherently reflects the evolution of all things, natural phenomena included, and is intricately interconnected with them. Such an argument is patently indefensible. Such a claim is clearly untenable.

If internal causes constitute a thing's inherent contradictions, then what exactly are the inherent contradictions of language? After correctly citing Engels' observation that "it would be difficult to explain the origin of the High German consonant shift... without falling into absurdity if one tries to give an economic explanation for a phonetic change that has turned a geographical barrier formed by the mountain range from the Sudetes to the Taunus into a formal schism in Germany"[1], Xu Qing demonstrates that linguistic changes cannot be mechanically correlated with social transformations. He also correctly notes that "the development of language has its internal contradictions as its foundational basis"[2], arguing that "the relative stability of langue and the absolute variability of parole constitute the fundamental internal contradiction of language"[3]. Should we agree with this thesis? I think not. Xu Qing's argument goes: "As a tool of human communication, language is characterized by sociality—a crucial aspect. On the other hand, since language serves as a communication tool, it is constantly being used concretely by people, which constitutes another important aspect. ...These two aspects are contradictory. As a tool for exchanging ideas, language is a relatively stable system. To maintain its communicative function, it regulates individual usage through normative

1 Engels, *Letter to Joseph Bloch*, in *Selected Works of Marx and Engels* (Russian edition), 1948, Volume 2, p. 468.
2 Xu Qing, *On the Internal Contradictions of Language and Their Development*, in *Chinese Language* (《中国语文》), 1961, No. 1, p. 7.
3 Ibid., p. 8.

power, requiring everyone to follow its rules." But on the other hand, the concrete use of language by individuals serves no other purpose than social communication. This requires speech to accurately, vividly, and richly express people's thoughts, which are continuously enriched by social development. These ever-evolving thoughts must find expression in speech, making it impossible for speech to merely repeat linguistic system components monotonously. Instead, speech introduces innovative elements alongside social progress and ideological enrichment, while also allowing for individual stylistic variations. ... As such, a contradiction arises between these two aspects. Is there a contradiction between language (langue) and speech (parole)? Certainly. But this contradiction pertains to langue as a system and speech as a whole. When considering the expressive elements within parole, langue does not contradict these elements; rather, it is largely consistent with them. Linguistic components are themselves elements of parole, standing in a relationship of generality to particularity with certain expressive elements in parole—specifically, some expressive elements in speech are universal linguistic components. What Xu Qing described as "the relative stability of langue and the absolute variability of parole" apparently refers to the so-called "introduction of innovative elements alongside continuous social development and ideological enrichment, as well as individual stylistic variations" in the expressive elements of parole. However, these "individual characteristics" are exceptional phenomena. The expressive elements in individual parole acts are predominantly universal linguistic components, with only extremely rare elements being purely individualistic. How many innovative expressive elements can an individual actually use in their lifetime? How often can one employ self-created expressive elements when using language to construct parole acts countless times? How many extra-linguistic expressive elements does one use across innumerable units of parole? Clearly, these are extremely limited. Parole acts are indeed infinitely variable, but the linguistic components within them are not infinitely variable—at least not in ways that violate linguistic norms. Therefore, Xu Qing's claim about the "absolute variability of parole" (in reality referring to the expressive elements in parole) is unfounded, and so too is the opposition he posits between "the relative stability of langue and the absolute variability of parole". That said, we do not deny the existence of contradictions between langue and parole. From the perspective of parole acts or utterances as a whole, there is clearly a tension between them and langue. When langue fails to adequately serve a speaker's communicative intentions, a contradiction arises between langue and parole acts, which can drive linguistic development. Similarly, when langue cannot sufficiently enable speakers to convey specific ideological contents in their utterances, contradictions between langue and parole emerge, naturally prompting linguistic change. The crux of the issue is whether such contradictions qualify as internal contradictions of language.

When we speak of "internal" in relation to a particular thing, the universe contains countless entities that, from the universe's perspective, are all "within" it and constitute its components. In this sense, there is no distinction between internal and external, for we cannot identify anything beyond the universe. However, for individual entities, the distinction between internal and external holds. For the solar system, Earth, Mars, Jupiter, etc., are internal components, while other constellations beyond the solar system are external. Internality and externality are also relative: within the solar system, Earth and Mars are internal, but from Earth's perspective, Mars is external. Similarly, within the category of social phenomena, language, economy, and politics are all internal components. But from the perspective of language alone, economy, politics, and other social phenomena are external. This is why we cannot regard other social phenomena as internal to language, even though we must recognize that language, economy, and politics are all internal to the broader category of social phenomena. So, what is internal to language? The use of language by humans and the speech products created through this use are distinct from language itself and belong to the realm of external phenomena. We would not consider a plant's absorption and use of water for nourishment as "internal" to the water itself, nor would we regard a house built with bricks (as a product of brick-using construction) as "internal" to the bricks. By the same logic, we cannot argue that human use of language and the speech products (i.e., utterances) generated through this use are internal to language itself merely because people use language to create them. The problem is evident: plants are not the only organisms that absorb water for nourishment—animals do too. If the use of water were considered "internal" to water, then every plant's, animal's, and individual's use of water would all be deemed internal to water. Some might claim that water's existence does not depend on plant or animal use, whereas language's existence does depend on human use, therefore human use of language is internal to language. But innumerable things depend on human use for their existence. Not only do all human-created tools and crafts rely on human use, but so do cultural products, scientific works, and literary art. Can we then say that human use of these things is internal to them? Language is a communication tool, as is semaphore; both are systems of symbols, and both depend on human use for their existence. Does this mean that human use of flag semaphore is internal to flag semaphore? If, as Xu Qing claimed, the internal contradiction of language is the conflict between the communicative tool and its use, then the internal contradiction of flag semaphore should logically be the same—so what distinguishes language from flag semaphore? This view clearly mistakes the relationship between language and external users (a relationship of use) for something internal to language, and confuses the connections between language and external phenomena with relationships among internal linguistic elements. Language is universal, while speech can exhibit class characteristics; these two certainly contain contradictions. But these contradictions arise primarily because language users have class identities, not because the language itself is class-based. The relationship between speech and its users is more fundamental than its relationship to the linguistic system. Why then define the contradiction between speech and users as external, yet insist that the contradiction between speech and language is internal? On this basis, the contradiction between language and speech cannot be considered an internal contradiction of language. The proletariat and the bourgeoisie have sharp contradictions, but we cannot therefore claim that this contradiction is an internal contradiction of the bourgeoisie. Rocks are natural objects, but artworks carved from them—such as the stone buddhas in Datong or the Monument to the People's Heroes in front of Tiananmen—carry class characteristics. There is a fundamental contradiction in characteristics between rocks and these artworks, but we cannot regard this as an internal contradiction of the rocks themselves. Similarly, while there is a contradiction between language and the speech produced through its use, this contradiction cannot be seen as internal to language. If the class nature of speech were to constitute one opposing aspect within language's inherent contradictions, could we still maintain that language itself lacks class character? Thus, the contradiction between language's universality and speech's class nature does not demonstrate that the conflict between language and speech is internal to language; on the contrary, it proves that this contradiction is between language and entities outside itself. For what is internal to classless language cannot be class-based speech.

The comparison between flag semaphore and language not only clarifies that the contradiction between a communicative tool and its use cannot be regarded as an internal contradiction of language but also reveals that apart from the contradictions among the constituent elements within the linguistic system, no other internal contradictions of language exist. Communicative tools with sociality can equally be language or flag semaphore; similarly, elements exhibiting class characteristics in human use can apply to both language and flag semaphore (and indeed, human use of all things carries class implications). Therefore, the specific contradictions distinguishing language from flag semaphore—their respective internal contradictions—cannot be the conflict between a communicative tool and its use. In reality, the internal contradictions of any entity in the universe reside in the conflicts among its internal structural elements: The internal contradiction of an atom lies in the conflict between its constituent positive and negative electrons; The internal contradiction of society is the conflict between opposing classes and other constituent social elements; The internal contradiction of the bourgeoisie resides in the conflicts among its individual members; The internal contradiction of an ideology lies in the conflicts among the constituent ideological elements within its system. Similarly, the internal contradictions of language are those among the various constituent elements of the linguistic system, for only these elements qualify as internal to the system they compose. It is for this reason that Guchmann (М. М. Гухман) and others stated in their *Laws of Internal Development of Language (Summary and Prospects of Research on This Issue)*: "The foundation of language development lies in the language system itself and the contradictory nature inherent to this system. It is precisely these specific contradictions that constitute the internal causes of linguistic change."[1]

It is true that internal contradictions can manifest in a thing's properties, leading some to argue that the internal contradiction of language lies in the conflict between the communicative function of linguistic elements and their material structure. However, this theory is untenable. The communicative function of linguistic elements is in fact an inherent property of those elements. Linguistic elements are not material structures; they are entities endowed with communicative capabilities. By definition, any linguistic element possesses communicative function—there can be no linguistic element devoid of this capacity. The arbitrariness of linguistic signs tells us that the connection between sound and meaning in language is arbitrary: in isolation, any phoneme can serve as a tool for expressing meaning and thus has communicative function; there is no question of one phoneme being "more communicative" than another. If a linguistic element loses its communicative function and thereby ceases to be a linguistic element, this is due to contradictions with other elements in the language system, not because the element inherently loses its function. For example, the Ancient Chinese particle "矣" (yǐ, already) gradually fell out of use

1 See Guchmann, Zvegintsev, Kuznetsov, and Serebrennikov, *Internal Laws of Language Development*, *Bulletin of the Karelian-Finnish Branch of the Academy of Sciences of the USSR*, 1954, No. 1.

because the later Chinese language developed the particle "了" (le, already/completed), which expressed the same meaning and contradicted yǐ. In the final analysis, it was the contradiction between yǐ and other linguistic elements that caused its gradual disappearance. Contradictions in properties must arise between different properties of the same entity. If language itself had both universal and class-based characteristics, or both communicative and non-communicative functions, we could indeed speak of these as internal contradictions of language. But no such conflicting properties exist within language. Language and speech are distinct entities, and the contradictory nature of their universality versus class-based characteristics cannot be construed as internal contradictions of the same thing. Sound is not equivalent to phoneme: the non-communicative nature of sound and the communicative function of language do not constitute internal contradictions of a single entity. Nor do the non-communicative nature of concepts and the communicative function of language form internal contradictions within the same thing. Language differs from flag semaphore in that it is a symbolic system of communicative tools composed of elements combining phonetics and semantics, whereas flag semaphore is a system of communicative tools formed by the coordinated movements of two cloth flags. This structural distinction is precisely why language serves as the most important communicative tool in human society: its specific communicative function arises from its unique symbolic structure. Without this specialized structural system, language could neither exist nor fulfill its communicative role. The sociality and universality of language reside in its unique symbolic system and constituent elements. Without this specialized system and its components, language would not exist at all, let alone exhibit social or universal characteristics. Functions are inherent to things—without the thing itself, where do functions come from? As an entity or existent, language is precisely a symbolic system composed of sound-meaning combinations serving as a specialized communicative tool. It is erroneous to view language's symbolic system as non-social, just as it is mistaken to deny that this unique system constitutes the defining feature that distinguishes language from other entities or even other communicative tools. A thing's internal structure is distinct from its origins. Humans evolved from apes, but the internal contradictions of apes or the relationship between apes and humans cannot be regarded as internal contradictions of humans. Houses are built by humans, but human internal dynamics or the relationship between humans and houses (whether constructive or utilitarian) do not qualify as internal contradictions of houses. Similarly, although language was created and used by human society, society's creation and use of language cannot be considered one opposing side of language's internal contradictions.

The fundamental cause of language development lies precisely in the opposition and contradictions among the various components or elements within the linguistic structure. Countless facts demonstrate this view. As communicative tools, different languages can develop differently in the same communicative environment—a phenomenon clearly evident in the historical records of societies using dual languages, as well as in cases where different social groups use the same language. When the Mongolian ethnic group established the Yuan Dynasty, Mongolians spoke two languages for daily needs: Mongolian and Chinese. For contemporary Mongolians, the social environment was identical, yet Mongolian and Chinese developed differently. Similarly, during the Qing Dynasty established by the Manchu people, the Manchus used both Manchu and Chinese, but these two languages did not undergo identical developments. The reason lies in the fact that Mongolian and Chinese, as well as Manchu and Chinese, each have distinct internal structures with different contradictions among their constituent elements. Even within the development of a single language, many changes cannot be directly explained by social phenomena external to language. For example, as Engels noted, "it is difficult to avoid absurdity" when attempting to explain the disappearance of entering tone endings from Middle Chinese to Modern Chinese solely through external social factors. The disappearance of entering tone endings was clearly triggered directly by contradictions within the phonological system: syllable-final sounds could not withstand the pressure from sounds in other syllabic positions, thus losing out in this phonetic struggle. The historical shift of some bilabial *p* sounds in Ancient Chinese to labiodental *f* sounds later on can be attributed to the influence of following rounded vowels. In their conflict with rounded vowel elements, the *p* sounds were encroached upon and transformed into *f*. Semantic changes follow the same pattern. The characters "江" (jiāng) originally referred exclusively to the Yangtze River, and "河" (hé) to the Yellow River, but both now generally denote "river". Yet the objective existence of these rivers has not fundamentally changed, nor have the conceptualizations of them in human cognition. Such semantic shifts are clearly driven by contradictions among components within the internal semantic structure of the language. The substitution of Ancient Chinese "矣" (yǐ) with Modern Chinese "了" (le) reflects no change in the objective world or subjective concepts. Its direct cause resides in the dynamics of the semantic system: as the character "了" (le) diverged into two functions—a verb meaning "to complete a task" and a grammatical particle indicating perfect aspect—it created functional redundancy with the archaic "矣" (yǐ). This semantic competition ultimately displaced "矣" from its original role in the linguistic hierarchy. In Ancient Chinese, "烟" (yān, smoke) referred to "gas rising from the combustion of matter," but later "烟" came to denote general vapor or mist, as seen in terms like "云烟" (yún yān, clouds and smoke) and "烟雾" (yān wù, smoke and fog). This semantic shift does not reflect changes in the physical phenomena themselves or in people's conceptualizations of these phenomena. Similarly, the Ancient Chinese term "墓" (mù, tomb) denoted "a place where humans are buried, with flattened earth mounds," whereas today it refers to any "burial place," regardless of whether the earth mound is flat or raised. This change also does not correspond to alterations in the objects or shifts in human concepts. Whenever a language absorbs foreign elements or creates new linguistic components, it does so in accordance with the internal structural contradictions of its own system. For example, when the Chinese language adopted the English word logic, it phonetically adapted it as “逻辑” (luó jí) according to the rules of the Chinese phonological system, rather than pronouncing it as [lɔdzik]. The creation of Modern Chinese neologisms such as “人造卫星” (rén zào wèi xīng, artificial satellite), “大字报” (dà zì bào, big-character poster), and “劳动模范” (láo dòng mó fàn, model laborer) clearly follows the internal logic of Chinese word-formation principles. The fact that the same new object or concept gives rise to different words in different languages, formed according to each language’s unique internal structural rules, further illustrates that each language has its own distinct system of internal contradictions. Language development arises precisely from the ongoing resolution of such internal contradictions. Since neither the objective world nor conceptual frameworks change in these cases, yet semantic shifts still occur, we must seek direct explanations within the structural contradictions of language itself rather than externally. Although Weiland’s understanding of language change was one-sided, his emphasis on internal causes was insightful. We can draw on his analysis to support our argument. Weiland posited that semantic change results from the positional dynamics of linguistic elements within phrases or compounds. When a component is elided, the remaining element assumes new meaning due to structural reorganization. For example, the semantic leap between German Korn (grain) and Korn (grain alcohol) lacks an obvious associative bridge, but this gap is filled structurally by the compound Kornbranntwein (grain brandy). Omission of -branntwein (brandy) leaves Korn to subsume the entire meaning, demonstrating how internal structural pressures drive semantic innovation. Another example is the German verb ablegen, which shifted from meaning “to set aside” to “to take off (a dress)” through ellipsis. In the phrase den Mantel ablegen (“to take off the coat”), omitting den Mantel (“the coat”) leaves ablegen to assume the specific meaning of “to take off a coat”.[1] While Weiland’s reduction of semantic change to ellipsis is one-sided, his examples illustrate that linguistic developments, as demonstrated in these cases, stem from internal causes. The evolution of Korn from “grain” to “grain alcohol”, for instance, did not occur because the referent changed or human concepts shifted, but rather as a direct result of structural ellipsis—specifically, the word’s positional dynamics within linguistic compounds.

Of course, this does not mean that external factors play no role in language development. In reality, internal causes operate within the framework of external conditions; without external context, internal mechanisms alone cannot function. The disappearance of entering tone

1 Cf. Weiland, *Ellipse in Semasiologisch Einheitlischer Verbindungen* (*On Ellipsis in Semasiological Unitary Compounds*), Uppsala, 1928, p. 9.

endings from Middle Chinese to Modern Chinese is clearly linked to the mechanics of speech organ movements. The semantic evolution of "江" (jiāng) is also tied to psychological aspects of cognitive activity. Thus, while we cannot directly attribute phonetic or semantic changes to physiological or psychological factors alone, these internal contradictions in language would not be activated without the presence of certain physiological or psychological conditions. The crux lies in the fact that specific physiological or psychological states do not unilaterally determine fixed phonetic or semantic changes. These external factors can only exert influence through the internal contradictions of the phonological or semantic system. From a physiological perspective, an [s] sound between two vowels might be expected to evolve into a sound like [r], but the internal contradictions of a language's phonological system may not permit such a change. For example, similar articulatory conditions led to the [s] > [r] shift in the development from Proto-Indo-European to Latin, but this same change did not occur in later stages of Latin or in the transition from Middle Chinese to Modern Chinese. As Stalin noted: "As production advanced, classes emerged, writing appeared, and the rudiments of the state developed. State administration required more systematic documentation, and the growth of commerce necessitated organized correspondence. The invention of the printing press and the emergence of published works—all these factors brought about significant changes in language development. [...] Later, the rise of national languages and nation-states, revolutions, and the replacement of old social systems with new ones all caused even greater transformations in language and its evolution."[1] The impact of social development on language is evident and profound. A look at the development of Modern Chinese since the founding of the People's Republic of China leaves no doubt about the enormous influence exerted by the rapid social progress of New China on the language. However, social development acts as an external factor affecting language; it drives linguistic change through the internal contradictions of the language's structural system. The development of language is concretely reflected in the changes or evolution of specific linguistic facts. Without changes or developments in specific vocabulary, grammar, semantics, or phonetics within the linguistic sign system, the concept of language development becomes meaningless. However, how does society influence these changes or developments in specific linguistic phenomena? Undoubtedly, in new social contexts, the emergence of new objects or new concepts formed by human thinking activities (as a social phenomenon) requires language—as a tool for communication and thought—to adapt and evolve. But how does language develop in response to social demands? The emergence of new objects or concepts does not necessarily trigger linguistic changes; people can resolve such needs through other means (e.g., using foreign languages without altering their native language). Nor does this demand necessarily

1 Stalin, *Marxism and Problems of Linguistics*, pp. 24–25.

require the creation of new words. Within the constraints of its internal structural contradictions, language can address this by adding a new semantic element to existing words. For example, the old word "跃进" (yuè jìn, meaning "leap") was repurposed to reflect the "leap-forward advancement" in China's socialist construction.

Social development may introduce new linguistic components into the sign system, such as "无产阶级" (wú chǎn jiē jí, proletariat). Why do different linguistic change outcomes arise from social development? This depends on the contradictions within the language's structural framework. If the old word "跃进" (yuè jìn) had not existed in opposition to "后退" (hòu tuì, retreat), or if adding the meaning "leap-forward advancement in socialist construction" had blurred the opposition between "跃进" and "后退" or caused sharp conflicts with other word meanings, the same social demand would not have resulted in this new lexical semantic element being added to Modern Chinese. The creation of the new term "无产阶级" (wú chǎn jiē jí) also unfolded in accordance with the internal contradictions of the Chinese language structure. Previously, people used the foreign loanword "普罗列塔利亚" (pǔ luó liè tǎ lì yà, proletariat) to denote this objectively existing phenomenon or the new concept emerging in modern society. Yet "普罗列塔利亚" (proletariat) has now fallen out of use, even though the social context that demands linguistic evolution to reflect this phenomenon or concept remains unchanged. The core social need—for language to adapt and serve modern communication by representing such concepts—has not diminished. The reason why the emergence of the same new concept leads to different semantic evolutions in different languages lies precisely in the fact that different languages have distinct internal contradictions. These observations clearly illustrate that society's influence on language must operate through the language's internal contradictions — in other words, external factors can only take effect through internal ones. Of course, the majority of language development is driven by social progress, which triggers the creation of new words, the decline of old words, and changes in the meanings of existing words. However, all these changes or developments must be realized through the internal contradictions of the language structure. It is for this reason that the specific development of a language is determined by its internal structural contradictions, not by social conditions external to the language. One might argue that the creation of new words would be impossible without social development, and this is certainly true. But the question is not whether new words could emerge without the condition of social development; rather, it is whether specific new words could come into being — and what form they would take — if social development alone occurred without passing through the internal contradictions of the language. The entire language is a creation of society, but creation itself is not equivalent to development. The generation of new words is indeed a form of creation, and newly created linguistic components do not yet constitute development. However, when new words are integrated into the old system, the old system undergoes changes and develops. Notably, the integration of new components must first conform to the internal contradictions of the language structure; it cannot be arbitrary. Throughout its historical development, Chinese has come into contact with many other languages. In adapting to the needs of social life, Chinese has needed to absorb elements from other languages, but how has this absorption occurred? When linguistic components expressing the same meaning already exist within Chinese, foreign linguistic elements are often rejected. For example, attempts were once made to adapt the Sanskrit words kara (ivory), timi (whale), acva (horse), grantha (scroll), and vibhāsa (commentary) into the Chinese loanwords "家啰" (jiā luō), "坻迷" (chí mí), "阿舍婆" (ā shě pó), "迦兰他" (jiā lán tā), and "毗婆娑" (pí pó suō). However, because these loanwords created sharp contradictions with existing Chinese words (象牙 xiàng yá, ivory; 鲸鱼 jīng yú, whale; 马 mǎ, horse; 卷 juǎn, scroll; 笺注 jiān zhù, commentary), they fleetingly appeared and quickly vanished, ultimately failing to be adopted by Chinese. Foreign elements can only take root in Chinese when they do not cause acute internal contradictions—this is why loanwords like "佛" (梵 Buddha, fó) and "薰陆香" (突厥 ghyungluk, xūn lù xiāng) succeeded in establishing themselves. The creation of non-loan new words follows the same pattern. New words can only enter the language if they do not disrupt the existing system's harmony, which is why some arbitrarily coined terms are rejected by Chinese. The very existence of new linguistic components is permitted only by the internal contradictions within the language's element system.

Thus, the development they trigger in the linguistic system must also unfold through these internal contradictions. Although society's influence on language development is mediated by internal structural contradictions, its impact is profound. First, social development inevitably prompts language—as a social communication tool—to change over time to adapt to new environments. When new linguistic components, permitted by the language's internal structural dynamics to meet this demand, enter the system, they create new internal contradictions and trigger further changes. For example, when "红" (hóng, red) acquired the new lexical semantic element "revolutionary", the lexical meaning of "白" (bái, white) shifted to include "reactionary". Similarly, the emergence of the new term "群众" (qún zhòng, masses) led to the gradual obsolescence of the original word "民众" (mín zhòng, common people). This linguistic shift manifested in the systematic replacement of compound phrases: "民众运动" (mín zhòng yùn dòng, popular movement) became "群众运动" (qún zhòng yùn dòng, mass movement); "民众教育" (mín zhòng jiào yù, public education) was replaced by "群众教育" (qún zhòng jiào yù, mass education); and "民众读物" (mín zhòng dú wù, public readings) transitioned to "群众读物" (qún zhòng dú wù, mass publications). Precisely for this reason, the same language can develop regional variants in different geographical areas. Under social conditions of regional fragmentation, the distinct social contexts of different regions lead to the emergence of unique new linguistic components or the decline of existing ones in their respective linguistic systems. Although these linguistic changes initially arise from the internal contradictions of the language, the divergence in new components or the attrition of old ones across regions—shaped by differing social conditions—introduces distinct new contradictions within the language's structure. These divergent contradictions drive the language to develop along different paths in separate regions. Thus, while we recognize society's influence on language as an external factor, we do not underestimate the profound role of social development in shaping linguistic evolution—for even internal factors require external conditions to operate. Ignoring either the internal or external causes of language development is one-sided. This is why we cannot endorse the mechanistic argument of scholars like Meillet, who claim that social development alone determines language change, nor the view of certain structuralists who seek to explain linguistic evolution solely through internal structural dynamics. In specific historical contexts, society can play a decisive role in language development. For example, the social transformations in China following the founding of the People's Republic have had an unprecedented impact on the evolution of Modern Chinese. As Chairman Mao taught, under certain circumstances, external factors can become decisive. Therefore, while clarifying that the social causes of language development are external, we must not belittle their significance. This is why Stalin instructed that linguistic research should be conducted in conjunction with the history of the people who use the language, even as he emphasized that "the primary task of linguistics is to study the internal laws of language development"[1].

From the perspective of external causes of language development, there are numerous such factors. Various causes of language development proposed by some linguists—such as changes in the speech organs, geographical and climatic conditions, variations in national psychological traits, analogical processes, rapid speech, language games, child language acquisition, ethnic separation and integration, diglossia, social differentiation and unification, etc.—all function as external causes of language development, sometimes even serving as decisive external factors. Additionally, the development of natural phenomena, as well as changes in human physiology and cognition, also act as external causes influencing language evolution. Not only do social changes find reflection in language, but natural changes are also mirrored in it: the development of natural phenomena prompts the creation of new linguistic components to denote these developments. Physiological conditions certainly affect linguistic change and growth. Anthropologists inform us that Javanese and Peking apes could only produce limited, slightly differentiated articulated sounds such as gutturals, back dorsal sounds, nasals, and ingressive sounds[2]. Later humans became capable of producing more and clearer syllables, and many

1 Stalin, *Marxism and Problems of Linguistics*, pp. 28–29. "The internal laws of language development" is identical to "the laws of internal development of language".
2 Cf. Bunak, *The Origin of Man and Ancient Human Distribution* (Russian edition), Academy of Sciences of the USSR, 1951.

phonetic evolutions are linked to the physical conditions of the speech organs during articulation, thereby altering the phonological systems of languages. The consequences of phonetic changes caused by the effort to conserve articulatory energy in various languages cannot be denied. The development of thinking certainly also drives language evolution. The emergence of new concepts and the refinement of logical thinking lead to the creation of new words and the precision of grammar, which are observable facts. However, these are external rather than internal causes of language development, for language is neither a physiological phenomenon nor equivalent to thinking itself; physiology and cognition exist outside the realm of language. Internally, the structure of language consists of lexical and grammatical components formed by phonological and semantic elements. Yet, phonological elements are not merely physiological sounds, nor are semantic elements identical to conceptual or logical relationships in thinking. For language, its internal contradictions reside in: conflicts within phonology (not mere sounds), such as among different phonetic features; tensions within semantics (not concepts or logic), such as among semantic components; contradictions among lexical items; frictions among grammatical structures; complex interactions between phonology, semantics, lexicon, and grammar. Sounds and concepts (or logical relations) are external to language. While physiological conditions of sound production and cognitive processes clearly influence language development, they cannot be regarded as internal causes. Without being mediated by contradictions within the phonological or semantic systems, physiological changes in sound production or shifts in thinking alone cannot drive linguistic evolution. For example, the same demand for articulatory economy may trigger different types of assimilation in different languages, or even no assimilation at all. Meanwhile, the emergence of identical new concepts may lead to divergent semantic changes across languages, or sometimes only alter semantic features without modifying semantic units. Therefore, it is also incorrect to claim that "effort-saving" constitutes an internal cause of language development, or to regard the clarifying expressiveness demanded by cognitive development as an internal driver. However, despite these diverse external causes, they do not all function equally; some are direct, while others are indirect. For example, the replacement of monosyllabic words with disyllabic ones to meet communicative needs is a consequence of direct external causes. Changes in nature, which prompt new linguistic reflections, are mediated by indirect external causes: natural changes must first be cognitively processed by the mind and then filtered through the communicative conditions for expressing thought before they can trigger the creation of new words to describe them. Since thinking itself is a social phenomenon, the influence of nature on language development that operates through cognition should be categorized under the broader impact of social phenomena on language. The direct external cause of language development can be summarized as social communicative conditions. As a tool for communication, the core function of language is to express thought, along with appended emotions and volitions. From its origin, langue has been a system composed of units that bind phonetic and semantic elements. The system's functionality embodies the connection between language's internal structure and social communication. Thus, both the physiology of speech organs and the processes of thinking can only influence phonetic or semantic changes in language through the mediating role of communicative needs. The role of "effort-saving" in language development observed by Bally in fact illustrates how the physiology of speech organs influences language development through communicative conditions: the drive to conserve articulatory energy operates only under the demand for communicative efficiency; without this demand, effort-saving would have no effect. Paul's observation of the role of analogical processes in language development also acts through communicative conditions: without the communicative need for clarity and consistency, analogy could not drive linguistic change. Similarly, Winter's noted role of associative functions in language development is mediated by communicative conditions: without the need to generate new semantic features through association or express required communicative content via association, this mechanism would not influence language evolution. The linguistic development triggered by the demand for expressiveness, as analyzed by Vendryès, further exemplifies this principle. For phenomena such as ethnic integration and contact, social differentiation and unification, or the development of various cultural sectors in society—in short, all socio-historical factors affecting language development—their influence must operate through communicative conditions is self-evident. Of course, communicative conditions vary widely, leading to diverse modes of impacting language development, sometimes even contradictory or mutually offsetting ones. Which mode prevails depends on the specific historical context of the language. All external causes are linked by communicative conditions, making them the most fundamental external factor and the core of external causes. However, communicative conditions themselves must act through the internal contradictions of language structure, just as these internal contradictions rely on communicative conditions to manifest. Although communicative conditions are the most fundamental external factor for language development, they are not the internal cause of language development. This is because communication is an act of people using language, representing a relationship between users and the used (i.e., between people and language). As such, it does not belong to language itself as a communicative tool and is not part of the internal structure of language.

Precisely because communicative conditions are the most fundamental external factor in language development, we can say that speech is the 'vanguard' of language development. This is because speech represents specific communicative acts, all of which occur under certain communicative conditions. In specific communicative contexts, speech becomes the "pathway" through which various direct or indirect external factors influence language development. Of course, this "pathway" can sometimes be blocked. For example, in speech acts that attempt to reflect the development of objective things or changes in physiological conditions, some "proposals" to alter language may fail to produce consequences for language development if they cannot adapt to or resolve internal contradictions within the language structure. Alternatively, they may not be able to "independently" make language evolve according to the will of the speaker. This is precisely why, although speech embodies the external factors of language development or serves as its "pathway", it remains only an external rather than internal cause of language development.

Section 3 Laws of Language Development

Language continuously develops under the influence of internal contradictions and external factors. This development follows certain laws. It is an important task for linguists to identify the laws of language development. However, what exactly are the laws of language development?

The laws of language development and the causes of language development are two distinct concepts. The causes of language development refer to the forces that drive language evolution, while the laws of language development refer to the directions in which language evolves. The former answers the question of why language develops, while the latter addresses what direction language development takes.

Since language functions as a tool for communication and thinking through a special symbolic system of sound-meaning combinations, its development is concretely manifested in the changes or expansions of this system—and the laws of language development thus refer to how and in what direction this system historically evolves. Without focusing on the direction or path of change or expansion of this symbolic system, there can be no discussion of the laws of language development. The laws of language development are objectively existent. As Stalin stated: "Marxism understands scientific laws—whether in natural science or political economy—as reflections of objective processes independent of human will. People can discover these laws, recognize them, study them, take them into account in their actions, and use them for societal benefit, but they cannot alter or abolish these laws, still less formulate or create new scientific laws."[1] The laws of language development are no exception. For this reason, the attempt by the Young Grammarians to study the laws of language development from the perspective of individual psychology was erroneous. The laws of language development are objective principles governing the historical processes of a special symbolic system of sound-meaning combinations serving as tools for communication and thinking. The Young Grammarians did emphasize the necessity of studying these

1 Stalin, *Economic Problems of Socialism in the USSR*, People's Publishing House, 1952, p. 2.

laws, but their so-called "laws" were atomistic. They took systematically recurring identical linguistic patterns (particularly in phonological development) within a specific language at a given time, reduced them to mere formulas applicable only to that language and period, and erroneously labeled these formulas as "laws of language development". In fact, as Zvegintsev noted, while these formulas certainly describe certain regular phenomena in language development, regular phenomena are not necessarily laws. This is because a law-like formula summarizes all the regularities of a phenomenon through comprehensive generalization, whereas "regularity" itself is broader than a law and cannot be fully encapsulated by such formulas. [1] For example, in Middle Chinese, whenever the consonant [k] appeared before [i], it inevitably changed to [tɕ] in Modern Chinese (e.g., kien 肩 > tɕien, kiem 兼 > tɕien, kieu 叫 > tɕiau, kiek 击 > tɕi, etc.). This is a regular phenomenon but not a law, as it only involves the single transformation from ki > tɕi and does not comprehensively generalize all regularities of the phenomenon. By contrast, the palatalization formula from Middle to Modern Chinese is a phonological law, as it synthesizes all regularities of the phenomenon. The palatalization formula integrates multiple regular phonological changes: not only did Middle Chinese kien (见) become tɕien, but ki (已), k'iwet (缺),

1 Cf. Zvegintsev, *Internal Laws of Language Development*, Times Publishing House, 1955, p. 6.

k‘iwen (劝), g‘iəp (杰), ka (家), etc., also evolved into syllables beginning with [tɕ-]. A law thus possesses not only necessity, defined as the ability to determine repeated phenomena under fixed conditions, but more importantly, the quality of embodying commonalities across individual regular phenomena. Therefore, we must distinguish between the hierarchical relationships among different regularities in language development and the interconnections between laws and their specific manifestations.

The development of language refers to the comprehensive formula of regular historical evolution within the objective symbolic system of language. Any phenomenon that does not involve the regular evolution of internal elements or components of the linguistic structure cannot be regarded as a law of language development. However, as both a social phenomenon and one of the countless existences in the universe, language also shares certain developmental laws with other social phenomena and entities. This is precisely why we must address the issue of internal laws of language development—those specific to the evolution of language's unique symbolic system, i.e., the historical laws governing the changes in and interrelations between the constituent elements of linguistic structure. For example, the palatalization process from Middle Chinese to Modern Chinese is an internal law of Chinese development, whereas the law that "language develops alongside society" does not belong to this category. The latter is a universal law shared by all social phenomena; language is governed by it not through its unique symbolic system, but through its identity as a social phenomenon. Other social phenomena also develop with society, yet they cannot undergo regular evolution like phonological palatalization as manifestations of a specialized symbolic system. Likewise, language is governed by the laws of dialectical development, but this governance arises not from the uniqueness of its symbolic system but from its status as an objective entity. All other entities in the universe, including natural phenomena, are subject to dialectical laws, yet none undergo regular evolutions, such as phonological palatalization, as part of a specialized symbolic system. In other words, laws governing the evolution of specific elements within the linguistic structure, such as phonological palatalization, are unique to language and thus qualify as internal laws of language development. As Zvegintsev noted: "Within the process of language development, various laws exist. Since language is a social phenomenon, the development of all languages exhibits regular reflections of processes inherent in the development of other social phenomena and of society itself. Because these phenomena arise within the course of social-historical development, they are uniquely reflected in language, which is closely intertwined with society... The internal laws of language development constitute a distinct category. These laws pertain to the characteristics that distinguish language as a social phenomenon from others."[1] His insights provide a valuable reference for our discussion.

However, the laws of language development mentioned here, which involve the developmental formulas of internal elements or components of the linguistic structure, do not imply that these laws are formulas for the evolution of such elements or components caused by the internal factors of language development. As previously stated, the external and internal causes of language development belong to the category of reasons for language development, while the laws of language development fall under the category of results brought about by these causes (i.e., the outcomes produced by these reasons). The two are not identical (cause and effect are not equivalent). Therefore, we must not confuse external/internal causes with the laws of language development or with the internal laws of language. In reality, both external and internal causes result in changes or expansions of linguistic elements/components and the symbolic system in language development. Consequently, the distinction between the laws of language development and internal language laws cannot be based on external/internal causes. Instead, it must be grounded in whether a law relates to the characteristics that distinguish language from other

1 Zvegintsev, *Internal Laws of Language Development*, pp. 29–30. Note: The phrase "语言的内部发展规律" ("internal development laws of language") in this translation is sometimes rendered as "internal laws of language development" in some Chinese translations.

phenomena (social or natural)—specifically, its status as a special symbolic system of sound-meaning combinations. As Engels noted in his letter to Schmidt (October 27, 1840): "When studying individual processes of labor or individual ideological superstructures, it is necessary to pay attention to the unique characteristics of their own movement and to the independent laws derived from nature or from the inherent traits of these phenomena themselves." What are the unique characteristics of language's inherent movement? As one of the objective existences, one of the social phenomena, and one of the symbolic systems, language shares some characteristics with all objective existences, all social phenomena, and even all symbolic systems (such as gestures, semaphore, etc.). However, language possesses special characteristics that distinguish it from any other things (including other symbolic systems). These characteristics are exclusive to language and precisely reflect the special features manifested by its unique structure, which differentiates it from other things. The internal laws of language development refer to the development laws inherent in this set of special symbolic systems unique to language and its structural interior. In their work *Internal Laws of Language Development (Summary and Prospects of Research on This Issue)*, Guchmann and others, while emphasizing that the internal laws of language development refer to the laws governing the unique characteristics that distinguish language from other social phenomena, argued that the internal laws of language development should be discussed in relation to language's fundamental function as a tool for human communication.[1] This formulation still requires further exploration. Language is undoubtedly a tool for human communication, but as Lenin noted, it is human's most important communicative tool, not a generic one. Beyond language, humans employ other communicative tools such as writing, semaphore, and gestures, all of which are also social phenomena. If the internal laws of language development pertain to the unique characteristics that distinguish language from other social phenomena, these laws should not be measured against the traits of general communicative tools but rather rooted in the specific features of this exceptional tool. What sets language apart from other communicative tools is its nature as a symbolic system combining sound and meaning for communication. Therefore, to elucidate the internal laws of language development, one must address the proprietary developmental laws within this specialized symbolic system and its structure as a communicative tool.

The linguistic sign system is structured around two "poles" (phonetics and semantics) and two "levels" (vocabulary and grammar), which in turn form interconnected subsystems within the language. The internal laws of language development thus involve these aspects of its structural makeup. Each component of the linguistic sign system also possesses its own internal developmental logic. This is why we can discuss the internal laws governing

1 See Guchmann, Zvegintsev, Kuznetsov, and Serebrennikov, *Internal Laws of Language Development*, Bulletin of the Karelian-Finnish Branch of the Academy of Sciences of the USSR, 1954, No. 1, p. 6.

phonetic development, semantic development, lexical development, and grammatical development. For example, the disappearance of entering tone endings represents an internal phonetic law in the transition from Middle Chinese to Modern Chinese; the emergence of classifiers such as "一个" (yīgè), "一头" (yītóu), "一匹" (yīpǐ), "一尾" (yīwěi) embodies an internal grammatical law from Ancient Chinese to Middle Chinese; and the proliferation of compound words reflects an internal lexical law from Ancient Chinese to Modern Chinese. However, the internal laws of language development are not merely the mechanical sum of these component-specific laws. Language is not a mere assemblage of elements but an organic unity, where all components are interdependent. As such, each component's developmental patterns must align with the characteristics of the entire linguistic system. Their internal laws interact and reflect the system's overarching traits. For instance, the massive growth of compound word formation from Middle to Modern Chinese was influenced by the disappearance of entering tone codas and other phonetic changes during this period.

Because each specific language has an internal structure distinct from that of other languages, every language also possesses its own unique internal developmental laws. It is precisely in this context that we must distinguish between the general and specific laws of internal language development. For example, the phonetic palatalization from Middle Chinese to Modern Chinese is a unique internal developmental law of

Chinese, while the phonetic palatalization from Old French to Modern French is a unique internal developmental law of French. Although both Chinese and French have undergone phonetic palatalization throughout their histories, the specifics differ significantly. In Chinese, palatalization is limited to sounds like [k], [k‘], [g], [k‘], [g‘] before phonetic elements ending in [-i] or those that changed from [-a] to [-ia], resulting in [ts-] or [tc^4-]. In French, however, the process is different: [k] (spelled c) before [-i] and [-e] palatalized early on to [ts-], which contracted to [s-] by the 13th century (e.g., cing “five” pronounced [sek], cent “hundred” pronounced [sa]). Palatalization of [k] (spelled c or ch) before [-a] occurred much later, becoming [tʃ] and contracting to [ʃ] by the 13th century (e.g., chat “cat” pronounced [ʃa]), while [k] before [-y] did not palatalize (e.g., cuve “wine barrel” remains [kyv]).

Phonetic palatalization is a general law of internal development common to all languages, but the specific manifestations in Chinese and French represent unique internal developmental laws for each language. The relationship between general laws and specific laws of internal development is one of generality and specificity. While all specific languages share general characteristics—as symbolic systems combining sound and meaning serving as tools for communication and thought—each language also has unique features, manifested in distinct sound-meaning integration systems. Precisely for this reason, they may possess unique internal developmental laws. Such laws are neither shared by any other language nor reducible to a more general formula with other languages' internal laws; they should be understood as internal developmental laws specific to an individual language, which "cannot be fully subsumed under the general" (Lenin). Yet they remain specific instances of internal developmental laws. However, general laws of internal development can only exist within specific ones, as "existence is only possible through the individual (i.e., the specific)" (Lenin). For example, the general phenomenon of phonetic palatalization can only manifest through specific instances like those in Chinese, French, and other languages. From this perspective, we cannot agree with the following argument by Zvegintsev. Zvegintsev stated: "However, the general internal laws of language development, regardless of their specific manifestations, remain universal to all languages as inherent principles. This is because they are governed not by the structural peculiarities of individual languages, but by the unique essence of human language as a social phenomenon exclusively dedicated to serving communicative needs. The law of unbalanced development in the speed of various components of language can serve as an example of such laws."[1] Here, Zvegintsev opposed internal development laws "constrained by the special essence of human language as a social phenomenon serving communication" to those "constrained by the structural characteristics of specific languages," using this as a criterion to distinguish between general

1 Zvegintsev, *Internal Laws of Language Development*, p. 22.

and specific internal laws of language development. In his co-authored work with Guchmann and others, *Internal Laws of Language Development (Summary and Prospects of Research on This Issue)*, Zvegintsev advanced the same argument. On the one hand, he asserted that "the internal laws common to all languages and the internal laws of specific languages are indivisibly unified... the general cannot exist without the specific or individual, and conversely, the general can be found within the individual"; on the other hand, while citing numerous specific cases to illustrate the internal developmental laws of phonetics, vocabulary, and grammar in specific languages, he maintained that general internal laws of language development include principles such as the gradualness of language change and the unbalanced development of structural components.[1] This does not adequately explain the relationship between the general and the specific. If the special essence of human language as a whole is "to serve human communication", can it be argued that individual languages do not share this same essential function? If specific languages have their own structural compositions, is there such a thing as a "general language" that exists apart from the structures of specific languages? In both functional and structural terms, general language is embedded within specific languages: the communicative essence of general language exists through the

1 Cf. Guchmann, Zvegintsev, Kuznetsov & Serebrennikov, *Internal Laws of Language Development*, Proceedings of the Karelian-Finnish Branch of the USSR Academy of Sciences, 1954, No. 1.

communicative functions of specific languages, and general language cannot fulfill its communicative role without the structures of specific languages. If the law of unbalanced development among language components is considered a general internal law of language development, then the manifestations of this unbalanced development in specific languages are equally entitled to be called specific internal development laws. For example, if the structural development of specific languages like English and German exhibits unique laws in their temporal categories—as cited by Zvegintsev—these distinct specific laws should still be generalizable into broader laws governing temporal category development. As Zvegintsev himself noted, the development of temporal categories in English and German shares "commonalities: the future tense forms are constructed according to the unified pattern of an auxiliary verb plus the infinitive of the main verb; and additionally, many modal verbs are used as auxiliary verbs, with certain shared semantic shifts occurring during their grammaticalization as auxiliaries."[1] Therefore, the general and specific internal laws of language development are unified, representing the general and specific aspects of the same laws. It is incorrect to separate the laws governed by the essence of language as a communicative tool from those governed by the structures of specific languages, labeling one as "general" and the other as "specific". This is because the development of specific

1 Zvegintsev, *Internal Laws of Language Development*, p. 22.

language structures is equally constrained by the need to serve communication, and a "general language" detached from specific structures does not exist. Moreover, there is no inherent connection between the law of unbalanced development of linguistic components and the essential characteristics of language as a communicative tool. Is the unbalanced development of components necessarily determined by the essence of being a communicative tool? In reality, countless things in the world exhibit unbalanced development of their components without being communicative tools. Of course, general laws may be further generalizations of specific laws. For example, phonetic assimilation can be seen as a broader generalization encompassing specific phenomena like palatalization, devoicing, and voicing. Even so, the general law of phonetic assimilation must still be embodied in specific laws such as palatalization, devoicing, and voicing. In reality, phonetic palatalization, devoicing, and voicing are simply different manifestations of phonetic assimilation. The relationship between phonetic assimilation and these specific processes (palatalization, devoicing, voicing) exemplifies the dialectical principle that the general resides within the specific, and the specific embodies the general. However, when Zvegintsev labeled the unbalanced development among language components as a "general internal developmental law" while categorizing the development of temporal categories in English and German as a "specific internal developmental law", he obscures the dialectical relationship between the general and the specific. We cannot discern any manifestation of the "law of unbalanced development" from the developmental patterns of English temporal categories, nor can we conclude that unbalanced development among components inherently dictates the evolution of temporal categories. The concept of unbalanced development refers to comparisons between the rates or directions of development across different components (e.g., phonetics vs. grammar), not to the internal development of a single component like temporal categories. Since these belong to fundamentally different logical categories, no general-specific relationship can be established between them.

The unbalanced development among language components should not be categorized as an internal law of language development. As Zvegintsev himself noted, internal laws of language development should refer to those unique to language. However, we observe that the unbalanced development of constituent parts is a phenomenon shared by nearly all evolving systems, not just language. Even if the unbalanced development of language components indirectly involves their specific evolution, a process unique to language, this does not resolve the issue. All laws of language development, by definition, must directly or indirectly relate to component development; for example, the law of language differentiation into dialects (which Zvegintsev excluded from internal laws) necessarily involves component development indirectly, as dialect divergence would not occur without differential changes in phonetics, semantics, grammar, or vocabulary. The crux of the matter lies not in whether a law involves component development, but in the perspective from which it is analyzed. Internal laws of language are those exclusive to language, distinct from developmental laws shared by other phenomena. The unbalanced development of constituent parts is a law common to countless non-linguistic systems. Thus, even though it indirectly relates to language components, it remains outside the scope of language's internal developmental laws.

The gradualness of language development and the law of its ever-expanding and improving scope also do not qualify as internal laws of language development, for they are not unique to language. Many other phenomena in the world unfold through "the gradual accumulation of new qualitative elements" and "the gradual decline of old qualitative elements". Stalin even stated that "generally speaking... the law of transition from old to new quality through explosion applies not only to the history of language development but often not to other social phenomena belonging to the base or superstructure."[1] This shows that gradualism in development is not exclusive to language. Countless other things in the world develop by continuously improving and expanding themselves. Although these laws indirectly involve the development of internal elements of language structure, they, like the unbalanced development among language components, are not unique to language and therefore do not belong to the category of internal laws of language development. These laws moreover

1 Stalin, *Marxism and Problems of Linguistics*, p. 26.

explain certain characteristics of language development, rather than defining its directional trajectory. They clarify the modes through which language realizes its developmental path, not the path itself; they describe how language manifests specific traits while following its inherent laws, not how the laws of development operate internally. These patterns can be considered "laws" in a secondary sense because they synthesize the recurring characteristics of how language development laws are implemented. However, they do not represent the internal laws of linguistic evolution; instead, they merely describe the features of how these fundamental laws are carried out in the process of language development.

To distinguish certain laws from the internal laws of language development, we may as well refer to these laws as the general laws of language development. The general laws of language development should be differentiated from both the general internal laws of language and the functional laws of language. The general laws of language development, along with the general and specific internal laws of language development, all fall under the category of language development laws, that is, the laws manifested in the historical transformation of language structure. However, the former pertains to the development laws shared by language and other phenomena. For instance, the law of gradual qualitative change is common to many phenomena, while the latter refers to the laws unique to language. The functional laws of language refer to how language exerts its communicative function and embodies thinking in accordance with certain rules. The activities of language are realized on the basis of the inherent structural characteristics of the language system. The functions of language are exerted in accordance with certain laws of the language system. These laws are static and belong to a different category from the historical laws of language development. Nevertheless, these two types of laws are mutually restrictive and interdependent. In the context of communication, new linguistic elements emerge and take shape as language fulfills its functions, thanks to the "advance guard" role of speech activities. The exercise of language functions identifies new societal demands on language, thereby driving its further development. Conversely, language development determines the emergence of new functional laws governing language. Therefore, while the developmental laws and functional laws of language are distinct in nature and must be distinguished, their interconnectedness cannot be severed.

Since language is a social phenomenon and the most important communication tool for people, it develops alongside societal progress. Although the general laws of language development are not unique to language, they are a concrete manifestation of its social essence. Understanding these laws is an indispensable condition for comprehending how language evolves. However, these laws also inherently involve the internal development of linguistic structures; without such internal development, they would be empty formulas. Yet, focusing solely on the internal laws of language development while neglecting the general laws would lead to a failure in recognizing language's social essence. This is precisely why Stalin, while emphasizing that "the primary task of linguistics lies in studying the internal laws of language development"[1], also stressed that "to understand a particular language and its developmental laws, it is possible only by conducting research in close connection with the historical development of society and the history of the people who created and use that language"[2].

The general laws of language development are primarily manifested in the law that language develops alongside societal development. The general regular phenomena of language development arising from the various relationships between language and society fall within the scope of this law. The differentiation of language as society differentiates and the unification of language as society unifies are concrete embodiments of this law.

1 Stalin, *Marxism and Problems of Linguistics*, pp. 28–29.
2 Stalin, *Marxism and Problems of Linguistics*, p. 20.

Chapter 3

The Prospects of Language Development

Section 1 The Progressiveness of Language

Since primitive humans created language, it has been continuously developing. Driven by internal and external factors, language has not only evolved continuously within its structural system but also differentiated into various languages and linguistic variants. At the same time, these variants have been unified into languages or different languages have merged into one. The phenomena of differentiation and unification simultaneously bring about various changes within the linguistic structure. The interplay of differentiation and unification presents a diverse landscape of languages: some new languages emerge due to historical conditions that foster differentiation, while others vanish as historical conditions drive unification. The entire history of human language is thus a record of the birth, decline, and evolution of linguistic structures shaped by this interplay. Historical comparative linguists, who emphasize language differentiation as the sole path of development, hold a clearly flawed view. The process of language differentiation is indeed proven by history. The fact that Latin split into French, Italian, Spanish, Portuguese, Romanian, and other languages is undeniable. Engels long ago addressed the phenomenon of language differentiation or division, stating: "...the formation of new tribes and new dialects through division occurred in America not long ago, and even today it may not have completely ceased."[1] Stalin also noted, "In fact, the kinship of languages cannot be denied; for example, the kinship among the various Slavic national languages undoubtedly exists."[2] The existence of related languages serves as evidence of language differentiation. However, it is erroneous to claim that differentiation is the only pathway for language development. History demonstrates that many regional dialects have unified into a common language, and many languages have merged into one. It is also a tangible fact that numerous dialects and languages were eliminated during the process of linguistic unification. History tells us that in ancient Greece, dialects such as Doric and Aeolic once existed, but these have become historical relics, unified into Koine (meaning "common language") based on the Attic dialect. Many archaeological discoveries, such as the Tocharian language found in Xinjiang, China, and the Hittite language discovered in Anatolia, as well as historical records in documents like the "National Language" (i.e., the Xianbei language) recorded in the *Book of Sui: Treatise on Classics* 《隋书·经籍志》 and Coptic language inscribed on Egypt's Rosetta Stone, all reveal how numerous languages vanished during the process of unification. While describing language division, Engels also noted: "Where two declining tribes merged into one, it

1 Engels, F. *The Origin of the Family, Private Property and the State*. People's Publishing House, 1955, p. 87.
2 Stalin, J. *Marxism and Problems of Linguistics*. p. 32.

sometimes happened, exceptionally, that two closely related dialects were spoken within the same tribe."[1] In most cases, tribal languages became unified. Stalin, while discussing the existence of related languages, also stated: "When two languages merge, one usually emerges as the victor, ... and the other gradually loses its essence and declines."[2] Therefore, language unification is also a pathway of language development. However, it is equally incorrect to emphasize unification as the sole path of language development. Marr, on one hand, argued: "Today, there is no language that has not been subject to fusion, and it is inconceivable that any formed spoken language could have originated without fusion: before fusion, there could be no spoken language... because there were no economic collectives before fusion." ...It can be seen that there have never been simple tribes or simple languages untouched by fusion—in essence, no unfused languages have ever existed.[3] On the one hand, he resolutely claimed that language unification through fusion represents the developmental path of all languages in all eras of human history, asserting that no other paths have existed or can exist.[4] According to Marr, when spoken language first emerged, there were many languages that immediately began to fuse with each other and follow the path of unification, leading to a gradual reduction

1 Engels, F. *The Origin of the Family, Private Property and the State*. p. 87.
2 Stalin, J. *Marxism and Problems of Linguistics*. p. 28.
3 *Selected Works of Marr* (Russian edition), Vol. 2, p. 65.
4 Cf. Bernstein, C. B. *On the Problem of Language Mixture*. In *Problems of Historicism in Linguistics*, p. 80.

in the number of languages. Marr's theory first fails the test of logic. If language was always fused from the start, then there must have been prior languages that were later fused. Were these latter languages also unified through fusion? If so, from which languages did they emerge? Pushing this line of questioning further, one must ultimately acknowledge the existence of unfused languages, for without them, there would be no source for language fusion and unification. Marr's theory also cannot withstand the test of facts. Despite his attempt to use the "four elements" theory to deny the existence of linguistic kinship and the process of language differentiation, his doctrine of the four elements lacks scientific foundation.[1] Even if, as Marr claimed, the analysis of any language can identify four elements—сал (A), бер (B), йон (C), рош (D)—this does not prove that language fusion or unification is the sole path of language development. Elements are merely the materials composing a language system; it is the system formed by these elements that constitutes a language. To determine whether a language contains components of other languages, one must examine whether it includes linguistic elements formed by these materials from other languages. It is insufficient to treat the discovery of such elements as evidence of fusion or unification with other languages, especially since the hypothesis of these four elements itself lacks scientific

1 Cf. Chikobava. *On the Problem of Historicism in Linguistics from the Perspective of Stalin's Works*. In *Problems of Historicism in Linguistics*, pp. 35–49.

basis. It is through the analysis of linguistic components themselves that historical comparative linguists have proven the developmental process of language differentiation. Facts stand on the side of historical comparative linguists in opposing Marr's theory. However, we should not deny the role of fusion or unification in language development due to Marr's errors. Languages do not exist in isolation from other languages. Despite the fact that in the era of primitive clans, languages spoken by various social units were distributed across vast regions, with "broad neutral zones"[1] existing between tribes — a situation that may have led to "language differences" due to the expanse of these zones, contradicting Marr's theory that all languages must fuse — there was still, over the long course of history, some degree of contact, whether direct or indirect, between the social groups using these languages. This made language fusion (or unification), at least partial fusion (or unification), a rather common phenomenon. Although languages develop according to their internal laws, the long-term accumulation of fusion can alter the complexion of their basic vocabulary and grammatical structures. Languages descending from the same parent language may differ sufficiently in basic vocabulary and grammatical structures to become distinct languages, thereby altering their internal development laws. For example, English, as one descendant of Proto-Indo-European, has departed from the internal development laws of its ancestor,

1 Cf. Engels, *The Origin of the Family*, *Private Property and the State*, p. 86.

shifting from a synthetic language to an analytic one. Even when languages develop according to their internal laws, the influence of long-term fusion can gradually transform them without shaking their most fundamental vocabulary and grammatical characteristics, thereby resulting in qualitative changes within the same language rather than the creation of mixed languages. Because in the course of their development, languages often both differentiate and undergo fusion with other languages, the systems of various languages exhibit diverse states. Therefore, in the study of language history, we must both analyze the phenomena of language differentiation and examine the impact of language unification (or partial unification) on language development, in order to complement the shortcomings of historical comparative linguistics.

Since language develops alongside societal growth and fades away with the decline of society, and since numerous instances of language replacement or extinction have occurred throughout history, we are confronted with a question: does language possess progressiveness in its developmental process? In the 19th century, historical comparative linguists once proposed theories of language degeneration. For example, Buber, a founder of historical comparative linguistics, put forward the concepts of the "organic period" and "inorganic period" of language. He argued that any sentence contains three indispensable components: subject, copula, and predicate, with the copula linking the subject and predicate. He claimed there is only one true verb in language—the copula— and that any verb is a product of the agglutination of a predicate component with substantive meaning and a certain form of the copula, even if the copula is implicit. For instance, the Latin word *dat* ("he gives" or "he is giving") includes -t (third-person subject), da- (predicate meaning "to give"), with the grammatical copula implicit. The verb *potest* ("he can"), however, reveals the copula explicitly, containing three components: -t (third-person subject), -es (copula), and pot- (predicate meaning "to be able"). The "agglutination" of these three components within the same word was seen as the origin of the "organic" elements of grammatical forms. The grammatical structure of ancient Indo-European was thus seen as a product of a certain "organic period" in language development, while the historical evolution of later Indo-European languages merely caused these "organic" structures to gradually fade from explicit to ambiguous forms.[1] Schleicher amplified Buber's views, arguing that languages are organic entities and dividing their "life cycles" into two distinct periods: the "prehistoric period" (an era of growth) and the "historical period" (an era of decline). He stated: "Within the historical scope, we observe that languages age in phonetics and form (i.e., grammar) according to specific laws of survival. The languages we speak today, like those of all significant historical nations, are descendants of ancient linguistic forms. All languages of civilized nations, as we know,

1 Cf. his *Comparative Grammar of Sanskrit, Sindhi, Armenian, Greek, Latin, Lithuanian, Old Slavic, Gothic, and German.*

are more or less in a state of degeneration."[1] He further claimed: "Languages were formed in prehistoric times and have been gradually dying out in historical times."[2] Schleicher argued that the Proto-Indo-European language represented the pinnacle of linguistic development in the prehistoric period. He called Sanskrit the "rose among languages" and posited that historical Indo-European languages were the result of gradual decline from this parent language. In his view, the ideal language was ancient Indo-European. This perspective typifies the theory held by many linguists who equated ideal language with ideal art in ancient classical languages—Greek and Latin. They claimed that Greek and Latin had reached the summit of linguistic perfection, with subsequent languages undergoing degeneration. This is clearly a flawed perspective. While language is indeed an organic system, it is not an organism. The "organicity" of a language system lies in the organic connections between its constituent components, rather than necessarily in the agglutination of the so-called three elements within a single word. The so-called "organicity" of modern national languages is in no way inferior to that of Greek and Latin, and the complex lexical systems of modern languages far surpass those of Greek and Latin. The theories of Buber and Schleicher clearly lack scientific

1 Schleicher, *Uber die Bedeutung der Sprache für die Naturgeschichte des Menschen* (*On the Significance of Language for the Natural History of Mankind*), Weimar, 1865, p. 27.
2 Schleicher, *Sprachvergleichende Untersuchungen* (*Comparative Language Studies*), Vol. 1, Bonn, 1848, Preface.

foundation. As for regarding Greek and Latin as ideal languages, this is evidently a mistake that confuses the artistic use of language by certain outstanding Greek and Latin authors with the inherent qualities of Greek and Latin themselves. It cannot be denied that the speech of classical authors such as Cicero serves as one of the paradigms for the artistic use of language. However, this does not mean that their employment of these languages defines the essence of Greek and Latin, even though Greek and Latin are embodied in their speech. Of course, we do not deny the beauty of Greek and Latin, but the question is not whether these languages are beautiful, but whether there has been a phenomenon of linguistic degeneration from Greek and Latin to the modern national languages. The facts clearly indicate otherwise. If Cicero's Latin exemplifies the elegance of the language, Balzac's French achieves an even higher level of refinement—not in spite of its Latin roots, but through the evolutionary transformation of those very roots. Therefore, between classical languages and modern languages, there is not only no so-called degeneration, but rather a process of further linguistic development and more progressive historical evolution.

Can language degenerate? For human language as a whole, it only develops forward, advancing on the path of progress. Although Vendryes criticized the idea of language degeneration, his own views were also flawed. He argued that from the perspective of language itself, linguistic development only manifests as meaningless transformations of linguistic forms. Vendryes stated: "...The same language exhibits various forms at different historical stages; its components change, revive, and shift. But in general, losses and gains can offset each other. We have explained why, due to natural development, a language never achieves logical perfection—the kind of logical perfection artificially imposed on all constructed languages. The various aspects of morphological development are like a kaleidoscope shaken countless times. Each time we obtain new combinations of its components, but nothing genuinely new is created besides these combinations."[1] Of course, as Vendryes pointed out, morphological changes are in many cases merely kaleidoscopic recombinations. For example, the disappearance of certain morphological features in ancient Indo-European languages (such as the loss of noun case endings from Latin to French) was compensated for by new grammatical forms (such as the emergence of prepositions in French), with no "extra" elements produced. However, language development is not limited to these so-called kaleidoscopic changes of mutual offset and compensation. The historical records of many languages demonstrate the emergence of new grammatical forms that do not merely replace old ones. The copula, regarded by Schleicher as one of the organic components of language, emerged relatively late in the history of Indo-European languages.[2] Unit words in

1 Vendryes, J. (1921). *Le Langage*. p. 412.
2 Cf. L. H. Gray, *Foundations of Language*, New York, 1939, pp. 230–232.

Chinese (such as "一个" (yīgè, one), "一棵" (yīkē, one tree), "一把" (yībā, one handle), etc. are also later developments in the history of the Chinese language, as are the articles in modern Indo-European languages. These phenomena do not replace obsolete grammatical elements but represent entirely new grammatical components. Therefore, Vendryes' views contradict historical facts, and his arguments lack scientific basis. When comparing the grammatical structures of modern national languages with those of the ancient languages prior to the slave era mentioned by Stalin, anyone can discern traces of progress. Why did Buber and Schleicher consider ancient Indo-European languages to belong to an "organic period" or "developmental era", believing that later languages degenerated? Why did Vendryes argue that no genuinely new elements emerge in language development? Because Buber and Schleicher equated morphological change with the entirety of grammatical content, while Vendryes confined linguistic development to mere kaleidoscopic morphological transformations. The truth is that morphological change does not constitute the whole of grammar, nor does grammatical development encompass all aspects of language evolution. A language may lose certain morphological features during its development but can simultaneously generate numerous new components in other grammatical forms—components that are not mere substitutes for the old but entirely novel. Comparative studies of the grammatical structures within the Sino-Tibetan language family show that Proto-Sino-Tibetan clearly possessed certain morphological features

(Tibetan, for instance, retains abundant inflections), while modern Sino-Tibetan languages like Chinese have lost most of these. Does this mean Chinese has degenerated? Obviously not, as the complexity of Chinese syntax is notoriously difficult for even Europeans to master. Thus, we cannot judge the progressiveness of grammar solely by its morphological state. Language is an integrated system, in which grammatical structure is inseparably linked to the lexical system. A language's nationality may lead it to use lexical forms to express meanings that other languages convey through grammatical forms—for example, Chinese employs lexical components like "男" (nán, male), "女" (nǚ, female), "阴" (yīn, yin), and "阳" (yáng, yang) to express the concept of "gender", which Indo-European languages convey through morphological changes. Therefore, there is no basis for measuring a language's progressiveness solely by its morphology or grammatical structure. Zvegintsev stated: "When discussing language development, one must not fixate solely on changes in linguistic forms, such as the increase or decrease of suffixal inflections and other formal modifications. ... We should not forget that language is closely intertwined with thought. In the process of its development, language 'records and consolidates the results of human mental activities and cognitive achievements in words and sentences composed of words, thereby making the exchange of ideas in human society possible.'[1] Therefore, the necessary prerequisites for language development include not only the perfection of its forms but also the richness of its content."[2] His words can serve as a reference for us.

Jespersen also approached the question of progress in language development from a morphological perspective but arrived at conclusions diametrically opposed to those of Buber and Schleicher. After comparing the grammatical structures of various languages and their historical development, he concluded that modern languages exhibit superiority in the following aspects:

(1) Shorter forms, which save muscular effort and require less articulation time;

(2) Fewer forms that do not overburden memory;

(3) More regularized word-formation;

(4) Syntax that likewise shows fewer irregularities;

(5) Greater analytic and abstract characteristics, which enhance expressiveness by enabling combinations and constructions that were once impossible or inelegant;

1 Zvegintsev quoted Stalin's statement, as seen in *Marxism and Problems of Linguistics*, p. 20.
2 Zvegintsev, *The Internal Laws of Language Development*, p. 15.

(6) The elimination of cumbersome repetitions categorized as "agreement", leaving only vestiges;

(7) Clear and unambiguous comprehension ensured by regularized word order.[1]

From this perspective, he posited that analytic languages represent progress whereas synthetic languages are regressive, citing English as a paradigm of linguistic advancement. English gradually evolved its grammatical structure from synthetic to analytic, a trajectory mirrored by other Germanic and Romance languages. He further claimed that the analytic nature of Chinese also demonstrates its progressiveness. It was under the influence of Jespersen's views that Gao Benhan (Bernhard Karlgren) argued: "Earlier theories classified Chinese (i.e., the Chinese language) as a 'primitive' language, claiming it had not reached the stage of inflection. This is precisely contrary to the truth. In fact, Chinese has followed the same evolutionary path as Indo-European languages: the suffixes (i.e., word endings) of synthetic languages gradually vanished, appealing instead to the pure logical analytic power of listeners (or readers). Modern English may be the most highly evolved language in the Indo-European family in this regard; yet Chinese has advanced even further."[2]

1 O. Jespersen. 1922. *Language: Its Nature, Development, and Origin*. p. 364.
2 Gao Benhan. 1933. *Chinese Language and Chinese Script* (S. Zhang, Trans.). Commercial Press. p. 27.

Gao Benhan abstractly praised Chinese while concretely denying its superiority, revealing a contradiction in his views on the language.[1] The issue is not whether Chinese is a progressive language, but what constitutes the criterion for a progressive language. Following Jespersen, Gao Benhan held that the analyticity of grammatical structure is the yardstick for measuring linguistic progress. However, this criterion is unreliable. Although opposing the standards proposed by Buber and Schleicher, Jespersen and Gao Benhan made the same mistake as their predecessors: they all took the presence of formal changes in language as a yardstick for measuring linguistic progress, a criterion that is fundamentally hypothetical. Language is a combination of sound (phonetics) and meaning (semantics). Changes in form do not necessarily indicate grammatical changes. Although synthetic and analytic languages differ in structure, they can express the same meanings. Therefore, the distinction between synthetic and analytic languages cannot be used to judge the "progress" or "backwardness" of a language. From a formal perspective, each language follows its own developmental path, as linguistic structures evolve according to their unique internal laws in different directions. However, even if the paths of formal change diverge, from the standpoint of the union of sound and meaning, all languages are advancing along their own paths of improvement. Historical

1 Gao Mingkai. 1960. *The bourgeois academic ideology of French Sinologists in Chinese language research*. In *Linguistic Research and Criticism* (Vol. 2, pp. 341–345). Higher Education Press.

comparative linguists, approaching language from a formalistic standpoint, proposed that linguistic development progresses through three stages: isolating, agglutinative, and inflectional. They derogatorily labeled Chinese, as an exemplar of isolating languages, a "primitive" language while elevating Sanskrit, a quintessential inflectional language, to the status of the "rose of languages". Their theory is demonstrably flawed. Although Jespersen and Karlgren correctly argued that Chinese, an isolating language, is progressive, their arguments, like those of the historical comparativists, still measure linguistic advancement by grammatical form.

Language certainly has distinctions between progress and backwardness, just as the cultures of various nations do. However, when using the concepts of "progress" and "backwardness", we must distinguish them from "superior" and "inferior". "Progress" and "backwardness" only describe states in the historical development process, not inherent "nobility" or "inferiority". In the overall history of human language development, the languages of primitive humans were clearly backward, while the languages of modern nations are clearly progressive. But this does not mean primitive languages were "inferior" or modern languages are "superior". For each specific language, its development also proceeds in a progressive direction. Ancient Chinese was clearly less progressive than Modern Chinese and was relatively backward. The crux lies in the criteria for linguistic progress. As noted above, language is a tool for national communication and abstract thinking. For any tool, its progressiveness is determined by its utility value—and language, as a tool for communication and thought, is no exception. This is why Vendryes' claim that "the arithmetical and practical problems of language cannot be counted toward the question of linguistic progress"[1] is incorrect. A language's structure is the very vehicle for its functions; this structure evolves under the influence of social communication needs, even if such needs are only external factors in language development. The progressiveness of this structure is manifested in how effectively it fulfills its roles as a tool for national communication and thought. Certainly, at every moment, as Vendryes observed, "language never refuses to serve those who express ideas."[2] Generally speaking, at any stage of social development, language is capable of serving people of that era, expressing the thoughts they wish to convey. However, in the process of social development, society itself exhibits differences in progressiveness and backwardness. Consequently, along with the distinction between the progressiveness and backwardness of societies in different eras, languages—as tools for national communication and thought in each era—also show differences between progress and backwardness. The criterion for this division lies in whether a language can function as a tool for national communication in a progressive society. The essence of language as a tool for national communication lies in its ability to enable all

1 Vendryes, J. 1921. *Le Langage*. p. 407.
2 Vendryes, J. 1921. *Le Langage*. p. 406.

members of society to exchange ideas with one another. Therefore, whether a language is progressive depends on whether it can express rich thoughts, facilitate precise thinking, and—above all—whether it maintains universality[1]. This is because language is not merely a communicative tool but a tool for national communication. Stalin stated: "The existence and creation of language serve the whole of society as a tool for human communication; they make language something common to all members of society and something unified for society. It must serve all members of society equally, regardless of their class status. When language deviates from this all-people stance and adopts a position that favors one social group over others, it loses its essence, ceases to function as a tool for human communication in society, degenerates into the jargon of a specific social group, and ultimately disappears."[2] Thus, whenever language loses its universality and its function of serving as a tool for social communication among all members of society, it not only degenerates but may even eventually perish. Therefore, for individual languages, there are not only phenomena of degeneration but also the possibility of extinction. History shows that many languages have been eliminated, and it also tells us that when a language becomes a "jargon", its development ceases. This is what happened to Latin when it became the "jargon of Christianity". Since

1 The so-called "universality" includes the quasi-universality of local dialects, as local dialects serve as communication tools for all members of a regional society. Therefore, "communication tools for the entire population" also encompass local dialects.
2 Stalin, J. V. 1950. *Marxism and Problems of Linguistics*. p. 5.

language serves society by facilitating the exchange of ideas and functions as a tool for national communication and abstract thinking, a language that can express rich thoughts and assist people in precise thinking is a progressive language. Of course, the fulfillment of these functions depends on the internal structure of the "vehicle" (i.e., the language itself) that bears them. A language that can achieve universality, express rich ideas, and assist in precise thinking must possess a rich lexical system and a sophisticated grammatical structure. This is precisely why modern national languages are far more progressive than ancient languages, and why Chinese ranks among the most progressive languages in the world.

Section 2 The Prospects of Language Structure Development

The trends in language development throughout history, coupled with the trajectory of human societal evolution, allow us to anticipate the future of human language. While each language has its unique internal laws of development, there are also common developmental trends shared among languages. These trends are manifested both in the evolution of their internal structures and in their adaptation to societal progress, with the two being closely interconnected. In terms of the development of internal language structures, we can elaborate on our perspectives regarding the prospects of language development from the following aspects.

The internal structure of language is a symbolic system composed of lexical and grammatical components, and any lexical or grammatical component is a composite of sound and meaning. Although phonetics is inherently bound to semantics, forming the opposing poles of the internal contradiction within any linguistic component, both phonetics and semantics possess relative independence. Therefore, we can first examine the prospects of language development from the perspectives of phonetics and semantics.

For a long time, many linguists have maintained that phonetic simplification is a general trend in phonological development. Consequently, they argue that human languages will undergo phonetic simplification in the future. For example, Whitney once stated: "The process of development also includes obvious manifestations of a trend toward simplicity. Of course, new sounds are not inherently easier to produce than old ones; on the contrary, many experiments lead us to conclude that they are more difficult to articulate—they are not immediately learned or repeated by children, nor are they easily found in the general structure of human languages. However, for practiced speakers, they are easier to produce in the rapid flow of continuous speech, as this requires the vocal organs to make quick transitions constantly between vowels and consonants, and between more open and less open articulatory positions."[1]

1 Whitney, *The Life and Growth of Language*, London, 1889, p. 69.

"The trend of linguistic change is so decisively toward the abbreviation and attrition of words and forms that one may quite appropriately speak of 'phonetic decay'. Driven by the impulse for simplicity, the components of speech are first unified, then their structures are blurred and destroyed. The process of merging creates ample scope for this trend; had language remained in its primitive, simplistic state, the scope of change would have been vastly restricted, and its effects in terms of phonetic decay would have been far less pronounced."[1] As Whitney observed, in terms of individual phonation, the variety of sounds humans can produce has been steadily increasing, with newly emerged sounds being more challenging to articulate. If apes can produce more sounds than other animals, and primitive humans could generate more than apes, there is no reason to doubt that humans would develop the capacity to produce even more sounds as they evolved. The developmental history of Indo-European languages bears this out. Proto-Indo-European had fewer vowels and consonants than its descendant languages, and newly arisen sounds in modern Indo-European languages (such as English [θ] and [ð]) are relatively more difficult to pronounce. The historical development of the Chinese language also bears this out. Ancient Chinese did not distinguish between light and heavy labial consonants, whereas Modern Chinese developed this contrast. Newly emerged sounds in Modern Chinese, such as [a] and [ts], and sounds like [B] and [4] in

1 Whitney, *The Life and Growth of Language*, London, 1889, p. 74.

Modern Chinese dialects, are also relatively difficult to pronounce. However, syllable structures have become simpler. The histories of both Indo-European languages and Chinese bear this out, as does the cumbersome syllable structure of more primitive languages. But does this allow us to conclude that phonological development is trending toward simplicity, leading to the abbreviation and attrition of word and grammatical forms—and that the brevity and attrition of the phonetic structures of words and grammar (so-called "phonetic decay") will characterize the future of human language phonology? Whitney argued that the pursuit of simplicity is a trend in phonological development, and continuous articulation leads to many mergers, i.e., phonetic assimilation. It is undeniable that phonetic assimilation is a common phenomenon in phonological development. But as we have argued, physiological sound changes are external factors in phonetic change, yet whether change occurs or how it proceeds depends on the internal contradictions within the language structure. Inside the linguistic system, phonetics and semantics form opposing poles of a contradiction. When sound changes exacerbate this contradiction to the point of undermining semantic expression, phonetic assimilation not only fails to occur; on the contrary, dissimilation arises instead. After collecting extensive historical data and analyzing phonetic change phenomena, M. Grammont concluded: "For scholars studying language evolution, distant dissimilation is the most significant of all phenomena. This is not because it is the most common—its frequency is far lower than that of assimilation—but because of its complexity and diverse manifestations."[1] Although dissimilation is less common than assimilation, its complexity surpasses that of assimilation. Neither contiguous dissimilation nor distant dissimilation occurs for the sake of articulatory ease; on the contrary, they often require greater phonetic effort. Therefore, the process of phonetic change does not always trend toward simplicity. Phonetic simplification can lead to difficulties in semantic expression, thus creating irreconcilable contradictions between sound and meaning. The notion that phonetic change results in the abbreviation and attrition of word and grammatical phonetic structures is also an unscientific conclusion derived from superficial observation. Of course, in individual cases, phonetic change may indeed shorten words, but historical evidence shows that due to the contradiction between sound and meaning, linguistically shortened words can also become longer. For example, the Latin words apis ("bee"), auris ("ear"), and sol ("sun"), due to their overly short phonetic structures, later evolved into longer forms: apicula, auricula, and solicula.[2] Between Ancient Chinese and Modern Chinese, such phenomena are innumerable: 友(yǒu, friend)→朋友(péngyou, friend); 家(jiā, home)→家庭(jiātíng, family); 道(dào, path/truth)→道理(dàolǐ, principle); 声(shēng, sound)→声音(shēngyīn, sound); 见(jiàn, see)→看见(kànjiàn, see); 乐(lè, joy)→快

1 Grammont, *Traité de phonétique*, Paris, 1933, p. 269.
2 Cf. Vendryes, *Le Langage*, p. 250.

乐(kuàilè, happy)... Countless cases of monosyllabic words evolving into disyllabic words like these demonstrate that phonetic changes do not necessarily shorten the phonetic structure of words. Moreover, from the perspective of lexical units, a compound word remains a single linguistic unit, and its phonetic structure is not only non-short but sometimes significantly longer. Modern national languages have widely produced compound words, all of which feature non-compact phonetic structures. Phonetic changes have indeed led to the loss of certain grammatical forms. For example, due to phonetic shifts, the Latin soror (sister), sororis (of the sister), and sorori (to the sister) evolved into soeur in French, losing their suffixal inflections. However, there are also numerous cases where phonetic changes give rise to new grammatical forms, and the inflections in many languages are the result of such changes. For example, the open-syllable *ŏ* in Latin became *eu* in French when under stress and *ou* when preceding stress, thus generating grammatical inflections in French: pouvons—peuvent (we can—they can), œuvre—ouvrier (work—worker), nouveau—neuf (new—inexperienced). Moreover, these grammatical changes are essentially just alterations in grammatical forms; when one grammatical form is lost, another often emerges to replace it. For instance, the simplification of suffixal inflections caused by the loss of post-stress sounds in the transition from Latin to French led to the proliferation of new grammatical forms in French, such as prepositions and articles. This demonstrates that "phonetic decay" does not exist. It should be noted that phonetics is not merely sound; as the sound component of linguistic elements, phonetics possesses sociality and expressive functions. If external causes induce phonetic changes, the contradiction between sound and meaning may intensify, thereby giving rise to other changes to resolve this conflict. The reason phonetics exist in human language is not for simplicity, but to combine with semantics, enabling language to serve as a tool for communication. If the purpose of phonetic changes in human language were to pursue simplicity, then, the simplest solution would be none other than to cease articulation altogether, allowing the speech organs to rest as much as possible. However, such "rest" would only lead to the nonexistence of language. Marx argued: "Language exists only because it is expressed through sound; the activity of thought can proceed without expression. [...] Language (vocal) has now begun to cede its functions to the latest inventions that absolutely conquer space, while thought rises by virtue of its unused past accumulations and new achievements, and can supplant and completely replace language. No language can hold its ground before it—not even spoken languages that remain connected to natural norms."[1] His "prediction" about the future development of speech sounds in language was entirely mistaken. The reason for this, as Stalin pointed out, is that Marr "divorced thought from language".[2] In fact, when viewed from the essence

1 As cited in Stalin, *Marxism and Problems of Linguistics*, pp. 37–38.
2 Ibid., p. 38.

of language—and from the perspective that language is a system integrating sound and meaning—phonetics will never develop toward extinction.

In summary, due to the influence of external factors, such as the development of human physiological states and the emergence of new sounds, human languages can evidently utilize new sounds as the phonetic material shell during their evolution. Additionally, due to the physiological constraints of the speech organs, languages may also undergo phonetic changes that facilitate articulation. These factors indeed make it possible for phonetics to develop toward simpler pronunciation in certain contexts. However, since sound is merely a constituent element of language, human languages primarily rely on the coordination and organization of sounds rather than their sheer quantity. The number of phonemes in different languages does not reflect linguistic advancement, and it is unimaginable how the number of phonemes in future human languages might become more complex. Physiological development is inherently limited: after hundreds of thousands of years of evolution, humans have not been able to produce significantly more sounds. Regarding the trend of phonetic development in sound coordination, it is true that physiological factors may lead to more articulatory convenience in future languages. However, this tendency will be counteracted to a considerable extent by the reactive influence of semantics: excessive simplification will inevitably lead to complexity in other aspects. Moreover, this is of minor significance, as phonetics constitute only one facet of linguistic components, not the entirety of language. Their development trend does not represent the overall direction of language evolution but merely that of one constituent element within the linguistic structure.

The development of semantics may appear to become increasingly complex, but this depends on the perspective from which it is viewed. As we have already stated, the semantic units in language are sememes, which are the semantic units possessed by morphs and taxemes, not the semantic components of words. From this perspective, although the semantics of language develop alongside the advancement of human thought, this development does not necessarily manifest in an increase in sememes. More often, it is reflected in the growing number of lexemic sememes formed by the combination of sememes. Morphs include roots, affixes, and inflections, while taxemes are units of word order. From the historical perspective of language development, the number of roots, affixes, and inflections does not always increase. Many roots in Indo-European languages have existed historically for a long time; while new roots do emerge, they are not abundant. The emergence of new concepts does not necessarily lead to the creation of new roots; generally, this is addressed through affixation or compounding. The gradual emergence of affixation in Chinese and the increasing prevalence of compounding reflect this trend in language development. However, despite the growing use of affixation, new affixes do not necessarily emerge rapidly. Moreover, during the process of development, old roots occasionally die out, and old affixes may cease to exist. These losses offset the gains, resulting in a less significant net increase in roots and affixes. As for inflections, while some languages may add inflections, there are at least as many cases of inflection loss; we cannot expect to see a consistent increase in their number. The possibilities for taxemes (word order units) are inherently limited, since word order involves only the sequence of elements (front or back). Although the complexity of sentences may increase the potential for word order variation, this remains bounded. Thus, while we cannot deny that the number of sememes, represented by the semantic components of roots, affixes, inflections, and word order, will gradually increase with social and cognitive development. However, this trend is slow and bounded. It is unimaginable that future human languages will contain a countless number of sememes embedded in roots, affixes, inflections, and word orders. Although the requirement to avoid excessive memory load is an external factor in language development, it plays a role by restricting the unlimited and rapid expansion of sememe numbers through the internal laws of language development. Human associative activities can generate various combinations of existing roots, affixes, inflections, and taxemes. Through mechanisms like affixation, compounding, and word order composition, these combinations create possibilities for new words and grammatical components that reflect cognitive development. New sememes can only be successfully generated when it is difficult to employ these means, and only some sememes can differentiate into distinct ones, because language cannot tolerate excessive homophony. While the number of sememes does not expand rapidly or infinitely, the structure of sememes becomes increasingly rich and complex. With the development of society and cognition, new concepts continue to emerge, and these concepts often evolve from existing ones. As a result, these new concepts often enter the sememes of original concepts as new semantic features (semes), enriching their content. Moreover, due to the increasing complexity of society, the growing precision of linguistic norms, the diversification of communicative contexts, and the enrichment of human emotions and imagination, semantic features related to rhetoric, style, emotion, and imagery within sememes have also increased. This has led to the multi-faceted development of sememes, with various semantic features continuously expanding and their content becoming increasingly rich and complex. Of course, due to the combination of semantics and phonetics, sememes containing excessive semantic features may conflict with phonetic structures, leading to the differentiation of sememes and their phonetic structures. However, the differentiated sememes will obviously continue to enrich their content over time. Nevertheless, just like phonetics, sememes are only one facet of linguistic components, and their development does not represent the development of language as a whole.

Since all linguistic components are combinations of phonetics and semantics, the basic units of language as building materials are words, and the structural patterns of language are grammatical components. The development of the lexical system composed of words and the grammatical system composed of grammatical components truly reflects the development of language. From a lexical perspective, it is predictable that future languages will become increasingly and rapidly enriched in their lexical systems. In particular, with the victory of the socialist system in its struggle against the capitalist system and the establishment of communism in future human society, the subsequent rapid development of all sectors of social culture will only serve to more quickly enrich the lexical systems of languages. The rapid development of the lexical system of Modern Chinese since the founding of the People's Republic of China can foreshadow an even more rapid enrichment of human languages' lexical systems in future societies. This enrichment is manifested both in the continuous increase in the number of lexemes and in the growing number of morphemes contained within lexemes. Although new lexical units represented by new stems are often formed by combining existing morphs (roots and affixes), they are new lexemes distinct from any past ones. To adapt to the rapid development of future societies, new lexemes will continue to emerge, which increasingly enriches the lexical system. As the culture of human society is the accumulation of human's achievements in transforming the world, and human knowledge is the historical record of human society's reflection of the objective world, although some words reflecting old cultural elements are eliminated, far more new words are created. Stalin stated: "In reality, the development of language does not occur by eliminating existing languages and creating new ones, but by expanding and improving the basic elements of existing languages."[1] This is precisely the case for the lexical system. We can also foresee the rapid enrichment of lexemes in future language lexical systems. This certainly does not manifest in the phonemes of lexemes, nor necessarily in the tagmemes of lexemes, but primarily in the sememes of lexemes. Lexemic sememes, represented by the simple or compound sememes of stems, will evidently generate new semantic features (semes) within the scope of lexemic sememes alongside the development of various sectors of social culture brought about by the victory of socialism and the formation of communism. After the founding of the People's Republic of China, many lexical sememes in Modern Chinese have acquired new lexical semantic features (semes). For example, the sememe of "东风" (east wind) has gained the semantic feature "全世界的人民的力量" (the power of the people worldwide); "西风" (west wind) now includes "全世界的反人民的力量" (reactionary forces worldwide); and "纸老虎" (paper tiger) contains "帝国主义" (imperialism) as a semantic feature. These examples all indicate the increasing enrichment of lexical sememes in future language development. Like sememes in general, the enrichment of lexical sememes will not only manifest in the growth of conceptual semantic features but also, alongside the increasing precision of linguistic norms, the diversification of communicative contexts, and the enrichment of human emotions and imagination. This gives rise to

1 Stalin, *Marxism and Problems of Linguistics*, p. 25.

numerous semantic features, such as rhetoric, style, emotion, and imagery, to develop their multi-faceted nature. From the perspective of how words reflect phenomena in the objective world, the universal lexical components of a language—those related to society, politics, economics, productive activities, and science and technology—will multiply rapidly as socialist and communist societies drive the universalization of social, political, economic, cultural, scientific, and technological life. They may even enter the scope of basic vocabulary. The current development of Modern Chinese has already demonstrated this trend in language vocabulary. Along with the development of human thinking, vocabulary also advances toward a path of high abstraction. As we have stated, language is the bearer of abstract thinking. Except for some lexical semantic features that express emotion, imagery, rhetoric, and style, the lexical sememes in language are all concepts solidified in words. Concepts are the materials or outcomes of abstract thinking; therefore, these lexical semantic features all possess abstractness. However, abstractness varies in degree and stage. Although humans have engaged in abstract thinking from the beginning, and this thinking has always developed within the realm of logical thinking, human thinking can still advance in terms of the degree of abstraction. Historical evidence shows that relatively primitive languages contained more words specifying minute differences between concrete objects. For example, Ancient Chinese had numerous terms for horses with specific characteristics:

A black horse with a yellow ridge was called 驷 (sì);

A horse with a white forehead was 驹 (jū);

A horse with a white left foot was 异 (yì);

A yellow-and-white dappled horse was 驱 (qū);

A blue-black horse with chessboard-like markings was 骐 (qí);

A red-and-white dappled horse was 瑕 (xiá);

A yellow horse with a black snout was 弱 (ruò);

A horse with alternating yellow and white patches was 貌 (mào);

A horse with a sunken abdomen was 骞 (qiān);

A horse with a white abdomen was 骠 (biāo);

A castrated horse was 骗 (piàn);

A horse with long hair was 鹑 (chún);

A horse standing six chi tall was 骄 (jiāo)...

Modern Chinese no longer has these distinct terms. Marcel Granet once used this to slander the Chinese language, claiming that its words do not express concepts. He cited as an example that Ancient Chinese lacked a single term for "elderly person", but instead had many words describing different types of aging: for instance, "耆" (qí) for those needing richer nourishment, "考" (kǎo) for those with breathing difficulties, and "老" (lǎo) for those over seventy showing specific infirmities. From these words, he concluded that Chinese words not only fail to denote concepts but are not even simple symbols, instead possessing the magical power of evocation.[1] This is clearly scientifically unfounded. If Ancient Chinese words did not express concepts, how could Confucius, Mencius, Gongsun Longzi, Zhuangzi, and others who used Ancient Chinese have written philosophically sophisticated works rare in the ancient world? In reality, words like "耆" (qí), "考" (kǎo), "老" (lǎo)... all possess abstractness and represent concepts in abstract thinking. However, it cannot be denied that the abstract thinking of primitive humans was less abstract than that of modern humans—in other words, less advanced in degree of abstraction. With the development of modern science and technology and the increasing abstraction of human thinking, modern languages contain more highly abstract words. It can be envisaged that in the future, with the victory of the socialist system, the establishment of an ideal communist society, and the advancement of science, technology, and all cultural sectors, a much larger proportion of highly abstract words will emerge in the lexical systems of human languages.

From a grammatical perspective, the grammatical structures of future human languages will develop toward greater precision and abstraction. The

1 Cf. Granct, *La pensée Chinoise*, Paris, 1934, pp. 34–42.

history of language development shows that when there is a need to distinguish certain logical relationships in the process of cognitive development, new grammatical components may emerge in language. For example, the verbs of Proto-Indo-European only had rich grammatical components for the aspectual category, but in Greek and Latin, numerous grammatical components developed to express the tense category.[1] This does not mean that Proto-Indo-European lacked linguistic elements for expressing tense; it simply means that Proto-Indo-European did not regard the nuanced distinctions of tense as urgently necessary in speech, nor did it elaborate such distinctions in detail. For example, Ancient Chinese often simply said phrases like "八佾舞于庭" (eight rows of dancers perform in the courtyard), without clarifying whether the performance was in the middle of the courtyard, on it, to the left of it, to the right of it, in front of it, or behind it. Later Chinese extensively adopted grammatical structures like "在……之中" (in the middle of...), "在……之上" (on...), "在……之下" (below...), "在……之左" (to the left of...), "在……之右" (to the right of...), "在……之前" (in front of...), and "在……之后" (behind...).[2] This certainly does not mean that Ancient Chinese lacked concepts of spatial orientation, but rather that precise spatial specifications were not felt as urgently necessary at the time. History also shows that grammatical

1 Cf. Vendryes, *Le Langage*, p. 415.
2 Cf. Gao Mingkai, *On the Historical Inheritance of Chinese Grammar*, in *Journal of Peking University* (Humanities), 1955, No. 1, p. 170.

components expressing less abstract concepts may gradually decline or even disappear in some languages. For instance, Proto-Indo-European originally had a "dual number" grammatical component. Sanskrit nouns and verbs both had a "dual number" category, as did ancient Greek and Old Slavic. In Modern Russian, два дома (two houses), три дома (three houses), and четыре дома (four houses) use the suffix -a, while пять или десять домов (five or ten houses) uses the suffix -OB. This distinction illustrates that the former is a vestige of the ancient "dual number"[1]. The dual number has disappeared in modern Indo-European languages. This is because, although primitive humans had abstract thinking, their generalizations were not broad enough—they had not yet subsumed "two" under "many". Later humans realized that concepts of two things and concepts of many things both belong to the category of "multiplicity". The gradual decline of the dual number demonstrates that as human abstract thinking developed in terms of generality, people progressively formed broader abstract concepts, such as the concept of "multiplicity". Some argue that the existence or disappearance of such grammatical components immediately reflects the advancement or backwardness of language development. However, grammar is an integrated system, and we must consider other factors before making judgments. For example, Modern Chinese is actually witnessing the gradual formation of "dual number" grammatical components, such as "我

1 Cf. Budagov, *Introduction to Linguistics*, pp. 186–187.

俩" (wǒ liǎ, we two), "咱俩" (zán liǎ, we two), "爷儿俩" (yér liǎ, father and son), "夫妻俩" (fūqī liǎ, husband and wife). These expressions are absent in Ancient Chinese. Does this prove that Modern Chinese is inferior to Ancient Chinese, or that grammatical development is not moving toward greater abstraction? It should be noted that Chinese speakers do not exclude "two" from the concept of "many". Not only does the Modern Chinese word "多" (duō, many) include the meaning of "two", but the grammatical component "们" (men, plural marker) also implies "two or more". We can equally use "我们" (wǒmen, we) or "咱们" (zánmen, we) to replace "我俩" or "咱俩". Thus, the generality of the Han people's abstract thinking is already expressed through other grammatical components. As for the formation of "俩" (liǎ), on the one hand, it is caused by the phonetic contraction of "两个" (liǎng gè, two)[1], and on the other hand, it is related to the psychological qualities of the Han people. The Han people customarily value paired or dual things. When indicating paired items, although they are also regarded as "many", the term "俩" is used, while in other cases, "们" (men) is used instead. For example, when referring to "two gentlemen", although it also means "two", we say "先生们" (xiānshengmen, gentlemen) rather than "先生俩" (xiānsheng liǎ). "俩" is only used to indicate paired or dual relationships, such as "公婆俩" (gōngpó liǎ, mother-in-law and father-in-law), "兄弟俩" (xiōngdì liǎ, two brothers), or "夫妻俩" (fūqī liǎ,

1 Cf. Gao Mingkai, *Treatise on Chinese Grammar*, p. 140.

husband and wife). It is also used in contexts like "我俩" (wǒ liǎ, we two) or "咱俩" (zán liǎ, we two) to denote paired relationships such as "brothers", "friends", or "spouses". This differs from the situation in ancient Indo-European languages. In Sanskrit, the "dual number" is used for "two", and the "plural number" (i.e., "many") is used for "more than two". Therefore, from the perspective of the entire grammatical system, the existence of "俩" in Modern Chinese does not reflect a lower degree of grammatical abstraction. Nevertheless, across the broader grammatical system, the general trend of grammatical development is toward greater generalization expressed by grammatical components that reflect the generality of abstract thinking. Therefore, we have reason to imagine that in future languages, there will be more grammatical components reflecting greater generality than in present-day languages.

Scholars often predict the future development of languages based on the evolution of grammatical forms. Some argue that future languages should increase morphological components in word-formation to enrich inflections, thus regarding morphological richness as the path or prospect of grammatical development. Some even "kindly" identify numerous so-called inflections in Modern Chinese to prove it is an advanced language progressing toward the forefront of grammatical development. Others believe the trend in grammatical form is the weakening of morphology and the strengthening of syntax. From the perspective of grammatical form alone, we maintain that the weakening of morphology and the strengthening of syntax represent the future of grammatical development—a trend proven by linguistic history. Of course, at certain stages of development, new morphological elements may emerge; for example, Modern Chinese has developed derivational morphemes like "子" (zi) and "儿" (er). But in general, the trend is toward reduced morphological complexity and enhanced syntactic structure. Compared to Ancient Chinese, Modern Chinese has fewer inflections. Ancient Chinese quite extensively employed consonant alternations between aspirated and unaspirated sounds, as well as tonal changes, to form new words, while Modern Chinese uses these word-formation morphologies less frequently. Although Russian is a highly inflectional language, its morphology has clearly simplified compared to Old Russian or ancient Indo-European languages. This is because the morphological system relies on one or two phonemes for construction, and these phonemes are extremely vulnerable to loss due to phonetic changes. Morphemes are mostly located at the end of words, placing them in a disadvantageous position within the internal contradictions of the phonological system, thus making them prone to disappearance. This is an inevitable result of the contradiction between phonetics and grammar. Therefore, we agree with Chikobava's argument that "the history of many languages demonstrates a trend toward the simplification of morphology (case and conjugation forms) and a shift of focus to syntax"[1], and we

1 Chikobava, *Introduction to Linguistics*, Volume 1, Part 1, p. 71.

maintain that future languages will follow the path of syntactic centrality in grammatical form—a path that the development of Chinese already exemplifies for the prospects of grammatical evolution.

However, the development trend of grammatical forms does not represent the overall trend of grammatical development, nor does it indicate the advancement or backwardness of grammar. The same content can be expressed by different forms. Historical evidence shows that the simplification of morphology goes hand in hand with the complexification of syntax, and morphological simplification does not imply grammatical simplification. As a tool for communication and thinking, the content embodied in a language's grammatical components is of greater significance. The complexification of syntax can equally fulfill the functions once served by lost morphological forms, while the simplification of morphology must be compensated for by syntactic complexification. Grammar evolves alongside the development of social life and thinking to serve subsequent societies effectively. With the progress of human society, human thinking clearly advances toward greater precision and generality. Therefore, regardless of form, any grammatical structure that adapts to societal needs, aligns with the trend of cognitive development, and achieves greater precision and generality embodies progress. Consequently, the grammatical structures of human languages invariably evolve toward increased refinement and abstraction in tandem with social development and cognitive progress.

In summary, the history of language development indicates that languages advance along the path of enrichment, abstraction, and precision. Both the lexical system (and its components) and the grammatical system (and its components) as internal structures of language will also evolve toward more multifaceted enrichment, greater abstraction, and higher precision. These "three evolutions" (enrichment, abstraction, precision) thus define the developmental prospects of future human languages.

Section 3 The Formation of a World Common Language

Driven by the developmental trend of the "three evolutions" (enrichment, abstraction, precision) in their internal structures, languages continuously diverge and converge under the constraints of social environments. From the history of human languages, it is evident that when primitive humans first created language, there was not a single language but multiple languages emerging simultaneously. When forming humans developed languages with preliminary basic vocabulary and grammatical structures through early speech activities, human society was in the primitive era. During this period, it was impossible to have many large social units, yet it was also unlikely that there was only one such unit. Like other species, forming humans could neither populate the entire globe nor live in a single location, as primitive living conditions forced them to migrate in groups to different regions for survival. The discovery of remains of human ancestors such as Java Man, Peking Man, and African ape-men proves that forming humans, who had preliminary speech abilities but had not yet developed languages with basic vocabulary and grammatical structures, had already migrated from the central birthplace of human to various regions. When these ape-men gradually refined their preliminary speech activities through labor to develop languages with essential linguistic characteristics, social units in different regions created their own distinct languages. These anthropological discoveries have forcefully refuted the fallacious monogenesis theories of language origin—such as the claims by medieval monastic scholars [1] and certain modern narrow nationalists [2] that human language originated from Hebrew or Dutch. Historical-comparative linguistic studies have also demonstrated the existence of language families whose common origins cannot be traced, while the failed attempts of some linguists to further establish a unified origin for all language families have further exposed the bankruptcy of such myths. However, we must also reject the view of Marr, who argued that countless languages existed from the outset and that the entire history of human language development involved only gradual reduction through continuous fusion. When studying the languages of the Caucasus, Marr observed the region's complex linguistic landscape and, based on

1 Even in the 17th century, some scholars still claimed that all languages originated from Hebrew—for example, E. Guichard.
2 An example is the Dutch missionary H.J. Goropius.

unfounded fantasies, concluded that language was fundamentally composed of four elements—сал, бер, йон, рош—and that humans created innumerable languages by manipulating these elements during language genesis. Marr argued that these four elements were the original combinations of sounds from which all languages derived. However, sound combinations alone do not constitute language. For instance, the Georgian word qel-qel means “hand”, while the Armenian qel-qel means “wisdom”, and qel means “foolishness”. This suggests that primitive humans regarded “hand” as a symbol of wisdom, likely because they had long relied on gesture language. When early humans began using their hands to create tools, they simultaneously developed vocal language. This coincided with the era of countless clan-based social units scattered across different regions, leading Marr to claim that languages were numerous from the start. This theory clearly contradicts reality. It is inconceivable that clan societies existed in large numbers from the outset, let alone that these units could have simultaneously created numerous distinct languages without any foundational basis, as if coordinating a unified uprising date. A reasonable assertion should be that primitive humans, due to their settlement in different regions, successively created diverse languages based on preliminary speech activities. As primitive clan social units could not have proliferated suddenly, the number of these languages was limited. Nor can we agree with Marr’s view that clan societies had contacts from the outset, leading to the claim that language fusion occurred from the beginning and that no language is free from being a fused language. Engels reminds us that the fundamental social organization in the clan era was the tribe, with each tribe characterized by a distinct (tribal) dialect. Between the regions occupied by various tribes, "besides the areas they actually inhabited", they "also held extensive territories for hunting and fishing. Beyond the boundaries of these territories lay a vast neutral zone extending to the borders of neighboring tribes"[1]. It was clearly extremely difficult for primitive human societies separated by vast neutral zones to make contact. On the contrary, the separation of social units was precisely the reason why each tribe had its unique language. Marx stated: "The tendency toward continuous differentiation originates from the elements within clan organizations. Under their social conditions (i.e., the tribal societies of the savage and barbaric eras) and the occupation of vast territories, this tendency toward continuous differentiation reinforces the tendency to form linguistic differences. Although the vocabulary of spoken language is relatively stable, especially in terms of linguistic structure, it cannot remain unchanged indefinitely. Geographic separation leads to the emergence of linguistic differences in space; this also results in the specialization of interests and complete independence."[2] Due to difficult living conditions, primitive culture, and population growth, early humans could not remain in

1 Engels, *The Origin of the Family, Private Property, and the State*, p. 86.
2 See *Marx-Engels Archive* (Russian edition), Vol. 9, p. 79.

one place or gather for food indefinitely. They needed to form groups and migrate to different regions for survival, which was the cause of clan society fragmentation. As clan societies split, the few primitive human languages diverged into many languages, making linguistic differentiation a defining feature of language development during this period. In the heyday of clan society, changes in living conditions gradually gave rise to tribal confederations, and thus some languages unified alongside tribal unification. However, the fundamental process during the clan society era was the continuous fragmentation of tribes and their languages.

When the clan system collapsed, there might have been isolated cases of further differentiation, but this was no longer a universal phenomenon. During the transition from classless to class societies, large-scale tribal confederations emerged. As a result, tribes speaking various tribal languages were unified, and their languages followed suit. Yakubinsky stated: "In the heyday of clan society and the classical period, tribal dialects or idioms constituted the basic linguistic units. However, during the phase of primitive classless societies—particularly on the eve of class society development—when confederation among related tribes became historically inevitable, linguistic unification occurred not through dialects but through common languages of tribal confederations. These languages, distinct from regional dialects, served as both the foundational linguistic strata and unifying tools characteristic of their historical era. As related tribes merged into confederations and then into ethnic groups, these common languages evolved into the languages of entire ethnic communities."[1] Nevertheless, isolated cases of linguistic differentiation still occurred during this period, as tribal confederations could disintegrate for various reasons, and individual tribes that had not yet formed confederations could still diverge. However, with the establishment of slavery and the incorporation of other tribes as captives-turned-slaves, linguistic unification became necessary between slave-owning tribes and enslaved tribes that originally spoke different languages. This gave primacy to the trend of language unification. In the subsequent feudal society, language further unified alongside the unification of ethnic groups. However, local separatism in the feudal era also contributed to linguistic differentiation at the regional level, which gave rise to local dialects. Meanwhile, the disintegration of feudal states could also lead to the emergence of new languages. Nevertheless, in general, if we exclude the emergence of local dialects, unification remained the dominant trend of language development, despite the persistence of isolated cases of linguistic differentiation. Under the conditions of nation development that accompanied the rise of capitalist society, the unification of local dialects into a national common language and the convergence among national languages became the prevailing trend. From this point onward, new local

1 Yakubinsky, *The Formation of Tribes and Their Languages*, Bulletin of Leningrad University, 1947, No. 1, p. 143.

dialects ceased to emerge, though existing ones did not necessarily die out, and language unification proceeded through the formula of linguistic fusion in which dominant languages sought to establish supremacy.

Today, we find ourselves in a new stage of development, with socialism having been established in many regions. Under these conditions of social development, how will human language evolve? As discussed above, the formation of nations gives rise to national common languages. Therefore, in today's social units struggling for national unity and independence, the unification of regional dialects into a national common language is an inevitable trend. In socialist countries, alongside the further unification of national common languages, there will also emerge phenomena of linguistic convergence among the various national languages within the country. However, this convergence belongs neither to the first formula nor the second, but rather to a third formula—which might be described as a transitional formula between the first and second. With the future victory of socialism on a worldwide scale, the establishment of communism, and the formation of a global communist family, the obvious trend in language development will be the creation of a world common language or linguistic unification within the global community. However, since the four elements of a nation will not disappear simultaneously, these elements—at least in terms of national psychological makeup—will not be completely eradicated before nations enter the communist family. This ensures that national consciousness will persist for a relatively long time.

Additionally, due to the uneven development among nations, various ethnic groups will continue to exist for some time. As Lenin reminds us, national differences among ethnic groups and state differences among countries "will continue to exist for a long time even after the establishment of the worldwide dictatorship of the proletariat"[1]. Therefore, the formation of a world common language will not occur anytime soon. But by what means will this world common language come into being?

Since language is the most important communication tool that people use at all times, it is impossible for them to suddenly switch to a new language. Therefore, imposing a world common language by force is unfeasible. The formation of a world common language must occur through "subtle and gradual influence", though human intervention can accelerate this process. In other words, it will be achieved through the gradual fusion of languages. Under new social conditions, however, this linguistic fusion will not follow the first formula but the second. As Stalin stated: "In this era, world imperialism will no longer exist, the exploiting classes will be overthrown, oppression of nations and colonies will be eliminated, national isolation and mistrust will give way to mutual trust and closeness among nations, equality of national rights will be realized, policies of suppressing and assimilating languages will be abolished, cooperation among nations will be established, and the languages of various nations will have the

1 *Selected Works of Lenin* (2 vols.), People's Publishing House, 1954, Vol. 2, p. 755.

possibility of enriching each other through cooperation..." Needless to say, under these conditions, there can be no question of some languages being suppressed and defeated while others triumph. Here, we are not dealing with two languages—one suffering defeat and the other emerging victorious in struggle—but with hundreds of national languages. Through the long-term economic, political, and cultural cooperation among nations, these languages will first give rise to the richest single regional languages, which will then merge into a common international language. This language will of course be neither German, nor Russian, nor English, but a new language that absorbs the essence of all national and regional languages.[1] Since language develops alongside social progress, changes in social conditions influence the way language evolves. The worldwide victory of socialism has brought about a qualitative change in the global social landscape, and thus, linguistic convergence will occur through cooperation—namely, by absorbing the best elements of various languages to create a new language. Of course, in the process of absorbing the essence of various languages, the essence of each language will not be absorbed in equal proportions. This has led some to doubt Stalin's assertion that this language will be neither German, Russian, nor English, arguing that the world common language must be a continuation of an existing language rather than a hodgepodge. This is, in fact, a misunderstanding of Stalin's words. The future world

1 Stalin, *Marxism and Problems of Linguistics*, pp. 53–54.

common language will certainly not be an existing national language like German, Russian, or English, but a new language that absorbs the essence of all languages. However, this does not mean that no language serves as a foundation in the development process. The key point is that during the capitalist era of national discrimination, linguistic convergence among national languages was marked by mutual distrust and struggle between nations, with languages resisting each other as national languages fiercely protected the essence of their characteristics. As a result, linguistic convergence did not produce a third new language but rather the victory of one language and the defeat of another; the victorious language absorbed certain useful elements from the defeated language and developed according to its own internal laws of evolution. Following the global triumph of socialism—a system that "not only safeguards the distinctive national identities of all peoples but actively fosters the genuine flourishing of socialist nations, their cultures, and languages"[1], the following developments will converge to facilitate the eventual emergence of a universal human language, i.e., intensified cooperation among nations, consolidation of the socialist economic order, deep-rooted integration of socialist principles into all ethnic communities, and growing practical recognition by all peoples that a shared global language offers greater utility than separate national tongues. These dynamics will progressively diminish

1 Chikobava, *Introduction to Linguistics*, Part 1, p. 98.

national distinctions and linguistic boundaries, paving the way for human's transition to a common world language.[1] Under these circumstances, the convergence among national languages does not occur through mutual struggle or resistance. In this process of convergence, since languages do not resist one another, their basic vocabulary and grammatical structures do not reject foreign elements—excellent components are gradually absorbed. This causes gradual changes within the internal structure of languages, ultimately altering the essence of their characteristics and giving way to new languages. With no mutual resistance among nations and no need for languages to resist foreign elements, the languages that once became interethnic lingua francas due to communication needs will naturally provide more components for the formation of a world common language to serve as the foundational languages for it. However, this foundational language is not the new language itself, just as a foundational dialect is not the national common language. For this very reason, the future universal language will be neither German, Russian, nor English. The process of linguistic convergence among China's domestic ethnic groups during the transitional period illustrates this point. Thanks to the traditional friendship and cooperation among ethnic groups, under the correct leadership of the Communist Party of China, these relationships have developed rapidly, even as each ethnic group continues to develop its own culture and language.

1 Cf. *Collected Works of Stalin*, Vol. 17, pp. 299–300.

With mutual trust established, Chinese has become the lingua franca among ethnic groups, and their languages are absorbing a large number of Chinese components while gravitating toward the Chinese language. Of course, these ethnic languages have not yet begun to fade away, nor have they lost the essence of their unique characteristics. This is due to three key factors: the limited time elapsed since the transitional period began, the continued presence of global imperialism, and the uneven cultural development rooted in each nation's historical legacy, alongside persistent national consciousness. They continue to develop by absorbing the fine elements of Chinese, and thus the formation of a universal language has not yet begun. However, this transitional scenario already indicates that future linguistic convergence will enter a new stage by gravitating toward a particular language. Due to the vastness of the world, the unique cultural and living conditions in different regions, and the gradual nature of language development, the formation of a universal language will occur through the establishment of regional common languages as an intermediate stage. These regional common languages will also develop based on a specific language. In the future, the evolution of these regional common languages into a universal language will likewise be grounded in a particular regional common language. The emergence of this new language will not violate the internal laws of language development. It should be noted that the phenomenon of qualitative change in a language through natural evolution is not only proven by historical facts but also acknowledged in Stalin's linguistic perspective. What Stalin opposed was the idea that a third new language could emerge abruptly through a linguistic upheaval, not the possibility of natural qualitative change in language—though such change is gradual, not abrupt. The transformation of Germanic into German and Latin into French clearly exemplifies qualitative change. After such changes, the internal laws of language development naturally differ as well. However, in the first formula, the absorption of foreign elements does not play a significant role in the qualitative change of the language. Although qualitative change occurs, it remains a historical transformation within the same language—a process that demonstrates the historical inheritance of its linguistic essence. In the second formula, while this qualitative change is also achieved gradually, it results from absorbing the quintessence of various languages. While one language provides the foundational basis, the absorption of significant linguistic components from other languages generates a new language distinct from all existing ones. This new language does not exhibit historical inheritance of the essential characteristics of any single predecessor. This does not mean, however, that it is a mere average conglomeration of linguistic components from various languages without any foundational language for development.

Since language, human's most important communication tool, is collectively created by society through gradual development and evolves over lengthy historical processes, artificial languages like "Esperanto" cannot serve as the world common language. Such constructed languages, unrooted in social life and not organically developed by communities, fail to meet society's comprehensive communicative needs. Abruptly replacing native languages with artificial ones also contradicts the natural conditions of human interaction. While Esperanto and similar projects cannot fulfill the role of a universal language, their utility should not be underestimated. Such constructed languages can assist people in conducting specialized communication under exceptional circumstances and function as international auxiliary languages. Until a universal language emerges, they can serve to connect the thoughts and emotions of people from different nations in specific cultural exchanges and political advocacy.

In the future world, with the global victory of socialism and the establishment of communism, languages will inevitably follow the path of forming a universal language, rather than diverging into local dialects or related languages. This does not mean, however, that all forms of linguistic divergence will be impossible. On the contrary, the differentiation of language into various societal dialects and speech variants will not only continue but also become more diverse. As human focuses on transforming nature and the world, human knowledge, culture, science and technology, and various aspects of social life will only grow increasingly prosperous. At that time, people will need to engage in frequent communication on a global scale while simultaneously occupying a greater variety of specialized labor roles. To adapt to this environment, a universal language will be used worldwide, while also diversifying into various societal dialects—such as those specific to scientific and technological communities or professional groups—though some outdated existing societal dialects will disappear alongside the communities they serve. Due to the multifaceted prosperity and development of society, communicative contexts will increasingly become complex. Therefore, to meet the requirements of different communicative situations, people will also develop more speech variants from the language. In summary, with the establishment of the communist community of nations and the unification of the world into a single social entity, alongside the increasing richness and prosperity of social life, human will both unify language into a universal common tongue for global use and diversify it into various societal dialects and speech variants. This represents a prospective trajectory for the development of human language.

www.ingramcontent.com/pod-product-compliance
Lightning Source LLC
LaVergne TN
LVHW010629110826
845149LV00014B/2815

9781965890813